The
ConciseEncyclopediaofWORLD

FOOTBALL

The ConciseEncyclopediaofWORLD

FOOTBALL

Tim Barnett • Ian Cruise • Glenn Moore • Mike Collett
Trevor Haylett • Conrad Leach • Charlotte Nicol

p

Acknowledgements
Art Director: Ron Samuels
Editorial Director: Sydney Francis
Managing Editor: Charles Dixon-Spain
Editor: Paul Barnett
Design: Digital Artworks Partnership Ltd

Picture Acknowledgements
All pictures by The Football Archive except the following:
Colorsport: 69 (inset), 71 (both), 135 (top), 244 (both)
Ronald Grant Archive: 132 (both), 133, 134
Empics sport photo agency 239
Page 1: Ronaldo in Brazilian colours
Page 2/3: Alfredo de Stefano scoring during Real Madrid's European
Cup win over Eintracht Frankfurt at Hampden park.
Cover photo © Getty Images
With special thanks to Peter Robinson at the Football Archive for all his help.

Football Archive

CONTENTS

The People's Game

For all its simplicity, football has ever been played on a grand scale. It began with whole villages playing each other in matches that lasted days at a time; now it involves the global village, with international competitions and worldwide television. Throughout, soccer has remained the ultimate people's game, capturing hearts and minds from Iceland to New Zealand, from Mexico to Saudi Arabia.

Though a similar game may have been played in ancient China, football is generally regarded as having started in medieval England. Frequently banned by local administrators for its rowdiness and national rulers because it distracted military archers from their practice – it nevertheless survived. Feast and Saint's Days were occasions for matches that sprawled over miles of English countryside. Some such matches still survive, although there is less bloodshed today.

These vast contests were, however, gradually eclipsed by smaller matches, played in towns and especially schools. Early 19th-century English schools were strong believers in the 'healthy mind in a healthy body' principle, as notably espoused by Rugby's Thomas Arnold. Sport was encouraged and football, or derivations thereof, was widely played. But the schools played according to different rules. This led to problems when schools wished to play each other, or when ex-pupils formed old boys' teams. There was thus the first codification of the laws, in Cambridge in 1848.

FACTORY FOOTBALLERS

The more formalized game gradually spread until, in 1863, the Football Association was formed – with a revised set of rules. This was primarily an upper-class body, as is reflected by the early winners of their first competition, the FA Challenge Cup. The picture changed as the game developed in the industrial English Midlands and North – often encouraged

Right: The People's Game reaches Argentina.

Opposite: Gary Lineker in red England strip.

7

Above: Juventus wear Notts County colours even today.

Opposite: The first World Cup Final in 1930 – Argentinian goal keeper Botasso foils Hector 'Mano' Castro of Uruguay.

by factory employers, who saw it as a way of organizing their workers' leisure time. The better clubs began to attract spectators and charge admission. They also began to pay players. Many Scots were attracted south of the border.

'Professionalism' was frowned upon by the FA hierarchy and was initially illegal. However, unlike the case with Rugby Football (which had derived from Association Football and was soon to split into the amateur Union and the professional League), an accommodation was found. The balance of power moved northwards, accelerated by the formation of the Football League in 1888.

Meanwhile, as the British Empire expanded, English and Scottish sailors, soldiers, railway workers and other émigrés were spreading the game across the world, notably to Europe and South America; the Anglicized names of many clubs (Everton in Chile, Athletic Bilbao in Spain, Athletic Club Milan in Italy, Newell's Old Boys in Argentina, etc.) reflect this influence. So do some colours: Bilbao began with a Sunderland strip and Juventus with Notts County shirts.

GLOBAL FOOTBALL

In 1904 FIFA was formed in France by seven nations – France, Belgium, Holland, Switzerland, Denmark, Sweden and Spain – to organize the sport on a global scale. The home nations (England, Scotland, Ireland and Wales) refused to join, the first example of an insularity which has never fully disappeared. Central Europe countries, in particular Hungary and Austria, came to occupy the vanguard of the European game, largely due to the evangelism of England's Jimmy Hogan.

Various small international competitions were created, and in the late 1920s the expanding FIFA decided to establish a World Cup. The first tournament, held in

Uruguay, was poorly attended, but the competition has never looked back. The World Cup is now the second biggest sports event after the Olympic Games, and FIFA now rivals the United Nations in terms of member countries.

The game boomed in many countries after World War II, and international competitions for clubs and countries were developed in South America, Europe and beyond. Soccer also became wealthier – particularly in Italy, where many industrialist investors were attracted by the game's mass popularity. In consequence, Italy's clubs were able to attract some of the world's best players by offering wages far above what they could have earned at home. This applied especially to Scandinavia, where for many years the game remained amateur, to the UK, where a maximum wage had been imposed, and to the South American countries, which were generally poorer. (Colombia attempted to buck the South American trend. In the early 1950s there was a Colombian attempt to set up a rogue league outside FIFA's jurisdiction. Players were attracted from Europe – one was the England centre-half Neil Franklin – and from other South American countries. The effort soon failed, with clubs going bankrupt. FIFA then re-established its iron control of the game.)

FREEDOM OF CONTRACT

In the late 1960s Italian soccer closed its borders to foreigners, aiming to improve the development of domestic players, and thus Spain became the most lucrative place to play – although England briefly attracted a number of foreign players in the late 1970s. Players across Western Europe were now paid the local going rate, and many had a measure of 'freedom of contract'. Eastern European nations generally prevented their players leaving the relevant country until late in their careers, although successful 'ambassadors for Communism' were relatively well rewarded. Meanwhile, the best South Americans played in Europe.

In recent years the sport has developed enormously in Africa and, more slowly, in North and Central America, Asia and

Right: Women's football has had an increasingly visible profile during the 1980s and 1990s, this is due, in some great part, to the Mundialito (or 'The Little World Cup') when women's national sides from all five continents compete.

Above: One of the all-time greats, Paolo Rossi. Caught up in scandal in the early 1980s, he extricated himself in time to represent Italy at the 1982 World Cup Finals.

Oceania. Even so, Western European club football has become ever more dominant. The transfusion of money from television has increased exponentially, and much of it has been passed on in the form of players' wages and transfer fees. Spain, England and Italy are now the venue of choice for any self-respecting footballer . . . and his agent. Fans in those countries have benefited through better facilities, while television coverage brings hundreds of games annually to armchair enthusiasts all over the world. In the more privileged countries the sport has never been so glamorous and successful as it is today.

THE WOMEN'S GAME
There has been a concomitant growth in women's football, especially in the USA – where the men are still struggling to introduce a professional outdoor league. Also in the USA, female-oriented off- shoots of the male game, such as beach football and indoor football, have professional circuits.

TWIN SHADOWS
There remain, however, two shadows on football: corruption and hooliganism.

Corruption has always been a problem. In the early days, underpaid players rigged matches to win on the fixed-odds betting. While this still occurs, the modern problem is on a bigger scale: clubs and, less often, national federations do sometimes rig matches, and in some

11

Above: South Africa: a young boy plays football.

Opposite: Paul Gascoigne celebrates with Teddy Sherringham during Euro 96.

cases, notably among the old Iron Curtain countries, the rigging has been done at governmental level.

Hooliganism has also always existed – games were certainly disrupted in the 19th century in England, and in earlier times many football matches were really just excuses for mass hooliganism: the players themselves were the hooligans. Until the late 1960s South America and Latin Europe were regarded as the worst areas, but most of the hooliganism was spontaneous. Then came a more sinister development, especially in England, with groups of fans organizing premeditated violence. This spread to other European countries and to South America but, unlike the case with England, most of it happened only in a domestic context. The English, by contrast, have long had serious problems with hooligans following club and national sides overseas – most tragically at Heysel in 1985 (see page 187) and more recently in Dublin in 1995, when an international match had to be abandoned, and in Marseille in 1998.

The irony is that domestic hooliganism has been largely eradicated in England, and the game there is now seen as an example to the world, offering some of the best facilities to the fans – not to mention the quality of the players. Having exported the game, followed by the good and bad of its national culture, England could justifiably say, when hosting Euro 96, that football was 'coming home'.

EVER THE SAME GAME

What the early pioneers – the university men who codified the rules in 1846, the establishment men who founded the FA in London 17 years later, and the businessmen who in 1888 met in a Manchester hotel to start the first League – would think of the modern professional game is anyone's guess. But show them a group of youngsters kicking a ball about on some open ground and they would recognize it: Africans playing with a rag ball on a dusty plain, US girls playing on a manicured pitch, or a couple of English boys using their jackets as goalposts after school. . . . It's all the same game, and that more than anything is what they would recognize.

GLENN MOORE
London, 1998

13

ON THE FIELD:
THE PLAYERS
AND MANAGERS

In each generation there are great players and managers and in the following sections we have tried to bring an objective eye to what is a subjective choice. But in each case we have tried to show why these men are worthy of inclusion, whether it is for individual brilliance, like Pelé, or for being the first black player in the English team, as Viv Anderson was. As for the managers, the sole criteria was success, whether under difficult circumstances and limited resources like Jack Charlton, or with a huge purse and high expectation like Helenio Herrera. Whether you agree with these choices is another matter, but then discussion and argument is one of the great pleasures of following the game.

A-Z of Players

Florian Albert

Born: 15 September 1941, Hungary

Club: Ferencvaros (Hungary)

Major honour: European Footballer of the Year 1967

Albert was, without doubt, his country's greatest player of the 'next generation' after the great Hungarian side of the early 1950s. A farmer's son, this hardworking centre-forward is best remembered for his inspiring displays at the 1966 World Cup in England.

Right: Lifting the World Cup is the high-light of any player's life.

Below: John Aldridge in action for the Republic of Ireland.

John Aldridge

Born: 18 September 1958, Liverpool, England

Clubs: Newport County (Wales), Oxford United (England), Liverpool (England), Real Sociedad (Spain), Tranmere Rovers (England)

Major honour: none

A proven goal-scorer at every level, Aldridge was part of the Republic of Ireland's international rise. Despite retiring from international football one goal shy of equalling Frank Stapleton's Irish record, Aldridge remained a prodigious striker at Tranmere Rovers, for whom he scored 20 goals in the 1996–7 season. Aldridge, who by then was acting as player-manager, had reached 471 goals in all comp-etitions in 882 games. Despite this magnificent scoring record, he was the first player to miss a penalty during an FA Cup Final at Wembley in 1988.

Ivor Allchurch

Born: 16 October 1929, Swansea, Wales

Clubs: Swansea (Wales), Newcastle United (England), Cardiff City (Wales), Swansea City (Wales)

Major honour: none

Grace and elegance were the watchwords of Allchurch, a mid-fielder who still holds the record for scoring the most League goals of any Swansea player (160). Tall and blond, perhaps inevitably

Above: Viv Anderson, the first black international for England.

he was known as 'Golden Boy', but he failed to gain just reward for his ample talents, as he spent his entire career playing for run-of-the-mill clubs. Only at the 1958 World Cup in Sweden did a wider audience get to appreciate his sublime talents. His younger brother, Len, also played for Wales.

José Altafini

Born: 27 August 1938, Brazil

Clubs: Palmeiras, São Paulo (Brazil), AC Milan (Italy), Napoli (Italy), Juventus (Italy), Chiasso (Switzerland)

Major honour: European Cup 1963

One of only four players to have appeared in a World Cup Finals series for two different countries – the others are Luis Monti (Argentina 1930 and Italy 1934), Ferenc Puskas (Hungary 1954 and Spain 1962) and José Santamaria (Uruguay 1954 and Spain 1962) – Altafini was a no-nonsense centre-forward; he was nicknamed 'Mazzola' because of his resemblance to the Italian player of the late 1940s. He represented Brazil at the 1958 tournament, where his display of power earned him a transfer to AC Milan, who insisted he play for the Italian national side in 1962.

Manuel Amoros

Born: 1 February 1961, Nîmes, France

Clubs: Monaco (France), Marseille (France)

Major honour: European Championship 1984

Holder of a French record 82 caps, Amoros was a key member of France's national side during the early 1980s, when it was widely considered one of the world's leading teams. Born of Spanish parents, the versatile Amoros was happy in either full-back position. As a youngster, he shone at rugby union.

Viv Anderson

Born: 28 August 1956, Nottingham, England

Clubs: Nottingham Forest (England), Arsenal (England), Manchester United (England), Sheffield Wednesday (England), Barnsley (England), Middlesbrough (England)

Major honours: European Cup 1979, 1980; European Supercup 1979

Viv Anderson broke through the taboos to become the first black player to appear in a full international for England, making his senior début against Czechoslovakia in 1978. However, this classy full-back or central defender and his excellent ball-skills deserve to be remembered for more than just that. During a long and glittering career with some of England's leading clubs, he won everything the domestic game had to offer. Anderson is now assistant manager to Bryan Robson at Middlesbrough.

José Leandro Andrade

Born: 20 November 1898, Uruguay

Clubs: Bella Vista (Uruguay), Nacional (Uruguay)

Major honours: Olympic Gold 1924, 1928; World Cup 1930

José Leandro Andrade was one of the mainstays of the great Uruguayan side of the late 1920s and early 1930s, but his career looked as though it was destined to finish prematurely when injury struck in 1929. However, he battled back, and his experience was a vital factor when the South Americans won the inaugural World Cup in 1930.

Nicolas Anelka

Voted Young Player of the Year in 1999 by the Football Writer's Association, he has already played for some of the top clubs in Europe – Arsenal, Real Madrid, Paris St Germain, Liverpool and Manchester City. At international level he has yet to prove himself – he was left out of the France 2002 World Cup squad, but could he have made the difference and saved them from an early return?

A-Z OF PLAYERS

Above: Ossie Ardiles playing for Spurs.

Roberto Baggio

Born: 18 February 1967
Vicenza, Italy

Clubs: LR Vicenza (Italy), Fiorentina (Italy), Juventus (Italy), AC Milan (Italy), Bologna (Italy), Internazionale (Italy), Brescia, (Italy)

Major honours: UEFA Cup 1993; European Footballer of the Year 1993; World Footballer of the Year 1993

At one time regarded as the world's greatest player, Roberto Baggio's record transfer from Fiorentina to Juventus sparked three days of riots by disgruntled fans in Florence. His early career was blighted by a series of knee injuries, but the 'Divine Ponytail' – thus nicknamed because of his hairstyle and Buddhist beliefs – recovered sufficiently to lead his country to the World Cup Final in 1994. Although blessed with almost perfect poise and control, Baggio missed a spot-kick in the penalty shoot-out, thereby condemning

Osvaldo Ardiles

Born: 3 August 1952, Cordoba, Argentina

Clubs: Huracan (Argentina), Tottenham Hotspur (England), Paris St Germain (France), Tottenham Hotspur (England), Blackburn Rovers (England), Queen's Park Rangers (England), Swindon Town (England)

Major honours: World Cup 1978; UEFA Cup 1984

Together with fellow countryman Ricardo Villa, 'Ossie' Ardiles took English football by storm in the wake of the 1978 World Cup. His sparkling skill made him the play-making star of Argentina's mid-field;

Right: Roberto Baggio, regarded as one of Italy's greatest players.

no sooner had he received his winners' medal than he and Villa were snapped up by Tottenham Hotspur in what, at the time, was a highly unusual transfer of foreign stars into a domestic side. Intelligent and thoughtful both on and off the pitch – he was studying for a degree in Law when football took over – Ardiles helped Spurs to FA and UEFA Cup triumphs.

With fellow countryman Ricardo Villa, 'Ossie' Ardiles took English football by storm in the wake of the 1978 World Cup.

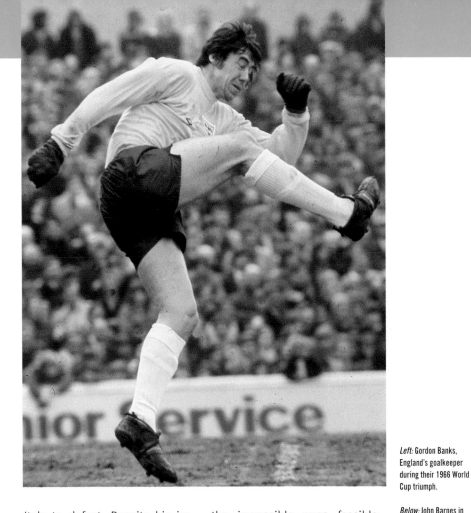

Left: Gordon Banks, England's goalkeeper during their 1966 World Cup triumph.

Below: John Barnes in action for England.

being an outstanding performer for Italy. His penchant for bringing the ball out from the back to help create attacking options revolutionized the way the sweeper's role was perceived. Along with Roberto Baggio, Baresi missed a penalty in the 1994 World Cup Final shoot-out – a cruel end to an otherwise faultless international career.

John Barnes

Born: 7 November 1963, Jamaica

Clubs: Watford (England), Liverpool (England), Newcastle United (England)

Major honour: none

Born in Jamaica to a high-ranking military family, John Barnes scored one of the most memorable England goals of all time – yet he is viewed more as a great talent gone to waste rather than as simply a great talent.

At club level, his play at the height of his career was matchless; his effortless control, touch and craft uniquely earned him back-to-back Footballer of the Year titles in 1988 and 1989 as well as two League titles, the FA Cup and the League Cup with Liverpool. But, that wonderful solo effort against Brazil in the Maracana aside, he never quite pulled it off for England, thereby frustrating fans and managers alike.

Later, Barnes moved to Newcastle, under the managership of former team-mate Kenny Dalglish.

Ironically, John Barnes played as a winger before eventually finding his *métier* in the mid-field where he shone for team and country throughout the late 1980s and 1990s.

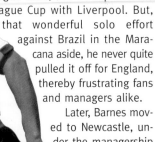

Italy to defeat. Despite his immense talent, he has struggled to gain the full faith of the national managers, with Azeglio Vicini, Arrigo Sacchi and Cesare Maldini all expressing doubts about his ability.

Gordon Banks

Born: 20 December 1937, Sheffield, England

Clubs: Chesterfield (England), Leicester (England), Stoke City (England)

Major honour: World Cup 1966

Destined to be forever remembered for a miraculous one-handed save from Pelé in the 1970 World Cup Finals, Gordon Banks was the rock upon which Alf Ramsey had built the side that won the World Cup four years previously. Brave and strong, with an uncanny knack of being in the right place at almost all times, Banks had a knack of making the difficult saves look mundane and

the impossible ones feasible. He was on the losing side in two FA Cup Finals with Leicester, but his international career far over-shadowed an unfashionable club life. A car accident in 1972 cost him the sight of his right eye and forced his retirement from the game.

Franco Baresi

Born: 8 May 1960, Travagliato, Italy

Clubs: AC Milan (Italy)

Major honours: European Cup 1989, 1990; European Supercup 1989, 1990; World Club Cup 1989, 1990

A gifted and forceful sweeper with an almost telepathic ability to read situations, Baresi was the defensive force behind the all-conquering AC Milan side of the late 1980s and early 1990s, as well as

A-Z OF PLAYERS

Franz Beckenbauer

Born: 11 September 1945, Munich, West Germany

Clubs: Bayern Munich (West Germany), New York Cosmos (USA), Hanover (West Germany), New York Cosmos (USA)

Major honours: European Cup Winners' Cup 1967; European Championship 1972; European Footballer of the Year 1972, 1976; World Cup 1974; European Cup 1974, 1975, 1976; World Club Cup 1976

The only man to have lifted the World Cup as both team captain (1974) and manager (1990), Franz Beckenbauer is the most successful footballer of all time. Known as 'Der Kaiser', he was an inspirational captain for Bayern Munich and West Germany for many years, enjoying glory and success at every turn of his career. Deceptively quick in both thought and deed, he was a tremendous passer of the ball, and almost single-handedly invented the position of sweeper in modern-day football, having operated initially as a left-winger and later in mid-field. The 1966 World Cup was the making of Beckenbauer's reputation: his grace and elegance marked him out, and his defensive skills negated the not insubstantial threat of Bobby Charlton in the final. Critics have suggested that by marking Charlton so well, Beckenbauer neglected his own attacking instincts and cost the Germans the match – but the defeat proved to be the only blip in an extraordinary career.

After helping Bayern achieve the greatest successes of their history, he and Pelé inspired the brief 1970s soccer boom in the USA. Having retired from playing in 1982, Beckenbauer moved into the media world, only to be approached by the German FA in 1984 to succeed national coach Jupp Derwall. So it was that a man with no coaching experience or qualifications at all led West Germany to two World Cup Finals (1986 and 1990).

Dennis Bergkamp

Born: 10 May 1969, Amsterdam, Holland

Clubs: Ajax (Holland), Internazionale (Italy), Arsenal (England)

Major honours: European Cup Winners' Cup 1987; UEFA Cup 1994; Premiership 1998, 2002

Bergkamp made his European début while still at school. By the time he had reached his late twenties, a chronic fear of flying appeared to be his only flaw. He starred at Ajax, struggled at Internazionale, and reached his peak at Arsenal. This gifted striker, with sublime passing and shooting skills and a priceless ability to find space, was the major reason Arsenal gained a league title in 1998.

George Best

Born: 22 May 1946, Belfast, Northern Ireland

Clubs: Manchester Utd (England), Dunstable Town (England), Stockport County (England), Cork Celtic (Republic of Ireland), Fulham (England), Los Angeles Aztecs (USA), Fort Lauderdale Stikers (USA), Hibernian (Scotland), San Jose Earthquakes (USA), Bournemouth (England), Brisbane Lions (Australia)

Major honours: European Cup 1968; European Footballer of the Year 1968

Lightning pace, mesmerizing footwork, instant control, a fierce shot, deceptive strength and a snappy tackle – George Best had it all. The fact that he also blew it all in the spectacular self-destructiveness of his private life is well documented, but perhaps the biggest 'crime' of all is that Best, a Northern Ireland international, was never able to display his sumptuous talents on the global stage. At his peak, he was a gifted, charismatic entertainer.

David Beckham

Born: 2 May 1975, Leytonstone, England

Clubs: Manchester United (England), Real Madrid (Spain)

Major honours: Champions League Final winner 1999; Premiership 1996, 1997, 1999, 2000, 2001, 2003; FA Cup 1996, 1999; Toyota Cup 1999; Runner up World Footballer of the Year 1999, 2001

Infamously sent off against Argentina in World Cup 1998, the lowest point of his career, he has risen during World Cup 2002 to a world football icon. As England captain he has led by example, and against the odds recovered from a broken foot to play in the first England match in World Cup 2002.

He has been an integral part of the Manchester United success during the past ten years, but has now moved to star-studded Real Madrid for an estimated £25 million.

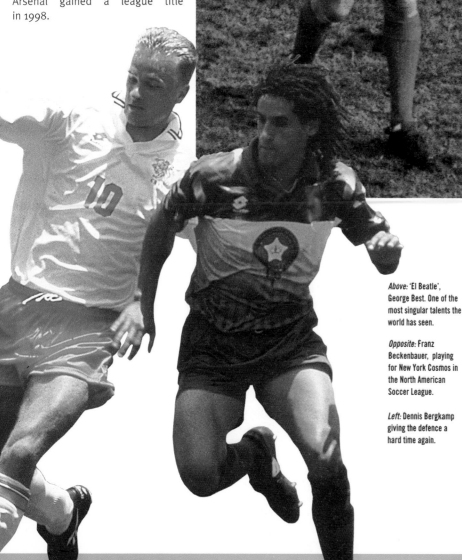

Above: 'El Beatle', George Best. One of the most singular talents the world has seen.

Opposite: Franz Beckenbauer, playing for New York Cosmos in the North American Soccer League.

Left: Dennis Bergkamp giving the defence a hard time again.

Danny Blanchflower

Born: 10 February 1926, Belfast, Northern Ireland

Clubs: Glentoran (Northern Ireland), Barnsley (England), Aston Villa (England), Tottenham Hotspur (England)

Major honour: European Cup-Winners' Cup 1963

A deep thinker on and off the field, Danny Blanchflower was the creative hub for the great Tottenham Hotspur side of the early 1960s. Earlier he had led Northern Ireland to their finest hour, at the 1958 World Cup in Sweden. The unfancied Irish reached the quarter-finals, disposing of Italy en route. As captain and principal play-maker for Spurs, Blanchflower made history in 1961 by guiding the White Hart Lane club to the first League/Cup double of the 20th century; a string of other trophies included the 1963 European Cup-Winners' Cup. On retirement, Blanchflower became a highly respected and forthright writer on football, then made an ill-starred attempt at management (with Chelsea) in 1978. He died in December 1993. His younger brother, Jackie, was seriously injured in the dreadful Munich air disaster of February 1958.

Oleg Blokhin

Born: 5 November 1952, USSR

Clubs: Dynamo Kiev (USSR), Vorwarts Steyr (Austria)

Major honours: European Cup-Winners' Cup 1975, 1976; European Super Cup 1975; European Footballer of the Year 1975

Blokhin, a very quick striker, was the first Soviet player to pass a century of caps. His European Player of the Year award came as recognition of his influence on Dynamo Kiev becoming the first Soviet side to win a European trophy. Oleg Blokhin's mother was a sprint hurdler. Blokhin himself could run 100m in 10.8 seconds.

Steve Bloomer

Born: 20 January 1874, Cradley Heath, England

Clubs: Derby County (England), Middlesbrough (England), Derby County (England)

Major honour: none

Bloomer was English football's first genuine star. In the game's relative infancy, he set records that would go unbroken until well into the 1950s; he had to survive plenty of rough treatment from defenders along the way. His England record speaks for itself: he scored in each of his first ten internationals, eventually achieving the astonishing record of 28 goals in just 23 games for his country.

Zbigniew Boniek

Born: 3 March 1956, Poland

Clubs: Zawisza Bydgoszcz (Poland), Widzew Lodz (Poland), Juventus (Italy), Roma (Italy)

Major honours: European Cup-Winners' Cup 1984; European Supercup 1984; European Cup 1985

Poland may have enjoyed their greatest international renown in the mid-1970s, but it is a player from the next generation who can lay claim to the title of his country's best. Zbigniew Boniek hit the world headlines at the 1982 World Cup, when a crisply taken hat-trick against Belgium earned him a big-money move to Juventus. In Italy, Boniek's predatory skills made him the outstanding performer in a side that was at the peak of its powers.

Jean-Marc Bosman

Born: 4 June 1962, Belgium

Clubs: Standard Liège (Belgium), RFC Liège (Belgium), St Quentin (France), St Denis (Réunion), Olympic Charleroi (Belgium), Vise (Belgium)

Major honour: none

If it weren't for his efforts in the European Court of Justice, Bosman would be no more than a footnote in Belgian football history. As it is, he shook the European game to its very foundations. In June 1990, Bosman was an out-of-contract mid-fielder with RFC Liège in Belgium. Liège cut his wages by 60 per cent. He was offered a move to Dunkerque. Liège demanded a fee of £533,000 – which the French club declined to pay – then refused the player a transfer

Below: Peerless for Poland in the early 1980s, Zbigniew Boniek.

and suspended him. After a legal battle, finally resolved in December 1995, the European Court of Justice announced that UEFA's system of transfers and limit on foreign players was illegal.

Paul Breitner

Born: 5 September 1951, West Germany

Clubs: Bayern Munich (West Germany), Real Madrid (Spain), Eintracht Braunschweig (West Germany), Bayern Munich (West Germany)

Major honour: World Cup 1974

Perhaps unusually for a player who began as a left-back, Paul Breitner is best described as a flamboyant, imaginative performer. He was superb for West Germany in the World Cup of 1974 – taking the penalty that levelled the score in the final – and in 1982 when again he scored at the last stage. He insisted on moving into midfield after joining Real Madrid; the consequent bust-up with the German authorities saw him miss the 1978 World Cup.

Emilio Butragueno

Born: 22 July 1963, Spain

Clubs: Castilla (Spain), Real Madrid (Spain)

Major honours: UEFA Cup 1985, 1986

Bloomer was English football's first genuine star. In the game's relative infancy, he set records that would go unbroken until well into the 1950s.

Below: Emilio Butragueno in action for Spain.

Nicknamed 'El Buitre' ('The Vulture') because of his predatory instincts, Butragueno overcame the early disappointment of being told by Real Madrid that he was not good enough to make it at the top level. Madrid's nursery club, Castilla, thought otherwise, and their careful nurturing turned him into a scoring sensation. He netted on his Spanish début (against Wales in 1984) and leapt into the public consciousness when he scored four times in a 5–1 thrashing of Denmark in the 1986 World Cup in Mexico.

Left: Paul Breitner scored in the 1974 and 1982 World Cup Finals.

alike in a string of bizarre incidents. His premature retirement from the game tells us a great deal about the man who craved perfection in everything he did. Disappointed in the 1996–7 season by what he saw as his own slipping standards, he led Manchester United to their fourth League title in five years and then simply walked away.

Careca

Born: 5 October 1960, Campinas, Brazil

Clubs: Guarani (Brazil), São Paulo (Brazil), Napoli (Italy), Hitachi (Japan)

Major honour: UEFA Cup 1989

One of the most feared strikers in the world during the 1980s and early 1990s, Careca missed the 1982 World Cup after injuring himself training on the eve of the tournament. A quite superb leader of the line, he made up for that disappointment by scoring five goals at Mexico 86 and subsequently was voted Brazil's Sportsman of the Year. His place in football's hall of fame was duly secured by a thrilling attacking partnership with Diego Maradona at Napoli. Surprisingly, he quit Brazil's squad in the build-up to the 1994 World Cup, moving to the Japanese club Hitachi. Careca won his first Brazilian championship at 17. He signed for Napoli for £3M.

Eric Cantona

Born: 24 May 1966, Paris, France

Clubs: Martigues (France), Auxerre (France), Marseille (France), Bordeaux (France), Montpellier (France), Leeds United (England), Manchester United (England)

Major honour: none

Above: The talented Eric Cantona, playing for Manchester United.

Flamboyant, often controversial, lavishly gifted and a great team player – Cantona was all of these

and more, and his influence transformed Manchester United from a good side into a great one. A career beset by anomalies saw the Frenchman revered in England as a world great, but largely ignored in his native France where, at the peak of his powers, he couldn't hold down a place in the national team. The highs as he led first Leeds United and then Manchester United to League titles were countered by the lows as he vented his anger against opponents, spectators and officials

Flamboyant, often controversial, lavishly gifted and a great team player – Eric Cantona was all of these and more, and his influence transformed Manchester United from a good side into a great one.

Left: Careca celebrating one of the many glorious goals that have adorned his career.

Jan Ceulemans

Born: 28 February 1957, Belgium

Clubs: Lierse (Belgium), Club Brugge (Belgium)

Major honour: none

Perhaps the most surprising thing about Jan Ceulemans' career was that such an outstanding player never sought fame and fortune outside his own country. The foundation stone of Belgium's national side for a decade, initially as a forward and later dictating from the mid-field, he was on the brink of a move to AC Milan in 1981, but was persuaded – by his mother, legend has it – to stay in Belgium. He won a record 96 caps for Belgium, scoring 26 goals in the process.

Below: Jan Ceulemans – his mother persuaded him to stay in Belgium for his entire career.

Stephane Chapuisat

Born: 28 June 1969, Lausanne, Switzerland

Clubs: FC Malley (Switzerland), Red Star Zurich (Switzerland), Lausanne (Switzerland), Bayer Ürdingen (Germany), Borussia Dortmund (Germany)

Major honour: European Cup 1997

Chapuisat is one of Switzerland's finest strikers of all time. The son of the former Swiss international Pierre-Albert Chapuisat, he has helped revive Borussia Dortmund's fortunes since arriving from Ürdingen in 1992. His partnership with Karl-Heinz Riedle helped fire Dortmund to their unexpected European Cup triumph over favourites Juventus in 1997.

John Charles

Born: 27 December 1931, Swansea, Wales

Clubs: Leeds United (England), Juventus (Italy), Leeds United (England), Roma (Italy), Cardiff City (Wales)

Major honour: none

Arguably the greatest-ever Welsh player, 'Il Buon Gigante' ('The Gentle Giant') – as he was known in Italy – packed a massive talent inside his huge frame. Standing at 6ft 2in (1.9m) and weighing 14 stone (90kg), John Charles had great presence in the air, and he allied his strength to a surprisingly delicate and precise touch. Capped by Wales 38 times (his brother Mel won 31 caps), Charles was versatile enough to perform as an outstanding central defender on the international stage while setting scoring records as a centre-forward with Leeds United: the 42 goals he scored for them in the League (during the 1953–4 season) remain a record to this day. Charles became one of the first – and best – UK exports to Italy when he

transferred to the Italian side Juventus for £67,000 in 1957, and he went on to score an astonishing 93 goals in 155 League games in Serie A. However, perhaps the most remarkable statistic of John Charles's remarkable career is that not once in all those games was he sent off or cautioned.

Bobby Charlton

Born: 11 October 1937, Ashington, England

Clubs: Manchester United (England), Preston North End (England)

Major honours: World Cup 1966; European Footballer of the Year 1966; European Cup 1968

If ever a real-life player embodied the comic-strip character Roy of the Rovers, then that was Bobby Charlton. Famed for his fearsome shot and his pinpoint long-passing, Charlton is known throughout the world as an ambassador for his sport. He joined Manchester United in 1953 and remained with the side for 20 years, during which time United became the most powerful club in the UK, and Charlton won everything the English, European and world games had to offer.

A 'Busby Babe', Bobby Charlton scored twice on his début, against Charlton Athletic in 1956. Aged 19, he survived the horrific 1958 Munich air disaster to become a key player with the England national side and with Manchester United. Originally a left-winger, Charlton moved into a central and deeper position to help England achieve World Cup victory in 1966, and United to become England's first winners of the European Cup two years later.

Rarely can a sporting knighthood (he received the honour in 1994) have been more richly deserved or more warmly received. He is the brother of fellow World Cup winner Jack Charlton, and the nephew of the former Newcastle forward Jackie Milburn.

Johan Cruyff

Born: 25 April 1947, Amsterdam, Holland

Clubs: Ajax (Holland), Barcelona (Spain), Los Angeles Aztecs (USA), Washington Diplomats (USA), Levante (Spain), Ajax (Holland), Feyenoord (Holland)

Major honours: European Cup 1971, 1972, 1973; European Footballer of the Year 1971, 1973, 1974

Three times European Footballer of the Year, Johan Cruyff was one of the greatest players the sport has ever known – and he has gone on to earn his place among the all-time best managers. He had his mother to thank for his start in the game: a cleaner at Amsterdam's mighty Ajax club, she pestered the coaching staff into taking a look at her ten-year-old son. Over the next 20 years, Cruyff went on to perfect the dazzling ball-skills and great football mind that made him a huge success both on and off the field. It was Cruyff's vision, intelligence and versatility that allowed the principle of 'total football' to work so brilliantly. Based on basketball's 'full-court press', 'total football' relies on every player having the skills to play in a number of different positions and the wit to swap roles at will. Nominally a centre-forward, Cruyff was as unorthodox as the number 14 he wore suggests – and this unpredictability helped make him a legend. Dogged by controversy throughout his playing career, owing to his sometimes outspoken opinions – he famously refused to play in the 1978 World Cup after a bust-up with the Dutch authorities – Cruyff again caused a storm with his decision to move

Opposite: The England player Bobby Charlton playing for Manchester United.

into management: Dutch coaches complained that he did not have the necessary qualifications. He countered by guiding first Ajax (1987) and later Barcelona (1989 and 1992) to European glory. His son Jordi moved from Barcelona to Manchester United in August 1996 and then back to Spanish football with Mallorca.

If ever a real-life player embodied the comic-strip character Roy of the Rovers, then that was Bobby Charlton. Famed for his fearsome shot and his pinpoint long-passing, he was knighted in 1994.

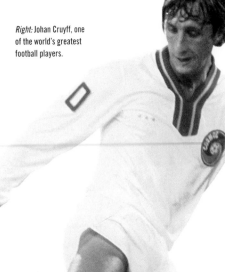

Right: Johan Cruyff, one of the world's greatest football players.

Kenny Dalglish

Born: 4 March 1951, Glasgow, Scotland

Clubs: Glasgow Celtic (Scotland), Liverpool (England)

Major honours: European Cup 1978, 1981, 1984; European Supercup 1987

Few people in the history of world football can match the achievements of this quiet Glaswegian as both player and manager. Already a legend at Celtic – the club he joined straight from school in 1967 – Dalglish was given the seemingly impossible task of replacing Kevin Keegan when he moved to Liverpool for a record £440,000 in 1977. But replace him he certainly did. In total, Dalglish played more than 500 games for the Anfield club, scoring 173 times in the process and winning everything the domestic and European games had to offer. As a manager, he has won still more admirers, both for his achievements – League titles with Liverpool and Blackburn – and for his dignity in the wake of the 1989 Hillsborough stadium tragedy, in which 96 Liverpool supporters were crushed to death.

William 'Dixie' Dean

Born: 22 January 1907, Birkenhead, England

Clubs: Tranmere Rovers (England), Everton (England), Notts County (England)

Major honour: none

The goal-scoring feats of this legendary Evertonian are unlikely ever to be matched. After he had scored 27 goals in 27 games in his first season with Tranmere Rovers, it was inevitable that the powerful Dean – he hated the nickname 'Dixie', which was an allusion to his dark colouring – would move on to bigger and

Above: Alberto Di Stefano scoring during Real Madrid's 1960 European Cup win over Eintracht Frankfurt at Hampden Park.

spell with Real Madrid, where he scored only 35 goals in a total of 85 appearances.

Dean's extraordinary 60-goal haul in the 1927–8 season, achieved when the legendary Evertonian was just 21 years old, remains a record to this day.

Alfredo Di Stefano

Born: 4 July 1926, Buenos Aires, Argentina

Clubs: River Plate (Argentina), Huracan (Argentina), River Plate (Argentina), Millonarios (Colombia), Barcelona (Spain), Real Madrid (Spain), Espanol (Spain)

Major honours: South American Championship 1947; European Cup 1956, 1957, 1958, 1959, 1960; European Footballer of the Year 1957, 1959; World Club Cup 1960

Considered by many the greatest player of all time – surpassing even Pelé – Di Stefano was the inspiration behind Real Madrid's run of five successive European Cups, and just for good measure he scored a goal in each of the first four finals and a hat-trick in the fifth, a 7–3 win over Eintracht Frankfurt. His transfer to Spain from South America was shrouded in controversy, and FIFA ordered that he spend a year at both Barcelona and Real Madrid. But Barcelona were unimpressed by his quiet start there and gave up their option; within days, he scored a hat-trick against them. Phenomenally fit – a result, he claimed, of road-racing in Buenos Aires as a child and working on his parents' farm – he was capable of defending one moment and popping up on the edge of the opposition's area to score a goal the next. Alfredo Di Stefano played international football for both Argentina and Spain without ever making it to a World Cup Final.

better things. He duly travelled across the Mersey to Goodison Park – and into the record books. His extraordinary 60-goal haul in the 1927–8 season, achieved when he was just 21 years old, remains a record to this day. In addition, he scored 18 times in just 16 games for England, 12 of those strikes being obtained during his first five matches. Unfortunate not to have gained more caps, Dean's outspokenness may have counted against him.

Kazimierz Deyna

Born: 23 October 1947, Poland

Clubs: Starograd (Poland), Sportowy Lodz (Poland), Legia Warsaw (Poland), Manchester City (England), San Diego (USA)

Major honour: Olympic Gold 1972

Much of the credit for Poland's emergence as a major footballing power in the early 1970s can be accorded to the elegant Kazimierz Deyna. The creative hub of the Polish side throughout that period – when the country achieved a best-ever third-place finish in the 1974 World Cup tournament – Deyna carved out openings for the likes of the free-scoring Grzegorz Lato and other team-mates such as Andrej Szarmach and Robert Gadocha.

Didi

Born: 8 October 1928, Brazil

Clubs: Rio Branco (Brazil), Lencoes (Brazil), Madureiro (Brazil), Flueninese (Brazil), Botafogo (Brazil), Real Madrid (Spain), Valencia (Spain), Botafogo (Brazil)

Major honour: none

A mid-field play-maker with a supreme touch, and a free-kick expert, Didi (real name Waldyr Pereira) was instrumental in Brazil's 1958 and 1962 World Cup triumphs. The sole blemish on his career was a relatively unsuccessful

Opposite: The multi-talented Kenny Dalglish.

A-Z OF PLAYERS

was Sporting's great rivals, Benfica, who snapped up the young Eusebio on his arrival in Portugal – all but kidnapping him off the plane and forcing him to lie low in an Algarve fishing village until the fuss had died down. A hugely popular and sportsmanlike player, Eusebio was top scorer at the 1966 World Cup held in England, where his lightning acceleration and wonderful dribbling skills earned him global acclaim and a fearful battering from opposition defenders. Having scored 38 goals in 46 games for Portugal, he had to bring his first-class career to an end in 1974, when at the age of 32, he injured his knee so badly he was advised never to play again. He was the Portuguese League's top scorer for nine consecutive seasons.

Luis Figo

Born: 4 November 1972, Lisbon, Portugal

Clubs: Sporting Lisbon (Portugal), Barcelona (Spain), Real Madrid (Spain)

Major honours: Portuguese Cup, Cup Winners Cup 1997, European Super Cup 1997, Spanish Championship 1998, 1999, Spanish Cup (Copa del Ray) 1997, 1998

Duncan Edwards

Born: 1 October 1936, Dudley, England

Club: Manchester United (England)

Major honour: none

The outstanding player in a remarkable crop of youngsters at Manchester United in the 1950s, Duncan Edwards had a brief life, but one that burned blindingly bright. His awesome power and ability – as both a creator and a stopper – made him England's then-youngest cap this century. In a career lasting just six years, he won 18 full England caps, other honours (including two League Championships) and an FA Cup Final. His death in the 1958 Munich disaster left an unfillable gap for both club and country.

Above: Giacinto Facchetti – for a full-back he scored a remarkable number of goals in Serie A.

Right: Eusebio, man of the World Cup finals 1966 playing for Portugal.

Eusebio

Born: 25 January 1942, Lourenço-Marques (now Maputo), Mozambique

Clubs: Benfica (Portugal), Boston Minutemen (USA), Toronto Metros-Croatia (Canada), Las Vegas Quicksilver (USA)

Major honours: European Cup 1962; European Footballer of the Year 1965

Eusebio Ferreira Da Silva, to give him his full name, was the leader of the pack of African footballers who, in the 1960s, made a huge impact on the Portuguese game, both domestically and internationally. Born in Mozambique, which was then a Portuguese territory, he began his footballing career with Sporting Lourenço-Marques, a nursery club of Sporting Lisbon. But it

Figo has become one of the best European players of the decade. He came to international prominence during the 1998 World Cup. Outstanding in the 2000 European Championships, he helped Portugal to a semi-final place where they lost to eventual winners France.

Japan and Korea 2002 proved to be a huge disappointment, with Portugal surprisingly failing to qualify for the second round.

Tom Finney

Born: 5 April 1922, Preston, England

Club: Preston North End (England)

Major honour: none

English Footballer of the Year in 1954 and again in 1957, the 'Preston Plumber' spent his entire career with the Deepdale club, and consequently won far fewer honours than his talents deserved. Versatile off both feet, Finney was a strong tackler who also possessed great power in the air. In total, he won 76 England caps and scored 30 goals, despite the disruption caused to the game by World War II. He was knighted in the late 1990s.

Juste Fontaine

Born: 18 August 1933, Morocco

Clubs: AC Marrakesh (Morocco), USM Casablanca (Morocco), Nice (France), Reims (France)

Major honour: none

Moroccan-born forward Juste Fontaine made his international début in 1956, but he was still unsure of his place in the French side when France travelled to the World Cup Finals held in Sweden in 1958. By the end of the tournament, however, the 13 goals he scored had made him a household name and established his place in the World Cup record book.

When teamed with 1958's European Footballer of the Year, Raymond Kopa, the man he had been bought to replace at Reims, Juste Fontaine became part of legendary and lethal front-line force for the French team, one that still hasn't been surpassed, even with players like Platini and Eric Cantona gracing the French team.

Above: Juste Fontaine (right) battles for the ball during an international for France.

Benfica snapped up the young Eusebio on his arrival in Portugal, all but kidnapping him off the plane.

Enzo Francescoli

Born: 12 November 1961, Uruguay

Clubs: Wanderers (Uruguay), River Plate (Argentina), Matra Racing (France), Marseille (France), Cagliari (Italy), Torino (Italy), River Plate (Argentina)

Major honours: South American Footballer of the Year 1985

An exciting mid-fielder-cum-striker and Uruguay's leading light during the late 1980s and early 1990s, Enzo Francescoli kicked off his football career with Wanderers. Before long, however, he had been tempted to move to Argentina by the giant River Plate club, and he proceeded to become a top-scorer in the Argentine League during 1985. Then he made his way to Europe in search of fame and fortune. There, he won a French Championship with Marseille before moving on to Italy's Serie A, where initially he played for Cagliari.

Hughie Gallacher

Born: 2 February 1903, Bellshill, Scotland

Clubs: Queen of the South (Scotland), Airdrie (Scotland), Newcastle United (England), Chelsea (England), Derby County (England), Notts County (England), Grimsby (England), Gateshead (England)

Major honour: none

Like so many an outstanding sportsman before and since, Hughie Gallacher had quite a muddled private life. He was an alcoholic, and he committed suicide in 1957, on the day before he was due to appear in court to face a charge of maltreating his son. Nevertheless, Gallacher was a sublime footballer who packed extraordinary pace, power and skill into his diminutive 5ft 5in (1.65m) frame. A prolific scorer – he scored

22 goals in the course of 19 games for Scotland, twice scoring five in a single match – Hughie Gallacher was a member of the so-called 'Wembley Wizards' who thrashed England 5–1 in 1928; oddly, in that particular match, he failed to score.

Garrincha

Born: 28 October 1933, Pau Grande, Brazil

Clubs: Pau Grande (Brazil), Botafogo (Brazil), Corinthians (Brazil), AJ Barranquilla (Colombia), Flamengo (Brazil), Red Star Paris (France)

Major honours: World Cup 1958, 1962

As brilliant on the pitch as he was wayward off it, Garrincha lived ever in the spotlight. Born a cripple, the 'Little Bird' retained a distorted left leg after the operation to correct his problems – but this did not affect his delightful ball-skills. He scored twice in the 1958 World Cup Final and then replaced the injured Pelé in 1962, again helping Brazil to win the tournament. Manoel dos Santos Francisco, to give him his real name, retired from the game after being on a losing Brazil side for the only time – in the 1966 World Cup in England. Beset by marital and income-tax problems, Garrincha died of alcohol abuse in January 1983.

Gallacher was a sublime footballer who packed extraordinary pace, power and skill into his diminutive frame. A prolific scorer, he netted 22 goals in 19 games for Scotland, twice achieving five in a match.

Right: Enzo Francescoli, a well-travelled player who has had periods with River Plate, Marseille and Cagliari.

Opposite: Garrincha playing for Brazil, and displaying the suppleness and intensity of all the greatest Brazilian players.

Paul Gascoigne

Born: 27 May 1967, Gateshead, England

Clubs: Newcastle United (England), Tottenham (England), Lazio (Italy), Glasgow Rangers (Scotland), Middlesbrough, Everton (England), Burnley (England), Lanzhou Flying Horse (China)

Major honours: none

Without any doubt the most gifted English player of his generation, blessed with sublime ball-skills allied to good balance and an eye for the goal, Paul Gascoigne is a formidable opponent. He shot to fame during the 1990 World Cup, when he was rated as the tournament's best young player, and ever since then he has combined the sublime with the ridiculous in a career that permanently threatens to self-destruct. This was never illustrated better than during Spurs' run to the 1991 FA Cup. In the semi-final, Gascoigne's superb 35-yard (32m) free-kick stunned rivals Arsenal into submission. By contrast, the final saw him make a reckless (and foul) tackle in the early minutes of the game; major surgery was required, and this rush of blood to Gazza's head could quite easily have finished his footballing career.

Francisco Gento

Born: 22 October 1933, Spain

Clubs: Santander (Spain), Real Madrid (Spain)

Major honours: European Cup 1956, 1957, 1958, 1959, 1960, 1966; World Club Cup 1960

This left-winger achieved six European Cup Winners' medals and two runner-up medals in a glittering 800-match career with Real Madrid. He was awarded 43 Spanish caps, playing in both the 1962 and 1966 World Cups. A strong player with outstanding pace, he was popularly known as Paco Gento.

Jimmy Greaves

Born: 20 February 1940, London, England

Clubs: Chelsea (England), AC Milan (Italy), Tottenham Hotspur (England), West Ham (England)

Major honour: European Cup Winners' Cup 1963

A natural goal-scorer whose speed of thought and chilling efficiency more than made up for any perceived low work-rate. Greaves came alive in the penalty box and, despite his diminutive size, was a supreme taker of chances – as his haul of 44 goals in 57 appearances for England shows. A bout of hepatitis laid him low in 1965, while missing out on England's 1966 World Cup glory – he was replaced by Geoff Hurst – was a further blow. Greaves later fell into alcoholism, and his subsequent battle back to become a much-loved TV personality is an inspiration to others.

Ryan Giggs

Born: 29 November 1973, Cardiff, Wales

Club: Manchester United (England)

Major honour: League Cup 1999

To date, Wales' youngest full cap, Ryan Giggs, is one of the most exceptional talents UK football has seen. From the moment of his explosive arrival on the scene – scoring the only goal of the Manchester 'derby' at Old Trafford in May 1991 – it was obvious that he was someone special. By the age of 20, he had already won a fistful of medals and honours, including the English League/Cup double in 1993–4 and 1995–6. Tremendous skill on the ball, exceptional pace and power, and an eye for the goal all go to make him a formidable foe.

Above: Ryan Giggs, in action for Wales.

Opposite A young Paul Gascoigne during his time with North London's Tottenham Hotspur.

Right: Another great Tottenham player, Jimmy Greaves.

A-Z OF PLAYERS

Ruud Gullit

Born: 1 September 1962, Surinam

Clubs: Haarlem (Holland), Feyenoord (Holland), PSV Eindhoven (Holland), AC Milan (Italy), Sampdoria (Italy), AC Milan (Italy), Sampdoria (Italy), Chelsea (England)

Major honours: European Footballer of the Year 1987; World Footballer of the Year 1987, 1989; European Championship 1988; European Cup 1989, 1990; European Supercup 1990; World Club Championship 1990

Although he will go down in record books as the winner of a string of domestic and European trophies, Gullit will also be remembered for his intelligent and graceful insight into the game. Whether playing at sweeper or as attacking mid-fielder, he could see angles and make passes for which no one else had the vision. After several years with AC Milan and Sampdoria, he moved to Chelsea where, after the departure of Glenn Hoddle, he proved a shrewd coach before being dismissed in 1998. He moved to Newcastle, taking them to the FA Cup final, but was later replaced by Bobby Robson.

Gheorghe Hagi

Born: 5 February 1965, Sacele, Romania

Clubs: FC Constanta (Romania), Sportul Studentesc (Romania), Steau Bucharest (Romania), Real Madrid (Spain), Brescia (Italy), Barcelona (Spain), Galatasaray (Turkey)

Major honour: none

Glittering individual skills and a devastating turn of pace have made Gheorghe Hagi a big favourite with the fans at every club he has played for. He appeared for Romania's youth team at 15, was a Top Division player at 17 and a full international a year later. After finishing as the League's leading scorer two years running (1985–6), he was forcibly transferred to the 'state' club, Steaua Bucharest, at the demand of the Romanian dictator Nicolai Ceaucescu. A star performance in the 1990 World Cup tournament earned him a £2M move to Real Madrid.

Glenn Hoddle

Born: 27 October 1957, Hayes, England

Clubs: Tottenham Hotspur (England), Monaco (France), Chelsea (England), Swindon Town (England), Chelsea (England)

Major honour: none

A central mid-fielder with awesome ball-skills and a penchant for spectacular long-range goals,

David Ginola

This classy, flamboyant midfielder with sublime skills and breath-taking long-range shooting moved from Newcastle to Tottenham Hotspur in 1997, and single-handedly saved the club from relegation. He won a personal double in 1999, taking the PFA and the Football Writers' Association Player of the Year titles.

Hoddle proved an enigma to most England managers: they couldn't decide whether to leave him out or build the team around him. After more than a decade of turning on the style for Tottenham Hotspur, during which time he won two FA Cups, he took his talents to France, where he won a new legion of admirers. On returning to England, he launched a coaching career with Swindon. After a promising spell managing Chelsea, he became England boss in June 1996. He was sacked in 1999 for indiscretions.

Opposite: A Dutch international, Gullit capped a remarkably successful career with a début at Chelsea as manager.

Right: England's goal-scoring hero Geoff Hurst.

Below: The England manager for France 98, Glenn Hoddle had awesome ball skills and a shrewd tactical mind.

Geoff Hurst

Born: 8 December 1941, Ashton-under-Lyne, England

Clubs: West Ham United (England), Stoke City (England), West Bromwich Albion (England)

Major honours: European Cup Winners' Cup 1965; World Cup 1966

Strong and deceptively quick for a big man, Hurst seemed to save himself for the big occasion. If he had achieved nothing else in his playing career, his Wembley hat-trick in the 1966 World Cup Final earned him his place in English football's hall of fame. Hurst would never have played in that match if it hadn't been for an injury to Jimmy Greaves – but he did, and the rest is history.

Above: Jairzinho (right) playing for Brazil.

Pat Jennings

Born: 12 June 1945, Newry, Northern Ireland

Clubs: Newry Town (Northern Ireland), Watford (England), Tottenham Hotspur (England), Arsenal (England)

Major honour: UEFA Cup 1972

The softly-spoken Jennings was a giant of the world game, and one of the all-time great goal-keepers. A veteran of over 1000 first-class matches – including four FA Cup Finals – he played his record 119th international game for Northern Ireland (against Brazil) in the 1986 World Cup on his 41st birthday. He was twice voted England's Footballer of the Year, in 1973 and 1976. Joined Northern Ireland coaching staff in 1988.

Kevin Keegan

Born: 14 February 1951, Doncaster, England

Clubs: Scunthorpe United (England), Liverpool (England), Hamburg (Germany), Southampton (England), Newcastle United (England)

Major honours: UEFA Cup 1973, 1976; European Cup 1977; European Footballer of the Year 1978, 1979

What he lacked in natural talent, Kevin Keegan more than made up for in sheer hard work and will to win. The player who was told that he was 'too small to make it' as a professional footballer went on to captain England and win every club honour in the game – including twice being voted European Footballer of the Year. Keegan became manager of Newcastle United in 1992, managed to avoid relegation that season and finished second in the Premiership in 1996. After a rest he returned to successfully manage Fulham. He had a brief spell with England, and is now with Manchester City.

Jairzinho

Born: 25 December 1944, Caxias, Brazil

Clubs: Botafogo (Brazil), Marseille (France), Cruzeiro (Brazil), Portuguesa (Venezuela)

Major honours: World Cup 1970; South American Club Cup 1976

Jair Ventura Filho was the man who really shone in Brazil's awesome 1970 World Cup-winning side. With a goal in every round of the tournament – a record – his cannonball shot and electric turn of pace made mincemeat of the best defences. He had a brief spell in Europe with Marseille and went on to win over 80 caps for his country, also appearing in the 1974 finals. A professional at 15, he was in the 1966 finals with schoolboy hero Garrincha. He scored the crucial goal in Cruzeiro's 1976 Copa America win over River Plate.

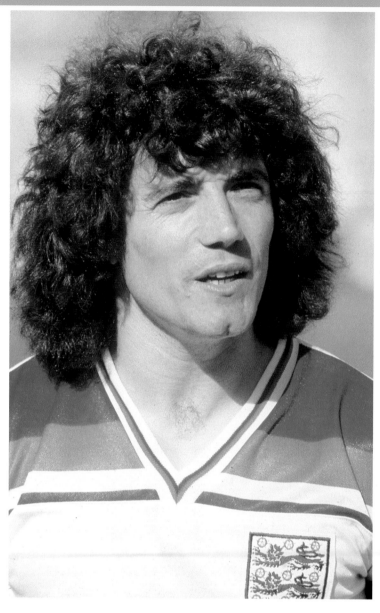

Left: Hard work and self-belief characterized both Kevin Keegan's playing style and his approach to management.

Jurgen Klinsmann

Born: 30 July 1964, Gîppingen, West Germany

Clubs: Stuttgarter Kickers (West Germany), VfB Stuttgart (West Germany), Internazionale (Italy), Monaco (France), Tottenham Hotspur (England), Bayern Munich (Germany), Tottenham Hotspur (England)

Major honours: World Cup 1990; UEFA Cup 1991, 1996

M ore than any other player, Klinsmann broke down the barriers of insularity that had surrounded English football since time immemorial. That he was a world-class player was self-evident, but he won over sceptical English supporters with his grace, intelligence and humour after signing for

Below: Jurgen Klinsmann showing his skill while playing for Germany.

Mario Kempes

Born: 15 July 1952, Cordoba, Argentina

Clubs: Instituto Cordoba (Argentina), Rosario Central (Argentina), Valencia (Spain), River Plate (Argentina), Hercules (Spain), Vienna (Austria), Austria Salzburg (Austria), Fernandez Vial (Chile)

Major honour: World Cup 1978

D espite playing in the 1974 World Cup in Germany, it was after transferring to the Spanish club Valencia that Mario Kempes really made his name. He finished his first two seasons as the Spanish League's leading goal-scorer and then became a household name around the world by scoring twice for Argentina during the 1978 World Cup Final. He was the only Europe-based player to earn selection by Cesar Menotti for that World Cup squad. He also played in 1982, making 18 World Cup Finals appearances in all. During his career, Kempes won 51 Argentine caps. Interestingly, he had been rejected by Boca Juniors as a boy. He trialled for Tottenham Hotspur in 1984 and later, bizarrely, managed Lusbijna of Albania before being forced to flee by the civil war.

Tottenham Hotspur in the wake of the 1994 World Cup. The fact that he spoke four languages fluently, contributed to Greenpeace and saw life outside the game as equally important did much to shatter the illusion that modern footballers are self-obsessed and ignorant. The only criticism that can be made of Klinsmann's first stay in England was its brevity.

Sandor Kocsis

Born: 30 September 1929, Hungary

Clubs: Ferencvaros (Hungary), Honved (Hungary), Young Fellows (Switzerland), Barcelona (Spain)

Major honour: Fairs Cup 1960

Top scorer in the 1954 World Cup, with 11 goals, Kocsis was nicknamed 'The Man with the Golden Head' thanks to his aerial ability. He scored a staggering 75 goals in 68 games for Hungary, and formed a devastating partnership with Ferenc Puskas for the Magyars. Following the crushing of the 1956 Revolution, Kocsis decided to stay abroad; he enjoyed further success at Barcelona.

Above: Grzegorz Lato, waiting to play at the 1974 World Cup Finals.

Ronald Koeman

Born: 21 March 1963, Zaandam, Holland

Clubs: Groningen (Holland), PSV Eindhoven (Holland), Barcelona (Spain), Feyenoord (Holland)

Major honours: European Cup 1988, 1992; European Championship 1988

At his best as a sweeper, with his good football brain and his ability to make laser-like long-distance passes and shots, Koeman was an outstanding performer for club and country. He scored one of the goals that ultimately was to deny England a place in the 1994 World Cup Finals. His brother Erwin was also a Dutch international.

Grzegorz Lato

Born: 8 April 1950, Poland

Clubs: Stal Mielec (Poland), Lokeren (Belgium), Atlante (Mexico)

Major honour: Olympic Gold 1972

Grzegorz Lato was top scorer in, and the inspiration behind, Poland's impressive showing in the 1974 World Cup Finals. The balding winger made 104 appearances for his country, scoring 45 goals in the process, and he was a regular member of the national side for over 13 years. After playing in the 1978 World Cup, he was allowed to leave the country and move to the Belgian club Lokeren.

Michael Laudrup

Born: 15 June 1964, Vienna, Austria

Clubs: Brondby (Denmark), Lazio (Italy), Juventus (Italy), Barcelona (Spain), Real Madrid (Spain), Ajax (Holland)

Major honours: World Club Cup 1985; European Cup Winners' Cup 1989; European Cup 1992

Elder brother of Brian, and son of ex-Denmark international Finn, Laudrup was the inspiration for a generation of Danish players. As a teenage sensation, he attracted interest from all Europe's top clubs, eventually choosing Juventus – who immediately sent him to Lazio on loan. A gifted striker, he fell out with national boss Richard Moller Nielsen and so missed Denmark's triumph in the 1992 European Championship.

Denis Law

Born: 22 February 1940, Aberdeen, Scotland

Clubs: Huddersfield (England), Manchester City (England), Torino (Italy), Manchester United (England), Manchester City (England)

Major honour: European Footballer of the Year 1964

A knee injury denied Law the possibility of his greatest triumph, forcing him to sit out of Manchester United's 1968 European Cup victory. Of only medium height and slim build, he became one of the most prolific goal-scorers of all time thanks to his superb athleticism and his iron will to win. A cavalier and entertainer, he was known as 'The King' to the fans, who adored him. He won two League titles and the 1963 FA Cup with United, as well as scoring 30 goals in a total of 55 games played for Scotland.

Tommy Lawton

Born: 6 October 1919, Bolton, England

Clubs: Burnley (England), Everton (England), Chelsea (England), Notts County (England), Brentford (England), Arsenal (England)

Major honour: none

Despite the fact that World War II robbed him of seven years of a glorious career, Lawton remains a hero of the game. His record says it all: a hat-trick on his League début at 16, the First Division's top scorer two seasons in a row, a League title at 19, 23 goals in 22 internationals for England, and 231

goals in 390 League games. One of the first players to realize his own value, Tommy Lawton moved clubs frequently. He added thousands to the gate of any match in which he played. He died in 1997.

Gary Lineker

Born: 30 November 1960, Leicester, England

Clubs: Leicester City (England), Everton (England), Barcelona (Spain), Tottenham Hotspur (England), Nagoya Grampus Eight (Japan)

Major honour: European Cup Winners' Cup 1989

Lineker was England's second highest goal-scorer of all time and is now a successful broadcaster; a missed penalty against Brazil left him one goal short of Bobby Charlton's national record

Above: Gary Lineker, one of England's most prolific goal-scorers.

(49). He burst into the limelight during the 1986 World Cup in Mexico, when six goals made him the tournament's top scorer and earned him a big-money move to Barcelona. No other player has headed the list of First Division scorers at three different clubs (Leicester, Everton and Tottenham Hotspur); no Englishman has surpassed his ten goals in World Cup Finals; and precious few have gone through a 16-year career at the peak of the game without collecting a single booking. He was twice voted Footballer of the Year (1986, 1992) and was an FA Cup winner in 1991.

Top scorer in the 1954 World Cup, Kocsis was nicknamed 'The Man with the Golden Head' thanks to his aerial ability.

Nat Lofthouse

Born: 27 August 1925, Bolton, England

Club: Bolton Wanderers (England)

Major honour: none

The archetypal 'old-fashioned' English centre-forward, Lofthouse was nicknamed the 'Lion of Vienna' after a typically courageous display for England in Austria in 1952. A battering-ram striker, he possessed a vicious shot from either foot and was peerless in the air. A one-club man, he won the FA Cup in 1958 and scored 30 times for England in 33 internationals. He is now President of Bolton Wanderers.

A colossus as captain of club and country, McGrain enjoyed a 20-year reign at the very top of Scottish football.

Above: Bolton hero Nat Lofthouse.

Left: Ally McCoist in action against Germany.

Ally McCoist

Born: 24 September 1962, Bellshill, Scotland

Clubs: St. Johnstone (Scotland), Sunderland (England), Glasgow Rangers, Kilmarnock (Scotland)

Major honour: European Golden Boot 1993

McCoist is a powerful and prolific striker. After leaving his first club, St Johnstone, for a club record £400,000 in 1981, he scored only eight goals in almost two seasons with Sunderland. Then he returned to his native Scotland to enjoy more than a decade of unprecedented success with Glasgow Rangers, winning countless trophies with them and scoring crucial goals for Scotland.

Danny McGrain

Born: 1 May 1950, Glasgow, Scotland

Club: Glasgow Celtic (Scotland)

Major honour: none

A colossus as captain of club and country, McGrain enjoyed a 20-year reign at the very top of Scottish football with all-conquering Celtic; injury robbed him of the chance to appear during the 1978 World Cup Finals, and he was sadly missed. An exceptional and versatile footballer – as well as a powerful and imposing figure – McGrain was one of the Celtic 'Quality Street Kids' of the late 1960s, growing up alongside the likes of Kenny Dalglish and Lou Macari. He suffered from diabetes throughout his career.

Dave Mackay

Born: 14 November 1934, Edinburgh, Scotland

Clubs: Heart of Midlothian (Scotland), Tottenham Hotspur (England), Derby (England), Swindon Town (England)

Major honour: none

A combative and inspirational leader on the field and off, Dave Mackay won a full set of Scottish medals with Hearts before he moved south to join Tottenham Hotspur in March 1959. He led them to their 1961 League/Cup double and to the 1962 FA Cup before, in 1963, suffering two broken legs. Always a battler, he returned to captain the club to the 1967 FA Cup before moving on to Derby; he led the Rams to the Division Two title and (with Tony Book) was voted joint Footballer of the Year in 1969. Later he enjoyed a successful career as a coach, the high point being to guide Derby to victory in the League Championship in 1975.

Below: Dave Mackay with the FA Cup in 1967.

Billy McNeill

Born: 2 March 1940, Scotland

Club: Glasgow Celtic (Scotland)

Major honour: European Cup 1967

With an impressive total of 22 medals to his name, Billy McNeill was captain of the most successful Celtic side of all time. Nicknamed 'Caesar' because of his imperious displays at the back and his buccaneering forward manoeuvres, he led the club to an unprecedented 'grand-slam' in 1967: with McNeill at the helm of Jock Stein's ship, 'The Bhoys' won everything they entered that year – the Scottish League, Scottish Football Association Cup, Scottish League Cup and, gloriously, the European Cup. Later he was employed as manager at Celtic (twice), Aston Villa and Manchester City, but without achieving any conspicuous success.

Josef 'Sepp' Maier

Born: 28 February 1944, West Germany

Clubs: TSV Haar (West Germany), Bayern Munich (West Germany)

Major honours: European Championship 1972; European Cup 1974, 1975, 1976; World Cup 1974; World Club Cup 1976

Famed as much for his habitual long shorts as for his tremendous goalkeeping skills, Sepp Maier was a frustrated tennis player who discovered that he was better at saving balls than serving them. He enjoyed a 19-year career with Bayern Munich, during which time he played in just under 500 League matches, 422 of them consecutively. Also noted for the large gloves that he wore, Maier was a member of West Germany's squad for four World Cups, from 1966 to 1978. Later he opened a tennis school to indulge his first love.

Paolo Maldini

Born: 26 June 1968, Milan, Italy

Clubs: AC Milan (Italy)

Major honours: European Cup 1989, 1990

The son of the former Italy manager, Cesare Maldini – himself an outstanding player with AC Milan in the 1960s – Paolo is widely regarded as one of the finest defenders in the world, and is a natural successor to the legendary Franco Baresi in the sweeper's role for AC Milan and Italy. The place of this cool, calm, cultured and quick player in the national side appears sacrosanct.

Diego Maradona

Born: 30 October 1960, Buenos Aires, Argentina

Clubs: Argentinos Juniors (Argentina), Boca Juniors (Argentina), Barcelona (Spain), Napoli (Italy), Sevilla (Spain), Newell's Old Boys (Argentina), Boca Juniors (Argentina), Deportivo Mandiyu (Argentina)

Major honours: World Cup 1986; World Footballer of the Year 1986; UEFA Cup 1988

Few players have provoked as many headlines as Maradona, the finest player of his generation. His talent lifted him above all others on the field, but off it he nearly ruined himself – he has had a succession of problems with drink, drugs and fire-arms. While his temperament may have been suspect, the stocky forward's ability to turn a game with a flash of unbelievable brilliance is beyond question. Born one of eight children to an impoverished family, in a classic 'rags to riches' story, he was playing for Argentinos Juniors before he was 16, led Argentina through four World Cups, and won a host of honours at club level before drug abuse led to the withering away of an exceptional talent.

Stanley Matthews

Born: 1 February 1915, Hanley, England

Clubs: Stoke City (England), Blackpool (England), Stoke City (England)

Major honour: none

Perhaps the first true legend of the game, Matthews was known as the 'Wizard of the Dribble' throughout his long and illustrious career; although short on trophies, he won admirers all over the world. Twice named Footballer of the Year (1948, 1963) – the second award came when he was 48 years old! – he is best remembered for his part in the 1953 'Matthews Final', when he inspired Blackpool, 3–1 down with 20 minutes left, to a remarkable 4–3 victory over Bolton to take the FA Cup. Obsessed with physical fitness, he created history when he played his final professional game (for Stoke) aged 50 years and five days; moreover, he completed his 33-year career without a single booking. He was knighted in 1965.

Sandro Mazzola

Born: 7 November 1942, Italy

Club: Internazionale (Italy)

Major honours: European Cup 1964, 1965; European Championship 1968

Sandro Mazzola chose to play with Internazionale to avoid the shadow of his father Valentino, who had been Italy's and Torino's captain; Valentino had died in the 1949 Superga air crash when Sandro was six. The younger Mazzola played successfully as an inside-forward and a centre-forward. He appeared 70 times for Italy, despite being rivalled by Luigi Riva. He made his international début at the age of 20.

Lothar Matthaus

Born: 21 March 1961, Erlangen, West Germany

Clubs: Borussia Mönchengladbach (West Germany), Bayern Munich (West Germany), Internazionale (Italy), Bayern Munich (Germany)

Major honours: European Championship 1980; World Cup 1990; World Footballer of the Year 1990; European Footballer of the Year 1990; UEFA Cup 1991, 1996

Leader of, and inspiration to, the German national side since the early 1980s, Matthaus started as a powerhouse mid-fielder and later moved back to sweeper – and was outstanding in both positions. A glittering career, spent largely with two of Europe's leading clubs, has seen him pick up many honours, but nothing can have surpassed captaining West Germany to the 1990 World Cup, where he was voted Player of the Tournament. He made a record 25 Finals appearances over five tournaments, the last, in 1998, at 37 years old.

Opposite: Diego Maradona showing his class while playing for Argentina.

Left: Paolo Maldini, Italy's top defensive player.

Right: Sandro Mazzola in action for Italy.

Below: Lothar Matthaus, Germany's outstanding captain, who led his country's team to World Cup victory in 1990.

Few players have provoked as many headlines as Maradona, the finest player of his generation.

A-Z OF PLAYERS

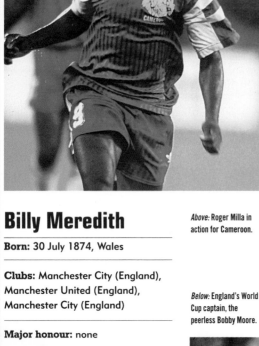

Billy Meredith

Born: 30 July 1874, Wales

Clubs: Manchester City (England), Manchester United (England), Manchester City (England)

Major honour: none

The 'Wizard of the Wing', as Billy Meredith was known, was one of the game's earliest major talents, and he was well aware of it: a former miner, he attempted to found a players' union. He was once banned for a year for being involved in a match-fixing scandal. Meredith was awarded 48 Welsh caps during his 25 years as a skillful right-winger.

Gunner Nordahl

The most successful of five footballing brothers, Nordahl was a prolific scorer in Sweden – he won four successive championships with Norrköping. He turned professional upon signing for AC Milan in 1948, thus denying himself the chance to play again for the amateur Swedish national side. Twice winner of the Italian Championship, and five times Serie A's top scorer, he scored 225 goals in 257 games.

Roger Milla

Born: 20 May 1952, Yaounde, Cameroon

Clubs: Leopard Douala (Cameroon), Tonnerre Yahounde (Cameroon), Valenciennes (France), Monaco (France), Bastia (France), St Étienne (France), Montpellier (France)

Major honours: African Footballer of the Year 1976, 1990

Having changed the spelling of his name from 'Miller' – he thought the new version sounded 'more African' – this shaven-headed striker shot to world fame with Cameroon during the 1990 World Cup, where his celebratory dances around the corner flag made a lasting impression. In 1982, he scored six goals in the qualifiers to lead Cameroon to the finals for the first time; in 1990, he netted four times to take the country to the quarter-finals. At 42, he became the oldest man ever to appear and score in the World Cup Finals, when he netted against Russia at USA 94.

Above: Roger Milla in action for Cameroon.

Below: England's World Cup captain, the peerless Bobby Moore.

Bobby Moore

Born: 17 April 1941, Barking, England

Clubs: West Ham United (England), Fulham (England), San Antonio Thunder (USA), Seattle Sounders (USA)

Major honours: European Cup Winners' Cup 1965; World Cup 1966

Arguably a better performer for country than for club, Moore remains the only man to have captained England to the World Cup. Blessed with good skill on the ball, and the ability to read the game and time a tackle to perfection, he was less strong in the air and short on pace – yet he was still a remarkable defender. Successive visits to Wembley brought him trophies of increasing importance: FA Cup (1964), European Cup Winners' Cup (1965) and ultimately World Cup (1966). His life after playing was less composed, with several ill-fated attempts at management and business. He died of cancer in 1993.

with tree-trunk thighs and a matchless speed of thought in the penalty area, Muller amassed a total of 628 goals in first-class football, including 365 for Bayern Munich during a 14-year career.

Alan Mullery

Born: 23 November 1941, London, England

Clubs: Fulham (England), Tottenham Hotspur (England), Fulham (England)

Major honour: UEFA Cup 1972

Mullery earned his place in history by being the first man to be sent off while playing for England. His moment of madness came in a European Championship match against Yugoslavia in Florence, on 5 June 1968. He was voted English Footballer of the Year in 1975, and later managed Brighton, Charlton, Crystal Palace, QPR and Barnet. He won a total of 35 England caps.

Michael Owen

Born: 14 December 1979, Chester, England

Clubs: Liverpool (England)

Major honours: PFA Young Player of the Year 1998; European Footballer of the Year 2001; FA Cup 2001; UEFA Cup 2001; Worthington Cup 2001, 2003

Michael Owen burst on to the international scene with 'that' goal against Argentina in World Cup 1998. It was no surprise; he had burst on to the Premiership stage as a 17-year-old in 1997, scoring on his debut against Wimbledon.

Famously he scored a hat-trick in England's 5-1 win in Munich in WC 2002 qualifying. He has been dogged by hamstring injuries recently but when fit is a player feared by every defender all over the world.

Stan Mortensen

Born: 26 May 1921, South Shields, England

Clubs: Blackpool (England), Hull (England), Southport (England)

Major honour: none

Known variously as the 'Blackpool Bomber' and the 'Electric Eel', Mortensen was the possessor of electric acceleration and a powerful shot, which earned him 23 goals in 25 appearances for England. He scored four times on his international début, a 10–0 win in Portugal, and also achieved the first FA Cup Final hat-trick, in the so-called 'Matthews Final' of 1953.

Gerd Muller

Born: 3 November 1945, Germany

Clubs: TSV Nordingen (West Germany), Bayern Munich (West Germany)

Major honours: European Cup Winners' Cup 1967; European Footballer of the Year 1970; European Championship 1972; World Cup 1974; European Cup 1974, 1975, 1976

With a staggering 68 goals in 62 games for West Germany during the 1970s, including the winner in the 1974 World Cup Final, 'Der Bomber' must go down as the greatest goal-scorer of the modern era. A stocky and powerful striker

Above: Alan Mullery in action for Spurs.

Emmanuel Petit

A distinctive figure on and off the field, Petit became an integral part of the French team, winning the World Cup in 1998 and the European Championship in 2000. He has played at Monaco, Arsenal, Barcelona and Chelsea.

Opposite:
Pelé, Brazil's greatest footballer.

Below: Daniel Passarella, who led Argentina to World Cup glory in 1978.

Ernst Ocwirk

Born: 7 March 1926, Austria

Clubs: FK Austria (Austria), Sampdoria (Italy), FK Austria (Austria)

Major honour: none

Strong and technically adept, the creative Ernst Ocwirk was the guiding force behind the powerful Austrian sides of the 1940s. Having made his name in his homeland, he moved to Sampdoria, spending five years there before returning to FK Austria – a team that he later coached to successive League titles in 1969 and 1970.

Daniel Passarella

Born: 25 May 1953, Argentina

Clubs: Sarmiento (Argentina), River Plate (Argentina), Fiorentina (Italy), Internazionale (Italy)

Major honour: World Cup 1978

Argentina's 1978 World Cup-winning captain, the powerful Daniel Passarella was an inspiration to his team. A thoughtful and creative central defender or left-back, he was often to be found stepping up into midfield to provide opportunities for the likes of Kempes and Ardiles, while he also possessed a fierce shot and power in the air. He became coach to his national side, then to Uruguay until he resigned in February 2001.

Pelé

Born: 21 October 1940, Tràs Coracoes, Brazil

Clubs: Noroeste (Brazil), Santos (Brazil), New York Cosmos (USA)

Major honours: World Cup 1958, 1970; World Club Cup 1962, 1963; FIFA's Gold Medal for Services to the Game 1982

Regarded by many as the ultimate player, Pelé had a blend of power, technique and flair that made him almost impossible to pin down. An outstanding prospect even as a child, he was soon transferred from Noroeste – his local side – to Santos, and was a Brazilian international by the age of 16. A year later, he had picked up his first World Cup Winners' medal, scoring a hat-trick in the semi-final against France, and then grabbing two more goals as the

A-Z OF PLAYERS

A-Z OF PLAYERS

Silvio Piola

Born: 29 September 1913, Italy

Clubs: Pro Vercelli (Italy), Lazio (Italy), Torino (Italy), Juventus (Italy), Novara (Italy)

Major honour: World Cup 1938

This aggressive and hard-working centre-forward was a great athlete, and surely would have boasted an even better record than his remarkable 30 goals in 24 games for Italy but for the fact that World War II disrupted his career. Later he admitted that his goal for Italy in their 2–2 draw with England in Milan in 1939 had been punched into the net.

Michel Platini

Born: 21 June 1955, Joeuf, France

Clubs: Nancy (France), Saint Étienne (France), Juventus (Italy)

Major honours: European Championship 1984; European Cup Winners' Cup 1984; European Cup 1985; European Footballer of the Year 1983, 1984, 1985; World Footballer of the Year 1985

France's brightest star and the man who put the country on the footballing map in the 1980s, Michel Platini was peerless as a creative mid-fielder: his record of 68 goals in 147 League games for Juventus is a remarkable total for a mid-fielder in Italy. Only the second player (after Johan Cruyff) to win three European Footballer of the Year awards, he captained France to the 1982 World Cup semi-finals.

Having scored the penalty winner for Juventus in the disastrous Heysel final of the European Cup in 1985, Platini was appointed to the position of French national coach in 1987, a post that he relinquished after the 1992 European Championship. He also acted as co-organizer of the 1998 France World Cup.

hosts, Sweden, were overrun in the final. Injury denied Pelé the chance of making the same dramatic impact at the 1962 World Cup; although he played his part in the early stages, jealous defenders resorted to stopping the great Brazilian any way they could. Things came to a head in England in 1966, when he was the victim

Above: Michel Platini in action for France.

Right: Ferenc Puskas, the captain of the 'Magical Magyars'.

of brutal fouls by players from Bulgaria and Portugal, and Pelé vowed never again to play in the World Cup. Happily, he changed his mind, and in the 1970 tournament he was magnificent as Brazil won again, allowing the great Pelé to announce his retirement from the international scene on a high. He scored more than 1000 goals.

Ferenc Puskas

Born: 2 April 1927, Budapest, Hungary

Clubs: Kispest (Hungary), Honved (Hungary), Real Madrid (Spain)

Major honours: Olympic Gold 1952; European Cup 1959, 1960

Captain of the great Hungarian side that lost just once between 1950 and 1956 – the 1954 World Cup Final was, ironically, their sole defeat – the 'Galloping Major' scored 83 goals in 84 games for his country. Surely it would have been even more but for the 1956 revolution, which saw him flee first to Austria and then to Spain, for whom he made four appearances. Two matches sum up the brilliance of this 'Magical Magyar'. He was the captain of the Hungarian side that defeated England 6–3 at Wembley in 1953, and he also scored four goals in Real Madrid's extraordinary 7–3 demolition of Eintracht Frankfurt in the 1960 European Cup Final. Weak in the air and totally left-footed, nevertheless Puskas scored more international goals than any other player except Pelé.

Antonio Rattin

Born: 16 May 1937, Tigre, Argentina

Club: Boca Juniors (Argentina)

Major honour: none

An inspirational mid-fielder for club and country throughout the 1950s and 1960s, Rattin is, sadly, best remembered for one unfortunate incident. In the 1966 World Cup, he refused to accept his dismissal for foul play during the game against England; his protests almost prompted a mass walk-off by his team-mates. Alf Ramsey famously described the Argentinians as 'animals' after the game, but Rattin always insisted he was a victim of circumstance.

A-Z OF PLAYERS

Frank Rijkaard

Born: 30 September 1962, Amsterdam, Holland

Clubs: Ajax (Holland), Sporting Lisbon (Portugal), Real Zaragoza (Spain), AC Milan (Italy), Ajax (Holland)

Major honours: European Cup Winners' Cup 1987; European Championship 1988; European Cup 1989, 1990; European Supercup 1989, 1990; World Club Cup 1989, 1990

Tall, powerful and quick, Rijkaard walked out on Ajax after a bust-up with coach Johan Cruyff in September 1987. He went on to become an automatic choice for AC Milan during their total domination of the game in the late 1980s. Rijkaard was a versatile player who could perform in defence, mid-field or up front with equal effect; he formed part of a deadly Dutch triumvirate with Ruud Gullit and Marco van Basten.

Luigi Riva

Born: 7 November 1944, Leggiuno, Italy

Club: Cagliari (Italy)

Major honour: European Championship 1968

Orphaned in early childhood, Luigi 'Gigi' Riva was never comfortable in the spotlight that his on-field achievements drew to him. He was a slow starter and took several years to reach Serie A, eventually making the top flight when he helped Cagliari to gain promotion in the 1963–4 season; the club followed up this achievement by winning the League in 1969–70. It has been the Sardinian club's only such success. Similarly, Riva's international career took time to build, but eventually he gained 35 goals in 42 games for Italy. Two broken legs prematurely terminated the career of this powerful-shooting left-winger or central striker.

Thomas Ravelli

Born: 13 August 1959, Vimmerby, Sweden

Clubs: Oster Vaxjo (Sweden), IFK Gothenburg (Sweden), Tampa Bay Mutiny (USA)

Major honour: none

Sweden's record cap-holder, the most-capped goalkeeper with more than 140 caps, Thomas Ravelli spent eight years with IFK Gothenburg, winning six League Championships and one Swedish Cup. He moved to the USA at the end of the 1997 season.

Above: Thomas Ravelli keeping goal for Sweden in the 1994 World Cup.

More than any other Brazilian player, Rivelino was admired for his prodigious long-range shot and his 'banana-bending' of free-kicks.

Right: Luigi 'Gigi' Riva scored 35 goals in 42 games for Italy.

Left: Italy's Gianni Rivera.

Bryan Robson

Born: 11 January 1957, Chester-Le-Street, England

Clubs: West Bromwich Albion (England), Manchester United (England), Middlesbrough (England)

Major honour: European Cup-Winners' Cup 1991

Below: Bryan Robson in action for Manchester Utd.

England's so-called 'Captain Marvel', and the nation's sole world-class outfield player during the side's barren years in the early 1980s, Robson was a workaholic mid-fielder who led by shining example. His return of 26 goals – often crucial – in 90 internationals shows his immense value. He captained his country in 65 successive internationals and, but for a nightmare collection of injuries (during his career, Robson suffered some 20 breaks and dislocations), he would have comfortably exceeded a century of appearances. Robson became the player manager of Middlesbrough. He signed Juninho and Fabrizio Ravanelli, and inspired them to their first FA Cup Final in 1997, before making way for Terry Venables.

Roberto Rivelino

Born: 1 January 1946, São Paulo, Brazil

Clubs: Corinthians (Brazil), Fluminense (Brazil)

Major honour: World Cup 1970

Perhaps more than any other Brazilian player, Roberto Rivelino was admired for his prodigious long-range shot and his 'banana-bending' of free-kicks. A star turn in Brazil's dazzling 1970 World Cup-winning side, he was also guilty of displaying some flamboyant histrionics after tackles on him, often completing a series of theatrical rolls to finish up inside the penalty area. He has been credited with scoring the fastest-ever goal, which was unofficially recorded as having taken three seconds. This was scored directly from the kick-off pass while the opposition goalkeeper was still completing his pre-match prayers.

Gianni Rivera

Born: 18 August 1943, Allessandria, Italy

Clubs: Alessandria (Italy), AC Milan (Italy)

Major honours: European Cup 1963, 1969; European Cup Winners' Cup 1968; World Club Cup 1969; European Footballer of the Year 1969

A graceful inside-forward, Gianni Rivera was a sublime passer of the ball, and he also packed a shot that was surprisingly powerful for one so slight. He made his international début in 1962, and thereafter a succession of managers built the Italian team around him. He played in three World Cups with Italy. On retiring, he briefly took on the role of president of AC Milan before becoming a politician.

A-Z OF PLAYERS

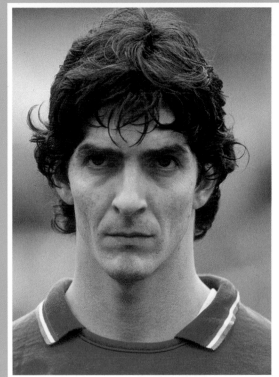

Paolo Rossi

Born: 23 September 1956, Prato, Italy

Clubs: Prato (Italy), Juventus (Italy), Como (Italy), Lanerossi (Italy), Vicenza (Italy), Perugia (Italy), Juventus (Italy), AC Milan (Italy)

Major honours: World Cup 1982; European Footballer of the Year 1982; World Footballer of the Year 1982

The soccer world was shocked when Rossi, having given a star performance during the 1978 World Cup, was banned in 1980 for four years because of a betting scandal. However, that ban was cancelled on 29 April 1982, and he responded by scoring six goals in Italy's last three games of that summer's World Cup to help his side take the trophy home. Small, quick and clever, he had been released by Juventus as a youngster because of knee trouble. His injuries did finally catch up with him and he had to retire in 1985.

A fearsome combination of power, pace and skill makes Ronaldo the most potent striker in the world game. . . . He has been described as the 'new Pelé'.

Ronaldo

Born: 22 September 1976, Rio de Janeiro, Brazil

Clubs: São Cristóvão (Brazil), Cruzeiro (Brazil), PSV Eindhoven (Holland), Barcelona (Spain), Internazionale (Italy), Real Madrid (Spain)

Major honours: European Cup Winners' Cup 1997; World Footballer of the Year 1997; World Cup 2002

Now with Real Madrid; Ronaldo created a storm in 1997 when he transferred from Barcelona to Internazionale. A fearsome combination of power, pace and skill marks him out as currently the most potent striker in the world game. A protege of former England boss Bobby Robson, he won the Dutch Cup with PSV Eindhoven before moving on to Spain for a fee of £13M. Japan and Korea was Ronaldo's third World Cup – he did not play in 1994, suffered illness prior to a dismal display in the 1998 Final, but 2002 was his renaissance. Once again he lead the line for Brazil with pace, skill and aggression.

Above: Italian striker Paulo Rossi.

Right: The renowned Brazilian star, Ronaldo.

Opposite top: Ian Rush at his prime when playing for Liverpool.

Opposite bottom: Star for Germany and Inter, Karl-Heinz Rummenigge.

Ian Rush

Born: 20 October 1961, St Asaph, Wales

Clubs: Chester City (England), Liverpool (England), Juventus (Italy), Liverpool (England), Leeds United (England), Newcastle United (England), Sheffield United (England)

Major honour: European Cup 1984

The seventh of seven sons, Ian Rush was the Welsh wizard whose ruthless streak in front of goal provided the driving force behind the mighty Liverpool machine of the late 1970s and early 1980s. His partnership with Kenny Dalglish was the cornerstone of the all-conquering Liverpool side. For nearly eight complete seasons, every time Rush scored, Liverpool failed to lose – and he scored often. His mutual love affair with Anfield was interrupted briefly in 1987, but after spending an unhappy season in Italy with Juventus, the hero returned home to guide the Reds to further glories.

Karl-Heinz Rummenigge

Born: 25 September 1955, West Germany

Clubs: Lippstadt (West Germany), Bayern Munich (West Germany), Internazionale (Italy), Servette (Switzerland)

Major honours: European Cup 1976; World Club Cup 1976; European Footballer of the Year 1980, 1981

Groomed as a right-winger by the small-town club Lippstadt, Rummenigge was transferred to Bayern for just £4,500 in June 1974. He went on to become a stalwart central striker for club and country, although injuries reduced his swashbuckling effectiveness after the early 1980s.

Hugo Sanchez

Born: 11 June 1958, Mexico

Clubs: UNAM (Mexico), Atletico Madrid (Spain), Real Madrid (Spain), America (Mexico), Rayo Vallecano (Spain)

Major honour: none

Renowned for performing a celebratory somersault following each and every goal he scored – a manoeuvre that was taught to him by his gymnast sister – Hugo Sanchez retained the position of top scorer in Spain for five successive seasons during the late 1980s and early 1990s, firmly cementing his place as one of the game's great strikers. Only Telmo Zarras of Bilbao has scored more than his 230-plus goals in Spain's top division. However, despite his undoubted talent and long career, Hugo Sanchez managed to participate in a total of only 50 matches for his native Mexico, thanks mainly to ongoing disputes with that country's FA.

Djalma Santos

Born: 27 February 1929, Brazil

Clubs: Portuguesa (Brazil), Palmeiras (Brazil), Atletico Curitaba (Brazil)

Major honours: World Cup 1958, 1962

The first Brazilian footballer to reach an official century of caps, defender Djalma Santos helped his nation to achieve back-to-back World Cup victories in 1958 and 1962. A thoughtful player who possessed excellent positional sense, he played for Brazil again in the 1966 tournament held in England, but by then his best years were already behind him.

Santos was one of the players who turned out for Rest of the World against England in the FA Centenary match of 1963.

Right: Hugo Sanchez, a Mexican player of such brilliance that it was a wonder he did not represent his native country more often.

Juan Schiaffino

Born: 28 July 1925, Montevideo, Uruguay

Clubs: Penarol (Uruguay), AC Milan (Italy), Roma (Italy)

Major honour: World Cup 1950

A vital member of the Uruguayan squad in the 1950 and 1954 World Cups, Schiaffino went on to represent Italy in the 1958 qualifiers. Nicknamed 'Pepe', initially he longed to play centre-forward, but was switched to inside-left by Penarol, where his range of passing and powerful left-foot shot made him a formidable opponent. He cost AC Milan a then record £72,000 when he transferred to Italy in 1954.

Salvatore Schillaci

Below: Salvatore Schillaci, a star of Italia 90.

Born: 1 December 1964, Palermo, Italy

Clubs: Messina (Italy), Juventus (Italy), Inter (Italy), Jubilo Iwata (Japan)

Major honour: none

The final player to be selected for Italy's 1990 World Cup squad, 'Toto' Schillaci shot into public recognition during that tournament. He first came off the bench to score against Austria, and his trademark wide-eyed celebrations were seen a further five times: he became the competition's top scorer. Dark rumours concerning Mafia involvement in his selection dogged him, but he was the 'Godfather of Goals' at Italia 90.

Peter Schmeichel

Born: 18 November 1963, Gladsaxe, Denmark

Clubs: Brondby (Denmark), Manchester Utd (England), Sporting Lisbon (Portugal), Aston Villa and Manchester City (England)

Major honours: European Supercup 1991; European Championship 1992; League Cup 1999; European Cup Winner 1999

Arguably the man who most inspired Manchester United to their domination of the English game. Schmeichel's £550,000 transfer from Brondby in 1991 must be one of soccer's all-time bargains. He is a superb shot-stopper, with excellent reflexes and total command of his penalty area. His final year at Utd (1999) was crowned by a host of home and international successes.

Enzo Scifo

Born: 19 February 1966, La Louviere, Belgium

Clubs: Anderlecht (Belgium), Internazionale (Italy), Bordeaux (France), Auxerre (France), Torino (Italy), Monaco (France), Anderlecht (Belgium)

Major honour: none

The son of Italian parents living in Belgium, Scifo decided to take up Belgian citizenship just in time to allow him to take part in the 1984 European Championship in France. A cultured mid-fielder with delightful passing skills and an eye for the goal, he helped Torino to the 1992 UEFA Cup Final before Torino's accountants sold him to Monaco to help balance their books.

Schmeichel is a superb shot-stopper with excellent reflexes and total command of his penalty area.

Above Top goalkeeper Peter Schmeichel, whose presence in club and national sides was an inspiration for his team-mates.

Uwe Seeler

Born: 5 November 1936, Hamburg, West Germany

Club: Hamburg (West Germany)

Major honour: none

A one-club man throughout his long and distinguished career, centre-forward Seeler was such an integral part of the West German national side that fans used his first name as their chant. He and Pelé are the only men to have scored at four World Cups, Seeler's goals having come during 1958–70. His never-say-die attitude won him many admirers, but surprisingly little silverware.

Right: England's most-capped player, Peter Shilton.

Alan Shearer

Born: 13 August 1970, Newcastle, England

Clubs: Southampton (England), Blackburn (England), Newcastle United (England)

Major honour: none

Top scorer at Euro 96 and regarded as one of the world's best strikers, Shearer is a powerful and hard-working front-man whose direct approach to goal-scoring makes him extremely difficult to stop. A succession of career-threatening injuries has limited his appearances, but he still ranks alongside his country's greatest. A title-winner with Blackburn in 1995, his transfer to his home-town club Newcastle in July 1996 set a then world-record price of £15M. He has scored a goal on every senior début he has made – from a hat-trick as a 17-year-old for Southampton in a match against Arsenal to netting on his first England appearance, against France, in 1992. Badly injured in August 1997, he returned for club and country by February 1998. He retired from inter-national football after Euro 2000 to concen-trate on playing for Newcastle and was back to his best scoring a total of 25 goals (in the 2002–2003 season).

Below: Alan Shearer, former England captain and striker, a typical English centre forward.

Peter Shilton

Born: 18 September 1949, Leicester, England

Clubs: Leicester City (England), Stoke City (England), Nottingham Forest (England), Southampton (England), Derby County (England), Plymouth Argyle (England), Wimbledon (England), Bolton Wanderers (England), Coventry City (England), West Ham (England), Leyton Orient (England)

Major honours: European Cup 1979, 1980; European Supercup 1979

Blessed with remark-able self-belief and an unquenchable thirst for improvement, Shilton placed himself at the pinnacle of the goalkeeping profes-sion throughout his long career and is England's most capped player (125 caps). Legend has it that as a child he used to hang from the banisters while his mother stretched his legs. Still playing in his 48th year, Shilton was famed for his fitness and single-mindedness.

Graeme Souness

Born: 6 May 1953, Edinburgh, Scotland

Clubs: Tottenham Hotspur (England), Middlesbrough (England), Liverpool (England), Sampdoria (Italy), Glasgow Rangers (Scotland)

Major honours: European Cup 1978, 1981, 1984

Despite his 'hard-man' image, Souness was a tremendous passer of the ball; he enjoyed a glorious career with Liverpool and Glasgow Rangers, where he won everything the domestic games had to offer. Having walked out of Tottenham Hotspur as a teenager, he developed to become a world-class mid-fielder who controlled games with his expert passing and ferocious tackling. As a manager he was successful with Glasgow Rangers, winning a string of Scot-tish titles and cups in the late 1980s and early 1990s. Then he moved to Liverpool, suffered a heart attack, recovered to win the 1992 FA Cup, but was sacked. Later he managed Galatasaray, Southampton, Benfica and Blackburn Rovers.

Left: Graeme Souness in action for Liverpool.

Hristo Stoichkov

Born: 2 August 1966, Plovdiv, Bulgaria

Clubs: CSKA Sofia (Bulgaria), Barcelona (Spain), Parma (Italy), Barcelona (Spain), CSKA Sofia (Bulgaria)

Major honours: European Cup 1992; European Footballer of the Year 1994

An outstanding member of Bulgaria's national side, this supreme goal-scorer was handed a life ban following a controversial Bulgarian Cup Final match between CSKA and Levski-Spartak in 1985. Only six months later, Stoichkov was back in action for club and country. A big favourite of Johan Cruyff, he was snapped up by Barcelona for £2M in 1990. He helped the Bulgarians to the semi-final of the World Cup in 1994.

Below: Neville Southall, the Welsh international goalkeeper, while playing for Everton.

Neville Southall

Born: 16 September 1958, Llandudno, Wales

Clubs: Bury (England), Everton (England), Port Vale – on loan (England), Everton (England), Southend United (England)

Major honour: European Cup-Winners' Cup 1985

An unlikely superstar, Neville Southall moved from working on a building site in Llandudno to playing for Everton in a little under two years during the early 1980s.

He was a major factor in their mid-1980s success and broke the club appearance record. An outstanding goalkeeper, he would surely have graced the very highest stage had Wales qualified for either of the major international tournaments during his career.

Shearer is a powerful and hard-working front man whose approach to goal-scoring makes him very difficult to stop.

59

A-Z OF PLAYERS

Marco Tardelli

Born: 24 September 1954, Italy

Clubs: Pisa (Italy), Como (Italy), Juventus (Italy), Internazionale (Italy)

Major honours: World Cup 1982; European Cup Winners' Cup 1984; European Supercup 1984; European Cup 1985; UEFA Cup 1990

Goal-scorer and man of the match in Italy's 1982 World Cup Final triumph, Marco Tardelli is one of only a select few to have won every major domestic European honour, plus that World Cup. An accomplished 'holding' mid-fielder who could also play in defence, Tardelli scored six goals in 81 games for his native Italy. Later he became assistant to manager Cesare Maldini.

Carlos Valderrama

Born: 2 September 1961, Santa Marta, Colombia

Clubs: Santa Marta (Colombia), Millonarios (Colombia), Atletico Nacional (Colombia), Montpellier (France), Valladolid (Spain), Medellin (Colombia), Atletico Junior Barranquilla (Colombia), Tampa Bay Mutiny (USA), Miami Fusion (USA)

Major honours: South American Footballer of the Year 1987, 1994

The distinctive, frizzy-haired Carlos Valderrama was Colombia's answer to Maradona or Gullit, with his outrageous skills and sublime goal-scoring. However, he failed to hit the heights during a spell in Europe and quickly returned across the Atlantic to South America. He inspired Colombia to a shock 5–0 win over Argentina in 1994 with his passing and reading of the game. Even at the age of 36, he remained one of Colombia's key players for the 1998 World Cup tournament. Valderrama passed a century of caps in 1997.

Marco Van Basten

Born: 31 October 1964, Utrecht, Holland

Clubs: Ajax (Holland), AC Milan (Italy)

Major honours: European Golden Boot 1986; European Cup Winners' Cup 1987; European Championship 1988; European Footballer of the Year 1988, 1989, 1992; World Footballer of the Year 1988; European Cup 1989, 1990; World Club Cup 1989, 1990

One of the finest goal-scorers of the modern era, Van Basten was a dangerous combination of power, pace and brains, with a large dose of athleticism thrown in for good measure. The scorer of one of the all-time great international goals, a gravity-defying volley for Holland against the USSR in the 1988 European Championship Final, he was both a huge fan and a protégé of Johan Cruyff. Sadly, his career ended prematurely because of an ankle injury, prompting FIFA to introduce changes in refereeing to protect such players.

Paul Van Himst

Born: 2 October 1943, Belgium

Clubs: Anderlecht (Belgium), RWD Molenbeek (Belgium), Eendracht Aalst (Belgium)

Major honour: none

Widely regarded as Belgium's greatest-ever player, Paul Van Himst also excelled as national team coach. He was selected as centre-forward for the Anderlecht first-team by the age of 16, and went on to win the League eight times, as well as picking up a host of other domestic honours, four times being voted Belgian Footballer of the Year. As a manager, Van Himst guided Belgium to the 1994 World Cup finals, having previously taken Anderlecht to UEFA Cup glory in 1983.

George Weah

Born: 1 October 1966, Monrovia, Liberia

Clubs: Young Survivors Clamtown (Liberia), Bongrange (Liberia), Mighty Barolle (Liberia), Invincible Eleven (Liberia), African Sports Abidjou (Ivory Coast), Tonnerre Yaounde (Cameroon), Monaco (France), Paris St Germain (France), AC Milan (Italy), Chelsea (England), Manchester City (England)

Major honours: World Footballer of the Year 1995; European Footballer of the Year 1995; African Footballer of the Year 1989, 1994

The powerful Liberian striker combines awesome power with a surprisingly deft touch for such a big man. A tremendous ambassador for Liberian and African football, George Weah, when his impoverished country competed in the African Championship held in South Africa in 1996, paid his team-mates' expenses out of his own pocket. Articulate and travelled, he owns property in New York.

Above: Norman Whiteside, who made his début as a World Cup player at the age of only 17.

Opposite: Marco Van Basten was Holland's top striker until injury forced his early retirement.

Norman Whiteside

Born: 7 May 1965, Belfast, Northern Ireland

Clubs: Manchester United (England), Everton (England)

Major honour: none

The man who stripped the World Cup's 'youngest player' record from Pelé, Whiteside was forced to quit the game before he reached his peak. He began as a striker, but was converted into a combative mid-fielder with an eye for the goal and the head for a big occasion, as his goals in League Cup (1983) and FA Cup (1985) Finals proved. He made his piece of World Cup history when he took the field against Yugoslavia in June 1982, aged 17 years and 42 days.

Van Basten was a dangerous combination of power, pace and brains, with a large dose of athleticism thrown in.

Billy Wright

Born: 6 February 1924, Ironbridge, England

Club: Wolverhampton Wanderers (England)

Major honour: none

England's captain through three World Cups (1950, 1954 and 1958), Wright won a total of 105 caps for his country, 90 as skipper. Not a naturally gifted player, he worked hard and led by example, showing good positional sense, waspish tackling and power in the air. Initially a wing-half, he moved into central defence for his 60th international, England v Switzerland, and was a revelation. A real-life *Boys' Own* hero, Wright completed his 'perfect life' by marrying Joy, the eldest of the Beverley Sisters. Less successful as manager of Arsenal, he moved into broadcasting. He died in 1994.

Lev Yashin

Born: 22 October 1929, Moscow, USSR

Club: Moscow Dynamo (USSR)

Major honours: Olympic Gold 1956; European Championship 1960; European Footballer of the Year 1963

Known as the 'Black Panther' because of the distinctive colour of his goalkeeping kit and his amazing reflexes and agility, Yashin was nearly lost to the world of football: in 1953, unable to force his way into Moscow Dynamo, he was on the verge of opting for a career in ice hockey. But the man described on his death in 1990 as 'the most famous Soviet sportsman ever' got his chance when an injury sidelined first-choice Tiger Khomich – and Yashin never looked back. He won the Supreme League six times and the Soviet Cup twice, and picked up a then-record 78 caps for his country. A brilliant goalkeeper

Above: Dino Zoff in action for Italy.

and a true sportsman, he was awarded his country's highest honour, the Order of Lenin, in 1968.

Zinedine Zidane

Born: 23 June 1972, Marseille, France

Clubs: Cannes, Bordeaux, Juventus, Real Madrid

Major honours: FIFA World Player of the Year 1998, 2000, European Footballer of the Year 1998, Italian Championship (Scudetto) 1997, 1998, Champions League winner 2002, World Cup winner 1998, European Championship winner 2000

Zidane, France's midfield maestro, made his international debut in 1994, scoring two goals against the Czech Republic. By World Cup 1998 he had moved to Juventus, helping them to two Champions League

finals. He moved to Real Madrid for a world record £48 million in 2001.

Probably the best player of his generation, he was pivotal in France's successes in France 1998 and Euro 2000. He started the Japan/Korea tournament injured, struggled to make the final group match, but could not prevent France being the first holders to go out in the first stages since Brazil in 1966.

Dino Zoff

Born: 28 February 1942, Mariano del Friuli, Italy

Clubs: Udinese (Italy), Mantova (Italy), Napoli (Italy), Juventus (Italy)

Major honours: European Championship 1968; UEFA Cup 1977; World Cup 1982

Goalkeeper Zoff is holder of a world record shut-out of 1143 international minutes, which he

achieved during the 1973–4 season. His career didn't fully take off until he was in his thirties. He was merely a promising goalkeeper in the lower divisions, but then he signed for Juventus for £400,000 in 1972 and embarked on a career that brought him five Italian Championships and two domestic cups, as well as the UEFA Cup, European Championship and World Cup. In 1982, when he captained Italy to the World Cup, he became the second Juventus goalkeeper to lift the trophy, his predecessor being Gianpiero Combi (1934). Later, as a manager, he spent a period at Lazio.

Opposite left: Zico, a man with prodigious talent, but who never once won a World Cup-winner's medal despite playing for Brazil.

Zico

A genius who somehow failed to win the World Cup with Brazil, despite three attempts (1978, 1982 and 1986). Great ball-skills, a sharp mind and a thunderous shot made him a favourite. On retiring, he became a politician, being appointed Brazil's Minister of Sport.

GAZETTE

Equipped for Change

Once footballs were so heavy they could be lethal, especially when wet. Today they are so light their movement in flight can leave the best of goalkeepers looking foolish. As with the ball, every other aspect of a footballer's equipment has undergone enormous changes over the decades since World War II.

Football is in essence a simple game: you have only to watch kids playing in a park to realize that all you need is a couple of coats to represent the goal and something (a taped bundle of rags will do) as a ball. That simplicity is the secret of soccer's worldwide popularity. But look at the catalogue of a sporting manufacturer and you might believe soccer was a rocket science – indeed, discoveries in space science are now used in the development of balls and boots.

Sports or Money?

While most of these developments have improved the game, many recent ones appear to be motivated more by considerations of profit and market share. Originally players simply nailed studs into their work

Above: **Until the advent of artificial fabrics, cotton was used for the team-strip.**

boots; later boots were specially made with fixed studs, out of leather and coated in dubbin. The introduction of lightweight materials, screw-in studs and moulded boots were revolutionary steps. Now, it seems, boots are not worth wearing if they do not have fins and wedges attached.

For the most talented players such developments can improve their performance (though many a player has signed a sponsorship deal with one company and worn another's boots disguised to look like the ones he is being paid to wear). For most players though,

the only serious question is whether a pair of boots is comfortable or not.

Comfort, again, has led to considerable changes in shirt and clothing design. The old heavy woollen jerseys were replaced first by cotton ones and then by shirts made of synthetic materials. Initially these latter were often of cheap, rash-inducing polyester and nylon, but there is now a range of 'breathable' fabrics in use.

Reinventing the Football

Goalkeepers are today the biggest fashion victims – some would not look out of

Above: **The pre-war Blackpool strip shows the woollen shirts players wore.**

BOBBY MOORE There should be a law against him. He knows what's happening 20 minutes before everyone else. – Jock Stein, manager of Celtic

place in a disco. Initially they wore the same kit as outfield players, being marked out only by a cap. In 1913 new legislation insisted they had to wear a distinguishing colour; until the early 1980s this usually meant plain got so heavy when wet. Many a defender had lace-marks embedded on his forehead after a game and, in a few tragic cases, players are said to have been killed by the impact of a wet, heavy ball.

Above: **With breathable fabrics, players are now much more comfortable.**

FACT FILE

FACT: The most exclusive soccer competition in the world is the football sector of the Island Games, open only to islands whose population is under 125,000. Anglesey won the 1999 competition, which was hosted by Gotland. The 2001 competition was on the Isle of Man.

FACT: Abel Resino, of Atletico Madrid, holds the club goal keeper's record for going the longest period without conceding a goal: 1,275 minutes, in the 1990–1 season — 21 hours and 15 minutes, or 14 full matches plus 15 minutes.

FACT: The 2002 World Cup was the first to be hosted by two countries jointly — Japan and South Korea.

green or yellow, or occasionally black (as with Lev Yashin) or white (as with Peter Shilton). Goalies' gloves have developed from plain cotton ones to ones made from commercial fabrics designed to enhance both stickability and marketability.

Balls, meanwhile, seem to change every time a major competition comes around: some even have different aerodynamic qualities depending on where the valve is placed! Such unpredictability may cause problems for the goal-keeper, but defenders are much happier than they were with the old leather ball, which

Playing at Pace

Pitches in most parts of the world are now much improved, the ball is easier to pass, and players are no longer weighed down by heavy clothing. The game has been changed by this modernization, and has become quicker and in some ways more skilful. One wonders just how much more bewitching players like Englishman Stanley Matthews might have been had they been able to parade their skills using modern equipment and kicking a modern ball ■

Glenn Moore

Above: **Zoff tips the ball over a crossbar. These were added to goalposts in 1875.**

STANLEY MATTHEWS One wonders how much more bewitching players like Englishman Stanley Matthews might have been had they used modern equipment...

Tactical Development

Tactics are at the heart of soccer. When a tiny country like Liechtenstein can hold the Republic of Ireland to a draw as in 1995, the effectiveness of well-planned defence – and the need for clever attack to defeat it – is obvious.

Tactics are not a new development. Early football games comprised little more than two collections of players running after the ball but, as soccer's rules emerged during the second half of the 19th century, formations soon appeared. The language of coaches quickly adapted to match this: the 'off-side trap' and the 'WM formation' being followed by 'catenaccio', 'split-strikers', 'wing-backs' and 'in the hole'.

Skills v System

Football, like most occupations, has spawned its own jargon, and no area of the game is more riddled with it than tactics. To some this is all rubbish – the game is about players, and good players will beat bad ones – but to others this attitude is tactically naïve. Darren Anderton, talking about life at Tottenham Hotspur during Ossie Ardiles's reign, once said: 'The football was enjoyable but Ossie used to say, "You are good players, go out and play."' Anderton added: 'The 11 best players in the world are not going to make a team. It depends how they gel.'

Systems alone do not make a team, but neither do players alone. Good players, if well organized, make a good team. These days, most good sides are based on defence and built around a strong spine which runs from the goalkeeper to the leader of the attack. How they are arranged depends on the coach's preference and the players' individual strengths. Some coaches, like Arrigio Sacchi at Italy and AC Milan, decide upon a system and then find players to fit it. Less well-financed coaches devise a system to fit the players they have. Other coaches vary the mixture according to circumstance.

Some teams, especially at higher levels or when playing stronger sides, adapt their system to counter the opposition. Other factors, such as the climate (high temperatures often lead to a slower match, high winds to a disjointed one) and the pitch (wide pitches favour wing players, frozen ones help forwards), can also affect the nature of the game.

Kick-and-rush

Teams may place an emphasis on set-plays. For many years the English Football Association officially backed the idea of 'direct play', a style which concentrates on moving the ball forward quickly and trying to score from subsequent corners, free kicks, etc. Some teams found success with these methods but, at times, it seemed little more than a refined version of schoolyard kick-and-rush. While many goals are scored from such set-pieces, and opposing teams need to be prepared for them, this philosophy works only up to a certain level. As players get better and defences more organized, greater subtlety is required. The Republic of Ireland, under Jack Charlton, gained a measure of success

Above: **Ray Houghton of Jack Charlton's Republic of Ireland at USA 94.**

TACTICS Selfishness, cowardice, indiscipline and stupidity can undo the best systems, and individual brilliance defeat them . . . tactics are really all about players.

with an adaptation of such a tactic, but was rarely able to beat the best teams. A range of tempo and technique, as practised by the Brazilians, is more penetrating and much more attractive to watch. By mixing up long and short passing, interspersing periods of passing with dribbles or shots, the Brazilians kept their opponents guessing.

National 'Tics'

Different nations developed different tactics from the earliest days. In England, where the game was all about dribbling, early formations consisted of a goal-keeper, a back, a half-back and eight dribbling forwards. This changed after the English were exposed to those Scottish clubs which entered the FA Cup between 1872 and 1887. These teams placed more emphasis on passing and, by the time the Football League was formed in 1888, clubs had begun to adopt the 2–3–5 formation (two backs, three half-backs, five forwards), which persisted until the change in the off-side law nearly 40 years later – the revised rule reduced the number of defenders required between a forward and the goal from three to the present-day two.

When that happened, in 1925, the immediate result was a huge increase in goals as forwards enjoyed their new freedom. The long-term result was a move to three defenders. Herbert Chapman, the legendary Huddersfield and Arsenal manager, is widely credited with the ploy; he developed the WM formation (3–4–3 or 3–3–4). There were variations on this formation – notably

Left: Johan Cruyff, (left) master and inventor of the 'sweeper system' which swept all but West Germany before it in the 1974 World Cup finals.

Don Revie playing as a deep-lying centre-forward – but over 30 years elapsed before there were further fundamental changes. Then, inspired by the success of Hungary and Real Madrid, coaches like Ron Greenwood and Dick Graham began to experiment with sweepers and more fluid formations. The most significant development for the English game, subsequently influenced by the tactic for decades, came when the national side won the 1966 World Cup under Alf Ramsey using a wingless 4–4–2 formation.

Catenaccio

Meanwhile, continental sides were moving in different directions. For them, defensive developments were highlighted by Helenio Herrera's introduction at Internazionale of catenaccio, using two markers and a sweeper. This was contrasted a decade later by the Dutch philosophy of 'total football', based on the talents of Johan Cruyff and positional flexibility. Two decades after that Ajax again led the way with an updated version, 1–3–3–3, with which they won the European Cup.

English clubs remained rooted in 4–4–2 for so long

> **English clubs remained rooted in 4–4–2 for so long that in the early 1990s a footballing magazine was named after it**

that in the early 1990s a footballing magazine was named after it. Ironically, this happened at just the same time as English clubs were beginning to adopt continental ideas and European sides like AC Milan were moving back to 4–4–2, rechristened 'pressing game'. There is now considerable diversity within some leagues, notably the English Premiership and the Italian Serie A. Several teams are happy to vary formations depending on whom they are playing, making use of what has come to be called the squad system. Many other teams find it easier, when playing away from home, to soak up the pressure within a tight unit, hitting their opponents on the counter-attack when the home side becomes stretched pushing forward.

Whatever system a team uses, their success or otherwise depends on attitude as much as formation: 3–5–2 can be ultra-defensive or very attacking, depending on the players' approach. Selfishness, cowardice, indiscipline and stupidity can undo the best systems, and individual brilliance defeat them. To that extent, tactics are really all about players ■

Glenn Moore

GLENN HODDLE You didn't have to go ten yards away and say: 'Here I am, I want the ball.' You could be a mile away and Hoddle would still find you – Cyrille Regis, fellow England international

67

European Cup Final, Glasgow, 18 May 1960

Double Hat-trick

Real Madrid 7 (Puskas 4, Di Stefano 3)
Eintracht Frankfurt 3 (Stein 2, Kress 1)

This match was the crowning glory of Real Madrid's domination of the early years of the European Cup, and the manner of their victory in front of 138,000 fans at Hampden Park guaranteed their lasting place in soccer's pantheon of the greats.

It is no exaggeration to say that no one had ever seen a match like this before, simply because no team had ever played the game the way Real Madrid played that night. What made Real's victory even more memorable was the fact that Eintracht themselves played some outstanding football, and against anyone else would probably have won at a canter. The Germans scored the first and last goals of the match – but unluckily for them, Real scored a sensational seven times between. It was Real's fifth successive Europeal Cup success ■

An Incredible Match

In the 1956–7 season Huddersfield Town, then managed by Bill Shankly, were leading Charlton Athletic 5–1.

With 20 minutes left of this English First Division match, Charlton staged a remarkable recovery to take a 6–5 lead with five minutes remaining, led by centre-forward and man-of-the-match Johnny Summers. Incredibly, Charlton had been reduced to only 10 men when Derek Ufton was injured after 15 minutes.

After the morale-sapping Charlton charge, the Huddersfield team recovered enough composure to level the score at 6–6 with just two minutes remaining on the clock, only for Charlton to score the winner. The last goal was Summers's fifth of the match, beating the goalkeeper to hit the back of the net deep in injury time ■

GOALSCORING RECORDS

BIGGEST WORLD CUP WINS

31–0 Australia v American Samoa (2001)

22–0 Australia v Tonga (2001)

19–0 Iran v Guam (2000)

17–0 Iran v Maldives (1997)

13–0 New Zealand v Fiji (1981)

BIGGEST WIN IN WORLD CUP FINALS

10–1 Hungary v El Salvador (Elche, Spain, 1982)

BIGGEST LEAGUE WINS IN ENGLISH DIVISIONS

Premiership: 9–0
Manchester United v Ipswich (1995)

Division 1: 12–0
West Bromwich Albion v Darwen (1892) and Nottingham Forest v Leicester Fosse (1909)

Division 2: 13–0
Newcastle United v Newport County (1946)

Division 3: 10–0
Gillingham v Chesterfield (1987)

Division 3 North: 13–0
Stockport County v Halifax Town (1934)

Division 3 South: 12–0
Luton Town v Bristol Rovers (1936)

Division 4: 11–0
Oldham Athletic v Southport (1962)

RECORD FIRST-CLASS SCORE

36–0 Arbroath v Bon Accord (1885)

RECORD FA CUP SCORE

26–0 Preston North End v Hyde (1887)

HUGO SANCHEZ He is a very dangerous man, as welcome as a piranha in a bidet.
– Jesus Gil, president of Atletico Madrid, on the Real Madrid striker

Left: Pelé scores for Brazil in the 1970 Mexico World Cup Final.

Inset: The celebrations for Brazil and the triumph of the beautiful game.

World Cup Final, Mexico City, 21 June 1970

The Beautiful Game

Brazil 4 (Pelé, Gerson, Jairzinho, Alberto), **Italy 1** (Boninsegna)

If Real Madrid's 1960 European Cup victory was the greatest ever performance by a club side, then Brazil's victory over Italy in the World Cup Final a decade later was the greatest performance by any international team; it was the pinnacle of Pelé's vision of the 'beautiful game'.

Pelé himself put Brazil on the way to victory with a headed goal after 18 minutes, thereby becoming only the second man after Vava to score in two finals.

Boninsegna equalized after 37 minutes, but Italy rarely threatened again. Brazil, inspired by Gerson, dominated a second half full of attacking brilliance. Gerson put Brazil back in front after 65 minutes, and five minutes later Jairzinho made World Cup history by becoming the first man to score in every round.

The fourth goal was the best of the match, and to this day is still one of the best ever: Pelé completed a dazzling build-up by laying off a perfectly weighted pass for Carlos Alberto, sprinting up the right wing. Without breaking stride the captain scored to secure the Jules Rimet Trophy. It was Brazil's third success and the trophy was awarded to them in perpetuity with a new one commissioned for the 1974 finals. Other members of this great Brazilian team were Roberto Rivelino, Everaldo, Clodoaldo and the brilliant Tostao. This is now regarded as Brazil's benchmark performance ∎

BRAZIL Brazil's victory over Italy in the 1970 World Cup final was the greatest performance by any international side . . .

East Meets West

For many the analogy between football and politics has become a cliché, but football has often been used for propaganda purposes, no more so than during the Cold War, when East and West vied for nuclear supremacy against a background of ideological and political paranoia. When East Germany and West Germany met in the 1974 World Cup finals, the world held its breath.

During the Cold War, East and West Germany met on the football pitch once, ironically on German soil in Hamburg, West Germany, during the 1974 World Cup. The East Germans, fearful of defectors, allowed a small party of vetted 'fans', mainly communist party officials, to be bussed into the match. Security was everywhere, to the extent that the East Germans had helicopters in the air.

Though East Germany was formidable in many sports, its football teams were weak. The domestic league was corrupt, with Dinamo Berlin run by the secret police and good athletes 'encouraged' to play other sports. The national team failed to reach any other finals but, incredibly, given their pedigree, defeated the West in this game with a late goal by Jurgen Sparwasser.

Despite this set-back the West German side still went on to win the tournament. Sparwasser later defected to the West ■

Glenn Moore

A Fix in 1978?

The Argentine junta of 1978 was one of those governments with the habit of making people vanish by the train-load.

This did not make FIFA withdraw the World Cup from them, but it did stop Johan Cruyff, then the best player in the world, from attending. He pulled out of the tournament as protest against Argentina's human rights record.

The tournament itself was a mixed success marred by poor refereeing and controversy, notably when Argentina, needing a big win to make the final, beat Peru 6–0. A brave Argentine journalist later discovered that, after the match, Argentina shipped food and, probably, weapons to Peru, and unfroze millions of dollars in credit for Peru. Argentine beat Holland 3–1 in an acromonious Final ■

Berlin 1938
English Players Use the Nazi Salute

In 1938, with war already brewing in Europe, England played a friendly against Germany in Berlin.

Following a diplomatic row two years before when English athletes had refused to give the Nazi salute at the Berlin Olympics, the FA agreed that this time England would do so.

English Triumph

The players did make the salute, though some later claimed that they were forced to do so. The action was decried by a very vocal English press, but the Nazi propaganda coup was limited. On the field, the German team, watched by such Nazi luminaries as Goebbels, Hess, Goering and Ribbentrop, were soundly thrashed 6–3 by a superior side, including Stanley Matthews, Cliff Bastin and Eddit Hapgood ■

Libya Withdraw

During qualifying for the 1990 World Cup, Libya withdrew from a home tie against Algeria.

This was a 'thank you' gesture for Algeria's continued support after the United States had bombed Tripoli, the Libyan capital. It was said at the time that the decision was made so late the Libyan crowd were awaiting kick off. Ironically, Algeria did not go on to qualify for the trials held across the Mediterranean in Italy ■

Football Wars

During qualifying for the 1970 World Cup, Honduras were drawn against neighbouring El Salvador – the situation was already volatile.

Relations had been tense for some time over the number and treatment of migrant Salvadorean workers in Honduras and mutual antipathy along the border. Though the matches were relatively trouble-free, rioting broke out elsewhere, along with border skirmishes after both legs and a play-off, staged in Mexico. This led to El Salvador invading Honduras, who immediately responded in kind. More than 2,000 people were killed.

El Salvador, having won the play-off and beaten Haiti, went on to the finals, only to lose all three matches without scoring a goal. Honduras later made the finals in 1987 ■

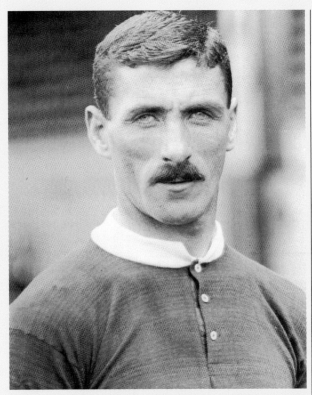

Above: Billy Meredith's career was not ended by the scandal.

England 1905

The Billy Meredith Scandal

The first truly sensational bribery scandal involved the Welshman Billy Meredith, the greatest footballer of his time.

When the scandal broke, Meredith was at the peak of his career with Manchester City. This didn't stop him being suspended for his part in offering inducements to an Aston Villa player to help throw a match (29 April 1905). Manchester City were in a two-horse race with Newcastle for the title, and were giving their players an illegal bonus of £10 a man if they could win the game against Villa – £10 was a lot of money in 1905. But the bribe failed: Villa won the match 3–2 and Newcastle in due course won the title. The fall-out of the scandal wrecked several careers. All Manchester City's directors were suspended, the secretary and chairman for life. Seventeen players were banned for seven months, and from ever playing for Manchester City again.

Meredith, who had scored the winning goal for the club in the 1904 Cup Final, was luckier than most of his peers at City: he resumed his career at his former club's local rivals, Manchester United, and in 1909 gained another FA Cup Winners' medal with his new team. He was later involved in another bribery scandal in 1915 ■

England 1915

Manchester United/ Liverpool Scandal

On Good Friday, 2 April 1915, just before English soccer belatedly closed down because of World War I, Manchester United beat Liverpool 2–0 in a game that was so obviously fixed the referee considered calling time long before he was due to blow the final whistle.

Players deliberately kicked the ball into touch, a United player kicked a penalty so far wide the crowd started laughing and booing because they could see what was happening, and the Liverpool players had only one shot at goal – when that hit the bar the player, not involved in the fix, was reprimanded by his team-mates for trying to score! It emerged soon after that the Liverpool winger Jackie Sheldon, a member of United's 1911 title-winning team, had conspired with some of his new and some of his former team-mates to throw the match and clean up at the bookmakers. The players' money was on United winning 2–0, and sure enough they pocketed large amounts through their 'predictions'. However, many bookies were suspicious and refused to pay. The authorities were equally suspicious, and eventually they banned one player for 12 months and a further eight players for life ■

Mike Collett

Above: **The Manchester United side involved in the rigged match against Liverpool.**

A-Z of Managers

Franz Beckenbauer

Born: 11 September 1945, Germany

Teams managed: West German national side, Olympique Marseille (France), Bayern Munich (Germany)

There were many dissenting voices when 'Kaiser Franz' was given the West German managership in 1984: after all, he had never managed any club before. Yet, within two years, he had taken a weak side to the 1986 World Cup Final. Deploying a swift counter-attacking style, Beckenbauer was excellent at getting the best out of his players. Efficient rather than flamboyant, the West German team eventually lost a dramatic final 3–2 to Argentina. In 1990, Beckenbauer became the first man to both captain and manage a World Cup-winning team, West Germany beating Argentina 1–0 in Rome. After a spell at Marseille as general manager, he returned to Munich in 1993 in an administrative role. The following year, he briefly went back to management, steering Bayern to the League title, before stepping up to become the club's president.

Below: World cup-winner as both manager and player, Franz Beckenbauer.

Matt Busby

Born: 26 May 1909, Bellshill, Scotland

Team managed: Manchester United (England)

For two-and-a-half decades, Matt Busby ran Manchester United and established the team's legend. His first side, which included the so-called 'Busby Babes', was destroyed in the 1958 Munich air crash, in which Busby came so close to losing his own life that the last rites were administered. However, he survived to reform the club and, building around the combined genius of George Best, Bobby Charlton and Denis Law, fashioned a team that brought home the European Cup in 1968. He retired in 1969 after 24 years at the helm, during which time he also won two FA Cups and five League Championships. Knighted in 1968, he died in 1994. Matt Busby was formerly a player with Liverpool, Manchester City and Scotland.

Above: Sir Matt Busby, the first of Manchester United's great managers.

Left: Fabio Capello in his playing days.

Fabio Capello

Born: 3 August 1947, Italy

Teams managed: AC Milan (Italy), Real Madrid (Spain), AC Milan (Italy), Roma (Italy)

Probably the most successful football manager working in Europe today, Fabio Capello took over the reins from Arrigo Sacchi at AC Milan in 1991 and won the League Championship four times during the following five seasons. He also gained the 1994 European Cup when his side beat Barcelona 4–0 in Athens. Fabio Capello's style of management has always been considered autocratic, and players who disagree with him can find themselves put on the transfer list. But there is no disputing his record in the game. He moved to Real Madrid in 1996 and steered the team to championship victory during the single season he spent there. After that, he returned to Italy and AC Milan.

Herbert Chapman

Born: 19 January 1878, Kiveton Park, England

Teams managed: Leeds City (England), Huddersfield Town (England), Arsenal (England)

England's greatest pre-war manager twice created teams that won a hat-trick of titles. In the 1920s, he did this with Huddersfield, leading them to their first two titles before moving on to Arsenal, where he built a famous side, only to die when it was part-way through winning its treble. He also won the FA Cup with each of the two sides. His achievements were not just about trophies, however. He was one of the great football visionaries, tactically and in broader terms. He was the first manager to use a central defender to bolster the defence, and he also experimented with varying systems at a time when most managers were not even thinking about such things. His Arsenal team was probably the most formidable pre-war club team in Europe, once providing no fewer than seven players to an England side that defeated the then World Cup holders, Italy, in 1934. Herbert Chapman is also notable for having persuaded London Transport to change the name of his club's local underground station from Gillespie Road to Arsenal.

Jack Charlton

Born: 8 May 1935, Ashington, England

Teams managed: Middlesbrough (England), Sheffield Wednesday (England), Newcastle (England), Middlesbrough (England), Republic of Ireland national side

When Jack Charlton moved into football management in 1973, he had achieved just about everything a player could hope for. As a manager, he took Middlesbrough from the lower Second Division to sixth place in the First Division within 12 months. Lack of finance at Middlesbrough saw him move to Sheffield Wednesday, whom he lifted out of the Third Division; this was followed by a brief spell at Newcastle before a short return to Middlesbrough. He took over as the Republic of Ireland's manager in 1986, and guided the side to its first ever European Championship in 1988, when it narrowly missed out in the semi-finals. The team went on to reach the World Cup Finals for the first time in 1990, getting to the last eight; it got as far as the finals again in 1994. Charlton retired after Ireland failed to qualify for Euro 96. Built around a solid defence and a pressurizing style of play, his teams were very difficult to beat, although it has to be said that they lacked flair.

Brian Clough

Born: 21 March 1935, England

Teams managed: Hartlepool (England), Brighton (England), Derby (England), Leeds (England), Nottingham Forest (England)

Brian Clough was an accomplished centre-forward with Middlesbrough, and good enough

Opposite: Jack Charlton at USA 94.

Below: Brian Clough made his name at Nottingham Forest in the late 1970s.

to win England recognition before injury brought an end to his career when he was in his late twenties. His first managerial job was at Hartlepool; then he moved to unfancied Derby County, with whom he won the League in 1972. After that, he had unsuccessful spells at Leeds United and Brighton and Hove Albion; his period at Elland Road is famous as one of the shortest in history – 44 days. It was with his move to Nottingham Forest, in 1975, that he cemented his reputation as one of the game's best managers. During an 18-year reign at Forest,

Brian Clough won two European Cups, the League Championship and four League Cups. He retired from the game in 1993 after Forest were relegated. Later he was charged by the FA with receiving illegal payments during player transfers. His son Nigel was selected to play for England.

Johan Cruyff

Born: 25 April 1947, Amsterdam, Holland

Teams managed: Ajax (Holland), Barcelona (Spain)

Apart from being the greatest Dutch footballer of all time, Johan Cruyff was an accomplished manager. As it had done during his playing days, his career centred on Ajax and Barcelona. He led the Dutch side to European Cup Winners' Cup success in 1987 and then, taking over at Barcelona, repeated the same feat with the Spaniards in 1989. More importantly, he steered Barcelona, for five years in the shadow of Real Madrid, to four La Liga titles between 1990 and 1994. Built around the attacking flair of Romario and Hristo Stoichkov, and the deadly shooting and passing skills of Ronald Koeman, the Barcelona side also won the 1992 European Cup. Cruyff, a heavy smoker, survived a heart attack before being sacked in 1996 in a power struggle.

Kenny Dalglish

Born: 4 March 1951, Glasgow, Scotland

Teams managed: Liverpool (England), Blackburn (England), Newcastle (England), Celtic (Scotland)

As a player, Kenny Dalglish had few equals. As a manager, he sought the same levels of perfection that he had achieved on the pitch. He took over the reins at Liverpool after Joe Fagan quit in the wake of the Heysel disaster. many people doubted Dalglish's ability to juggle playing and managing, but he confounded them by guiding the club to the League/Cup double in 1986 - and two further titles before he resigned. Dalglish returned to the soccer scene in 1991, leading Blackburn to the League Championship, before retiring again but coming back for a short spell at Newcastle in January 1997. He later became director of football at Celtic, but was fired in early 2000.

Alex Ferguson

Born: 31 December 1941, Glasgow, Scotland

Teams managed: St Mirren (Scotland), Aberdeen (Scotland), Scottish national team, Manchester United (England)

Having helped Aberdeen break the Celtic–Rangers stranglehold in Scotland and win the Cup Winners' Cup for good measure, Alex Ferguson took over the reins at Old Trafford in October 1986. He had briefly taken over as manager

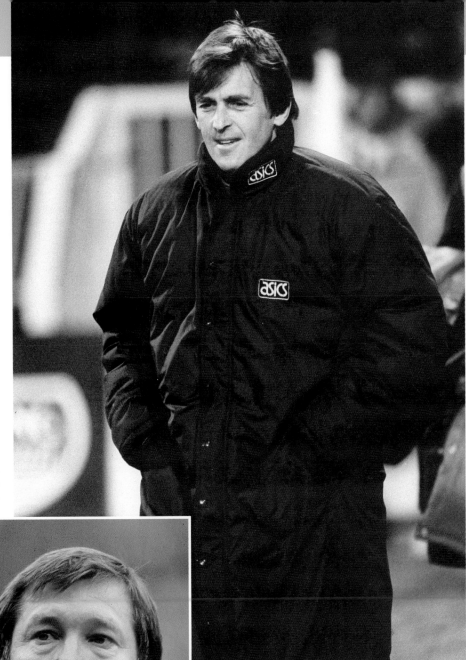

Above: Kenny Dalglish at Blackburn Rovers.

Opposite: Johann Cruyff in his managing days at Barcelona.

Left: Alex Ferguson.

of the Scottish national side after the death of Jock Stein, but it was with Manchester United that Fergie created a place in history. Under pressure to keep his job in early 1990, he went on to win the FA Cup and the European Cup Winners' Cup before, in 1993, taking Manchester United to their first League Championship in 26 years. Four titles followed in five years – the crowning glory coming in 1999 when Manchester United won the FA Cup, Premiership and Champions League.

Ernst Happel

Born: 29 June 1925, Austria

Teams managed: Feyenoord (Holland), Bruges (Belgium), Dutch national side, Hamburg (West Germany)

Happel's standing in the game was illustrated when Vienna's Prater stadium was rechristened in his honour after his death in 1992. As a player, he was a fine centre-back with Rapid Vienna and Austria, appearing in the 1958 World Cup Finals at the end of a 51-cap career. Once, he scored a hat-trick against Real Madrid in a European Cup tie.

The often dour Happel went on to become one of Europe's most successful coaches, working in several countries. He guided Feyenoord to the European Cup and the World Club Cup in 1970, and eight years later he not only took Bruges to the European Cup Final, but also managed the Dutch national side and led them to their second consecutive World Cup Final. In 1983, he steered Hamburg to European Cup success.

Sepp Herberger

Born: 28 March 1897, Germany

Teams managed: West German national side

Sepp Herberger was the first of the great German football managers. He was a keen student of the game and spent some time travelling the world to look at different systems of play. He became assistant manager of the German national side in 1932 and was appointed full coach in 1936. His hour of glory came during the 1954 World Cup tournament, when he took the bold step of fielding the West German reserve side against the mighty Hungarian team in the qualifying rounds; the reserves were soundly beaten 8–3, but West Germany gained revenge in the final, when Herberger sent out the first team, which went on to win 3–2.

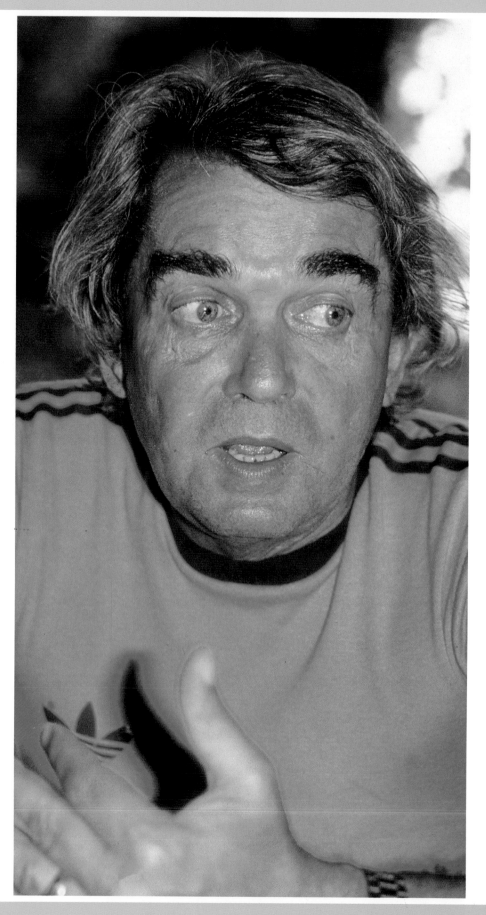

Helenio Herrera

Born: 17 April 1916, Argentina

Teams managed: Red Star Paris (France), Stade Français, Atletico Madrid (Spain), Valladolid (Spain), Sevilla (Spain), Belenenses, Barcelona (Spain), Internazionale (Italy), Roma (Italy), Spanish national side, Italian national side

As controversial as he was successful, Helenio Herrera had an impressive cv, managing Barcelona, Internazionale and the Spanish and Italian national sides, among others. It is not difficult to see why he was given the best jobs going: just look at his trophy haul. He won two championships while at Barcelona's Nou Camp, then three with Internazionale in

Italy, not to mention two Fairs Cups and two European Cups. He is credited as having introduced to world football the *catenaccio* system – the complete locking up of the defence whenever his team went into a one-goal lead. Team managers all over Italy rushed to copy his style, but few sides managed it as effectively as Herrera's Internazionale.

Marcello Lippi

Born: 1948, Italy

Teams managed: Napoli (Italy), Atalanta (Italy), Juventus (Italy), Internazionale (Italy)

The cheroot-smoking Marcello Lippi took Juventus back to the

Above: Sepp Herberger's World Cup campaign in 1954 was as idiosyncratic as his coaching philosophy was thorough.

Opposite: Ernst Happel, a coach and player whose influence was so great in his native Austria that they named a stadium after him.

peak of club football in 1996, only two seasons after having taken charge of Italy's greatest club. Following spells at Napoli and Atalanta, Lippi was appointed Juventus' manager in 1994, and the club immediately achieved victory in the League Championship, for the first time since 1986, and won the Italian Cup. In 1996, Juventus added the European Cup; however, Lippi then controversially sold off several leading members of the first team. Despite those changes, in the same year, Juventus went on to win the World Club Cup, the European Supercup and Serie A, although lost in the 1997 European Cup Final. Lippi left Juventus in 1999 to take the Inter Milan job, but returned to win the Scudetto in 2003 with Juve.

Valery Lobanovski

Born: 1939, Ukraine

Teams managed: Dynamo Kiev (USSR), USSR national side, United Arab Emirates national side, Kuwait national side, Dynamo Kiev (USSR)

Valery Lobanovksi's name is primarily associated with Dynamo Kiev. Having played for the side, in due course, he became its coach and guided it to domestic and European greatness during the 1970s and 1980s. He was the USSR's manager for the 1986 World Cup Finals. In the early 1990s, he took flight, accepting the position of manager of the national sides of Kuwait and the United Arab Emirates, but six years later, in 1997, he returned once more to Dynamo Kiev.

While we have yet to see how successful his new spell with the club will be, his first period there

Above: The Argentinian Cesar Luis Menotti – smoking as usual.

Opposite: Dutchman Rinus Michels – one of the game's great thinkers.

was astonishing. Lobanovksi was the inspirational and scientific coach behind Dynamo's run of 13 League and Cup titles between 1971 and 1987. In 1975, with a team starring striker Oleg Blokhin, he took them to their first European trophy, the Cup Winners' Cup, and he repeated the feat 11 years later – with Blokhin still in the side.

Hugo Meisl

Born: 1881, Austria

Teams managed: Admira Wacker (Austria), Austrian national side

Hugo Meisl was born into a wealthy Viennese banking family, but on becoming obsessed with football, he spurned the family business. He played inside-forward for FK Austria before retiring as a player to manage the Austrian club Admira Wacker. He

went on to become secretary of the Austrian Federation while simultaneously managing the national side, which became one of the great inter-war teams. Under his managership, Austria had their greatest achievement – and their greatest disappointment – when competing in the 1934 World Cup tournament. Widely tipped to win, they lost in the semi-finals to Italy, whom they had defeated in Turin just a few months earlier. Hugo Meisl died in 1937.

Cesar Luis Menotti

Born: 9 July 1934, Argentina

Teams managed: Independiente (Argentina), Argentinian national side, Barcelona (Spain), Valencia (Spain)

No manager was ever able to appear as highly strung as

Cesar Luis Menotti. He had already enjoyed a spell as the manager of Independiente when he took over the Argentinian national team.

During the 1978 World Cup Finals, he broke the mould of traditional Argentinian teams by going for all-out attack. Menotti declined to select the young prodigy Diego Maradona for this effort, but this was a decision for which he was heavily criticized. Nonetheless, his side survived some early hiccups to bring the World Cup home to Buenos Aires, beating Holland 3–1 in the final. Later he went on to manage Barcelona before moving to the Middle East and Mexico. Finally, he had a spell at Valencia.

Rinus Michels

Born: 9 June 1928, Holland

Teams managed: Ajax (Holland), Barcelona (Spain), Bayer Leverkusen, Los Angeles Aztecs (USA), Dutch national side

Breathtaking football was always a hallmark of the sides managed by Rinus Michels – as was an impressive collection of trophies. He discovered the brilliant young Johan Cruyff, and achieved victory in the Dutch Championship no less than five times with a team that played with breathtaking skill and vision. Ajax also lifted the European Cup three times in a row with Michels acting as their manager, while the Dutch national side reached the 1974 World Cup Final under his guidance.

In a later spell as national coach, he provided the guidance for a new set of Dutch youngsters that led to them gaining a place in the 1988 European Championships. Having lost to the hosts, West Germany, in the 1974 final, this time his team trounced the Germans in the semi-final.

Later Rinus Michels became one of UEFA's and FIFA's most respected coaching gurus. In this role, he worked as a special advisor to the Scottish Football Association among others.

A-Z OF MANAGERS

then the German side Eintracht Frankfurt 7–3 at Glasgow in a memorable final.

Bill Nicholson

Born: 26 January 1919, England

Team managed: Tottenham Hotspur (England)

Bill Ncholson holds the distinction of being the first manager this century to achieve the League/Cup double: he steered Tottenham Hotspur to League and FA Cup victory in 1961. He had already taken the League title with Spurs a decade previously when he was a player, and as a team manager he was equally relentless in his pursuit of excellence. During his reign at the club, Bill Nicholson picked up just about every trophy that was going: the League Championship in 1961; the FA Cup in 1961, 1962 and 1967; the League Cup in 1971 and 1973; the UEFA Cup in 1972; and the European Cup Winners' Cup in 1963. Only a controversial semi-final defeat during the 1962 European Cup prevented him from completing a grand slam. Nicholson remained associated with the club until into his eighties.

Miguel Munoz

Born: 15 September 1924, Argentina

Team managed: Real Madrid (Spain)

As a player, Miguel Munoz knew all about winning in Europe: he had captained the first two European Cup-winning sides put together by Real Madrid. He went straight into team management with the same club at the end of his playing career, and promptly conducted the side in what is generally considered to be the finest European Cup campaign of all time. Munoz's Spaniards completely destroyed Nice in the quarter-finals before beating their arch-rivals Barcelona both at home and away in the semi-finals, and

Above: Bill Nicholson standing at the gates of White Hart Lane.

Opposite: A proud Bob Paisley and the European Champions' Cup.

Right: Miguel Munoz managed perhaps the finest club side ever seen in Europe, Real Madrid.

Bob Paisley

Born: 23 January 1919, England

Team managed: Liverpool (England)

Bob Paisley was the most successful English club manager of all time, winning 13 major trophies during the period he spent in charge at Anfield. He won the European Cup three times, gained six League Championships and three League Cups, and lifted the UEFA Cup. As a player, he was a member of the Liverpool side that tasted victory in the League in 1947. Retiring in 1954, he joined the club's coaching staff, becoming assistant manager to Bill Shankly in late 1959. When Shankly retired in 1974, there were many who doubted that Paisley had the ability to take Liverpool's progress further. But they were wrong. Although he did not possess any of the dry wit of Shankly, what was more germane was his record, which stood for itself. After stepping aside in 1983, he became a director of the club, assisting Joe Fagan and Kenny Dalglish. Such was his popularity that all of Liverpool mourned when Bob Paisley died in February 1996.

Vittorio Pozzo

Born: 12 March 1886, Italy

Teams managed: Torino (Italy), Italian national side

Vittorio Pozzo discovered football when he visited England as a student before World War I. He was a very enthusiastic fan of English football in general, and of Manchester United in particular. In 1912, he was put in charge of the Italian team at the Stockholm Olympics, and it was there that he met Hugo Meisl. Pozzo later became an admirer of Arsenal boss Herbert Chapman. At club level, Pozzo was associated with Torino. At national level, he was able to guide Italy to victories in the 1934 and 1938 World Cups, and to Olympic Gold in 1936.

Alf Ramsey

Born: 21 January 1920, Dagenham, England

Teams managed: Ipswich (England), English national side, Birmingham (England)

The man who led England to their finest hour: Ramsey earned a knighthood for guiding Bobby Moore's side to the 1966 World Cup Final, where they beat West Germany 4–2.

As a player, Ramsey was an intelligent and creative right-back with Southampton and Spurs. On his retirement in 1955, he became manager of Ipswich, and by taking that club from the Third Division to the First Division title in the space of seven years he earned the England job in 1963. He left in 1973 when the side failed to qualify for the World Cup Finals. Later he had a brief spell at Birmingham. He died in 1999.

Bobby Robson

Born: 18 February 1933, Langley Park, Co. Durham, England

Teams managed: Vancouver Royals (Canada), Fulham (England), Ipswich Town (England), English national side, PSV Eindhoven (Holland), Sporting Lisbon (Portugal), Porto (Portugal), Barcelona (Spain), PSV Eindhoven (Holland), Newcastle Utd (England)

Below: Bobby Robson, an England manager who earned the job through a very good run with Ipswich.

As manager of Ipswich, Robson built a formidable team that made a real impression at home and in Europe, winning the FA Cup in 1978 and the UEFA Cup in 1981. He took over the English national side a year later, but received a panning when it failed to qualify for the 1984 European Championships. In 1986, he took England to Mexico where the side made the quarter-finals, losing arrowly to Argentina. After defeat by West Germany in the semi-finals of the 1990 World Cup, Robson moved to PSV Eindhoven, leading them to League Championships in 1991 and 1992. He also won League Championships for Sporting Lisbon and Porto before joining Barcelona, where he won the Cup Winners' Cup, Spanish Cup and European Supercup. He returned to PSV Eindhoven in 1998, but in 1999 returned home to Newcastle United.

Arrigo Sacchi

Born: 12 February 1947, Italy

Teams managed: Rimini (Italy), Parma (Italy), AC Milan (Italy), Italian national side, AC Milan (Italy)

Sacchi developed one of the greatest club sides of all time when in charge of AC Milan. From 1986, when he took over at the club, he immediately set about rebuilding its fortunes. In came Ruud Gullit from PSV Eindhoven; a year later, he signed Marco Van Basten and Frank Rijkaard. Sacchi mixed the three Dutchmen's skill in attack with the defensive capabilities of Paolo Maldini, Franco Baresi, Mauro Tassotti and Alessandro Costacurta, and the midfield guile of Roberto Donadoni and Carlo Ancelotti. Playing according to the English 'pressing' game, AC Milan proceeded to win the European Cup twice, beating Steaua Bucharest 4–0 in the 1989 final, and Benfica 1–0 a year later. Sacchi then left to take up the Italian national job, leading the side to the 1994 World Cup Final; although he brought it to within a penalty kick of the trophy, he had never been popular and, after

failing in Euro 96, returned to AC Milan, where this time he lasted only six months. A cobbler's son and moderate player, he was often criticized.

Tele Santana

Born: 26 July 1933, Brazil

Teams managed: Atletico Mineiro (Brazil), Gremio (Brazil), Flamengo (Brazil), Fluminese (Brazil), Palmeiras (Brazil), Al Ahly (Brazil), São Paulo (Brazil), Brazilian national side

Tele Santana led Brazil to the World Cup Finals of 1982 and 1986, and his teams were considered the most entertaining and attack-minded in the world. However, his insistence on attacking football was criticized as naïve after the national team went out to slick counter-attacking sides in those two World Cup tournaments. But he finally managed to silence his critics when he led São Paulo to the World Club Cup in both 1992 and 1993. Santana made enemies through never being afraid to point out corruption within the Brazilian game.

Above: Tele Santana, a combative and passionate manager.

Right: Arrigo Sacchi was the mastermind behind one of the greatest club sides of recent times: AC Milan.

A-Z OF MANAGERS

Helmut Schoen

Born: 15 September 1915, Germany

Teams managed: Saar (West Germany), West German national side

Above: Helmut Schoen's tenure as manager of West Germany included winning the 1972 European championships and the 1974 World Cup.

As a player, Helmut Schoen was a prolific goal-scorer at international level: he achieved 17 goals in 16 internationals between 1937 and 1941. He spent a brief period as manager of Saar before being appointed assistant manager of the West German national side in 1955, under the great Sepp Herberger. He took over from the latter in 1963, and went on to lead the team to the World Cup Final in 1966. Later, when under the guidance of Franz Beckenbauer, the side came third in 1970, then won the trophy in 1974. Under Schoen, West Germany were also European Champions in 1972 and runners-up in 1976.

Gusztav Sebes

Born: 21 June 1906, Hungary

Teams managed: Hungarian national side, Ujpest Doza (Hungary)

After developing a good playing career with Vasas and MTK Budapest, Gusztav Sebes went on to create the 'Magical Magyars', the Hungarian national side. Assisted considerably by the communist Hungarian government's policy of investing in the national side, Sebes combined the talents of Ferenc Puskas, Nandor Hidegkuti, Sandor Kocsis and others into an attacking team that was definitely ahead of its time. In 1953, the use of Hidegkuti in a deep-lying role was instrumental in inflicting on England that nation's first home defeat to foreign opposition. Hungary romped through the 1954 World Cup tournament and, until they lost 3–2 to West Germany in the final, they never looked like being beaten.

Gusztav Sebes resigned from his position as national team manager in 1957, after several of his top players had defected to the West. Known as 'Uncle Guszhi' by his players, he combined his job with being Deputy Sports Minister. He died in 1986.

Left: Bill Shankly, surrounded by the red of his beloved Liverpool.

Bill Shankly

Born: 2 September 1913, Glenbuck, Scotland

Teams managed: Carlisle (England), Grimsby (England), Workington (England), Huddersfield (England), Liverpool (England)

Bill Shankly played for Carlisle, Preston and Scotland during the 1930s, and began his managerial career at Carlisle. In 1959, he took over a fading Liverpool side, then stuck firmly in the Second Division; once Liverpool achieved promotion to the First Division in 1962, under his management, there was no stopping them. From 1964, Shankly steered the club to the League Championship, FA Cup and League Championship (again) in consecutive seasons. With the assistance of Bob Paisley, he laid the foundations that would make Liverpool the best football club in Europe. He retired in 1974 after achieving further FA Cup success.

Jock Stein

Born: 5 October 1923; Scotland

Teams managed: Dunfermline (Scotland), Glasgow Celtic (Scotland), Leeds United (England), Scottish national side

The first man to guide a UK team to European Cup glory, Jock Stein achieved just about every available honour in the game. He was manager of the Glasgow Celtic side that collected nine consecutive titles between 1966 and 1974, plus a tenth in 1977, but it was his side's European Cup triumph in 1967 that earned him his place in the managerial hall of fame: he guided a team that was made up almost entirely of Glaswegian players to victory over the favourites, Internazionale. After a brief spell in charge at Leeds, Stein took over as the manager of the Scottish national side. Tragically, he died of a heart attack during the match that ensured Scotland's qualification for the 1986 World Cup Finals.

Giovanni Trapattoni

Born: 17 March 1939, Milan, Italy

Teams managed: AC Milan (Italy), Juventus (Italy), Internazionale (Italy), Juventus (Italy), Bayern Munich, (West Germany), Cagliari (Italy), Bayern Munich (Germany), Italian national side

Giovanni Trapattoni spent his time as a player during the late 1950s and early 1960s; he was so highly regarded as a man-marker that he was spoken of as the only player who could mark the re-nowned Pelé out of a game. He attained two European Cups during his time with AC Milan. When his playing days were over, he made the move into coaching, eventually taking over the task at Juventus – where he was instrumental in winning the World Club Cup, the European Cup, the European Cup Winners' cup, the UEFA Cup, the European Supercup, seven Italian Championships and two national cups – all in the space of eight years! Later he managed a series of clubs without similar success before leading Bayern Munich to the Bundesliga title.

Louis Van Gaal

Born: 1951, Amsterdam, Holland

Teams managed: Ajax (Holland), Barcelona (Spain), Dutch National Team

Confident to the point of ar-rogance, Louis Van Gaal was the man who transformed Ajax's fortunes and was responsible for returning the famous Dutch club to their glory-days of the 1970s. He started his professional play-ing career with the same club, then moved on to Antwerp, Telstar, Sparta, and AZ 67 Alkmaar. He took over the task of managing Ajax from Leo Beenhakker in 1991. The team he assembled, compris-ing largely home-grown players, achieved victory in the UEFA Cup in 1992 and, after gaining the first of three consecutive League titles in 1994, lifted the European Cup in

1995. That year, his side swept all opposition before them: they also picked up the European Supercup and the World Club Cup.

Van Gaal moved to Barcelona in the summer of 1997. He was the Dutch National coach when they failed to qualify for WC 2002.

Terry Venables

Born: 6 January 1943, Dagenham, England

Teams managed: Crystal Palace (England), Queens Park Rangers (England), Barcelona (Spain), Tottenham Hotspur (England), English and Australian national teams, Crystal Palace (England), Middlesbrough (England), Leeds (England)

After becoming the only player to win England caps at every level from schoolboy to full, Terry Venables started his managerial career in the role of assistant to Malcolm Allison at Crystal Palace. Then, taking over from Allison, he built up a much-hyped team of youngsters during the early 1980s. Upon moving to Queens Park Rangers, he oversaw the installation of England's first artificial pitch. Under his management, Barcelona, having won the Spanish title, almost landed one of the biggest prizes of all: his team lost in a penalty shoot-out in the 1986 European Cup Final.

Next he took up a position with Tottenham Hotspur, with whom he gained the 1991 FA Cup, then he led a buy-out of the club, only to leave as a result of a dispute with his partner, businessman Alan Sugar. The feud with Sugar would bedevil Venables' subsequent career with the English national side; after the team had reached the semi-finals of Euro 96, he resigned. After that, he combined coaching the Australian national side with owning the English club Portsmouth.

He briefly joined Crystal Palace in 1998, acted as consultant manager at Middlesbrough and took over at Leeds United for part of the 2002–2003 season.

Mario Zagallo

Born: 2 July 1932, Brazil

Teams managed: Botafogo (Brazil), Fluminese (Brazil), Flamengo (Brazil), Brazilian national side, Kuwaiti national side, United Arab Emirates national side, Brazilian national side

Zagallo was the first man to attain the World Championship as both a player and, then, a manager. He was a very fit and successful left-winger with Flamengo and Botafogo, and his international career was equally impressive: he was in the sides that won the 1958 and 1962 World Cups. Known as 'Lucky', because he made those sides only through injuries suffered by others, he seemed to be equally blessed in his managerial career when it came to the players he could choose. Following Brazil's disastrous showing in England in 1966, he was given the chance of taking his country to the next World Cup. Gifted with a team of outstanding individuals, he allowed them to

express themselves in a way many coaches might not have done. The reward, in 1970, was the most famous of all World Cup wins. After failing to perform a repeat with a more physical side in 1974, Zagallo moved to the Middle East before assisting Carlos Alberto Perreira in Brazil's successful 1994 campaign. Thereafter, he became national manager again. A stern taskmaster, he led Brazil to the 1996 Olympic final, the 1997 Copa America title and the 1997 Confederational Cup.

Left: Mario Zagallo, castigated by the Brazilian press for Brazil's loss to Argentina on the eve of France 1998.

Right: From Crystal Palace to England, Terry Venables showed the same appetite for challenge he'd shown on the pitch.

Opposite: In Barcelona for 1997, Van Gaal has proved himself an inspirational coach.

GAZETTE

Law and Order

The laws of soccer are under constant revision, as the lawmakers seek to make the game ever more attractive to fans, sponsors and TV companies.

Within the past few years alone, for example, goalkeepers have been barred from picking up back passes or holding on to the ball for more than six seconds, but have become permitted to move along the goal-line during penalties, something disallowed before.

The International Board officially determines these changes. For historical reasons, the Board consists of representatives from the four home nations – England, Scotland, Wales and Northern Ireland – and four from the other 150-plus countries in FIFA, football's governing body; the identity of the latter rotates. The desire to retain this format is one reason why the UK does not enter a football team in the Olympics, as the four Football Associations might then have to offer a combined UK team in all competitions including the World Cup finals.

The laws were first codified in 1848 by representatives of the public schools, the first exponents of organized football. Until then, each school or club

had its own rules. Some permitted catching the ball and running with it (hence came rugby football), throwins with one hand rather than two, and even 'hacking' (the deliberate kicking of opposition players on the shins). These diverse rules were gradually adapted until, in 1863, the newly formed Football Association adopted a set of laws drawn up by Cambridge University.

In the early years there were a number of changes: the crossbar was introduced, handling was restricted to the goalkeeper, 'tries and conversions' were eliminated, etc., until, by the 1880s, the game became recognizably similar to today's.

Referees are the sole arbiters, but they have the help of assistants (formerly called linesmen). These officials traditionally wear black, though a variety of other colours is now used, especially in European and international matches. In some countries the officials wear kit dictated by sponsors. Women are allowed to officiate at men's matches; there is currently a female

Above: **The dreaded red card, signalling an early shower for someone.**

assistant, Wendy Toms, working in the English Premiership. A female referee will not be long.

Now that the game is becoming faster, consideration is being given to handing the responsibility for timekeeping to a fourth official in the stand, allow-

ing instant video evidence (as in Rugby League and cricket), having full-time referees, and having two referees and no assistants (as in hockey).

What follows is a précis of the 17 Laws and their associated advice. More detailed rules are available from your local soccer association.

RED CARD The fastest club sending-off was that of Giuseppe Lorenzo of Bologna, dismissed after 10 seconds of a Serie-A match against Parma after striking an opponent.

Law 1: The field of play

The pitch is rectangular in shape, 100–130 yards (90–120m) long by 50–100 yards (45–90m) wide. A halfway-line is marked, with a circle of 10 yards' (9.15m) radius at its centre. Most professional grounds measure about 115 x 75 yards (105 x 70m). The goal area, 20 x 6 yards (18.32 x 5.5m), extends from the goal-line and is enclosed within the penalty area, which is a 44 x 18-yard (40.32 x 16.5m) rectangle. Within that area, 12 yards (11m) from the goal-line and in line with the centre of the goal, is the penalty spot. An arc of radius 10 yards (9.15m), centred on the penalty spot, is drawn outside the penalty area.

Each of the pitch's four corners should have a flag at least 5 feet (1.5m) high placed on it and a quarter-circle, of radius 1 yard (90cm), drawn around it.

The goal consists of two upright posts, 8 yards (7.32m) apart, topped with a bar 8 feet (2.44m) from the ground. The goals should be anchored to the ground and have nets attached. If the crossbar breaks during a competitive match, the game cannot be resumed until it is replaced by another bar.

Law 2: The Ball

The ball is spherical and of circumference 27–28 inches (68.5–71cm). Its internal pressure should be 0.6–1.1 atmospheres and its weight 14–16 ounces (400–454g).

If the ball bursts or becomes deflated during play, the match is restarted with a dropped ball at the point at which the ball became defective – unless it was in the goal area, when the restart is on the edge of the goal area, parallel to the goal-line.

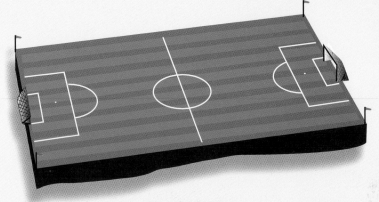

Above: A football pitch should measure between 100–130 yards (90–120m) by 50–100 yards (45–90m).

UK FOOTBALL

Only six teams have won the English League/Cup double:

- Preston (1888)
- Aston Villa (1897)
- Tottenham Hotspur (1961)
- Arsenal (1971, 1998, 2002)
- Liverpool (1986)
- Manchester United (1994, 1996, 1999)

In 1908 the Football Association attempted to introduce a transfer-fee limit of £350. The restriction, brought into practice following the £1000 transfer of Alf Common from Sunderland to Middlesbrough in 1905, lasted just four months.

Eight men have been knighted by Britain for services to the game: Sir Stanley Matthews, Sir Alf Ramsey, Sir Matt Busby, Sir Tom Finney, Sir Bobby Charlton, Sir Geoff Hurst, Sir Alex Ferguson and Sir Bobby Robson.

In 1961 Denis Law scored seven times in an FA Cup tie at Luton for Manchester City – and lost. He scored all six goals in the original match, which was abandoned due to flooding when City was leading 6-2. He scored again in the re-match, but this time City lost 3-1.

In 1930-1 Blackpool conceded a record 125 goals in the (old) First Division. They were not relegated.

In 1993 Hartlepool United went 13 matches (11 League, two Cup) without scoring a goal: 20 hours and 27 minutes.

Above: **Jimmy Greaves warms up, in the days when the ball was much heavier.**

PETER SHILTON He criticizes himself for goals the combined talents of Clemence, Banks, Southall and Grobbelaar in the same net could not keep out. – John Barnes, England team-mate

Law 3: Number of players

The team consists of no more than 11 players, one being the goalkeeper. There can be up to seven substitutes, but none of these can enter the field without the referees' permission and until the departing player has left. Substitutes should enter at the half-way line but their studs must be checked by the assistant.

If one team has or is reduced to under seven players, the match is invalid. If a player is sent off before a match begins he may be replaced, but only by one of the previously designated substitutes.

Law 4: Players' equipment

A player shall wear a jersey, shorts, socks, boots and shinpads (which must be covered by the socks). The goalkeeper shall wear a jersey coloured differently from those of the other members of the team.

Law 5: Referees

The Referee's authority begins as soon as he enters the field of play. His decision is final. He enforces the laws, plays 'advantage' when appropriate, records events in the game, and keeps time. He can stop or suspend the game if he deems necessary, signalling

Above: **A referee's assistant attracts the referee's attention.**

the recommencement after any stoppage. He should understand completely every law, be absolutely fair and impartial, and keep physically fit.

Law 6: Referee's assistant

The referee's two assistants shall indicate when the ball is out of play, which side is entitled to the subsequent

Above: **The referee is the sole arbiter on the pitch.**

PELÉ He was unselfish, a true team man. He was playing with blokes who'd spent their careers with Watford and Sheffield United but never thought himself above them. – Steve Hunt, team-mate at New York Cosmos

GOALSCORING RECORDS

ALL-TIME HIGHEST GOALSCORING AGGREGATE

1282: Pelé (1956–77: Santos, Brazil, New York Cosmos, 1365 matches – includes many in friendlies for Santos)

FASTEST GOALS

3.5 seconds: Colin Cowperthwaite, Barrow v Kettering (Alliance Premier 1979)

4 seconds: Jim Fryatt, Bradford PA v Tranmere (Division 4 1965); Gerry Allen, Whitstable v Danson (Kent League 1989); Damien Mori, Adelaide City v Sydney United (Australian National League 1995 – backed by film evidence)

FASTEST HAT-TRICKS

110 seconds: Maglioni (Independiente v Gimnasia de la Plata 1973)

2 minutes: Jimmy Scarth (Gillingham v Leyton Orient, Division 3S 1952)

FASTEST INTERNATIONAL HAT-TRICK

3 minutes: Willie Hall (England v Northern Ireland 1938)

HIGHEST SCORE IN INTERNATIONAL PENALTY SHOOTOUT

North Korea 11, Hong Kong 10 (Asian Cup 1975)

HIGHEST SCORE (AGGREGATE) IN EUROPEAN CLUB COMPETITIONS

21–0 Chelsea v Jeaunesse Hautcharage (Luxembourg), European Cup Winners' Cup, 1971

21–0 Feyenoord v US Ramelange (Luxembourg), UEFA Cup, 1972

HIGHEST SCORE IN ONE EUROPEAN CLUB COMPETITION MATCH

16–1 Sporting Lisbon v Apoel Nicosia, 1963

---

corner kick, goal kick or throw-in, and when a substitution is to be made.

In practice, assistants also signal off-side violations and other infringements the referee may not have observed.

Law 7: Duration of the game

Two periods of 45 minutes each, plus injury time to be added at the end of each respective half. Such added duration is to make up for time lost through substitutions, injuries and time-wasting; the precise period is at the referee's discretion only.

Law 8: The start of play

The choice of ends is decided by a toss of the coin. The team losing the toss kicks off. On the referee's signal, the game is started by the ball being kicked forward. Every player must be in his own half, and none of the non-kicking-off side may be within 10 yards (9m) of the ball. If any of the above regulations are not followed, the kick is retaken. The player who has kicked off cannot kick the ball again until another player has. If he does, an indirect free kick is given against him.

After a goal is scored, the conceding team kicks off in the same way. After half-time, the game restarts with a kick-off taken by the team other than the one which started the game. A goal can be scored from a kick-off.

After any stoppage not caused by an infringement or by the ball going out of play, the game is restarted by the referee dropping the ball at the place of the suspension – unless this is in

ATTENDANCE The greatest recorded attendance for a football match has been the 199,850 at the Maracana, Brazil, for the 1950 World Cup Final between Brazil and Uruguay (1–2).

the goal area, in which case the ball is dropped on the line marking the goal area parallel to the place of suspension. If the dropped ball is played before it hits the ground, it must be dropped another time.

Law 9: Ball in and out of play

The ball is out of play if it is wholly over the goal-line or touch-line, or if the referee has stopped play.

Law 10: Method of scoring

A goal is scored when the whole of the ball passes over the goal-line, under the crossbar and between the posts. A goal cannot be allowed if the ball has been stopped by an outside agent from going over the line; the game is restarted with a dropped ball. If a spectator comes onto the pitch as the ball is going into goal (as with Geoff Hurst's third in the 1966 World Cup Final) the goal is allowed unless the spectator has made contact with the ball or otherwise interfered

Above: **Players protesting against a yellow card.**

with play. In such a case a drop-ball is taken.

Law 11: Off-side

A player is in an off-side position if he is nearer to the opposition's goal-line than the ball unless (a) he is in his own half of the field or (b) he is not nearer to the goal-line than two of his opponents. He is declared off-side and penalized only if, in the referee's opinion, he is (a) interfering with play or an opponent or (b) seeking to gain an advantage by being in that position. He cannot be off-side from a goal kick, corner kick or throw-in.

Law 12: Fouls and misconduct

Nine offences, if committed intentionally, are punished by a direct free kick (penalty kick if in the opposition's penalty area). These offences are as follows:

- kicking or attempting to kick an opponent
- tripping an opponent
- jumping at an opponent
- charging an opponent in a dangerous or violent manner
- charging an opponent from behind (unless the opponent is obstructing)
- striking, attempting to strike or spitting at an opponent
- holding an opponent
- pushing an opponent
- handling the ball (the exception being that the goalkeeper may handle the ball when within his area, subject to certain limitations – see below)

FACT FILE

FACT: The USA hosted the first World Cup match played indoors when it played Canada in the Seattle Kingdome in a 1976 qualifier. A month before, the same teams had contested the first World Cup match to be played on artificial turf – in Vancouver, Canada.

FACT: The fastest World Cup sending-off was when José Batista of Uruguay, playing against Scotland in Mexico 86, was dismissed within 54 seconds. The match ended 0-0. There were no further dismissals.

FACT: The youngest player to appear in a World Cup finals tournament is Norman Whiteside who was 17 years and 42 days when he played for Northern Ireland at España 82. Whiteside is also the youngest goalscorer, at 18 years, 19 days, in an FA Cup Final (1985, Manchester United v Everton, 1-0).

STANLEY MATTHEWS His name is symbolic of the beauty of the game, his fame timeless. A magical player, of the people, for the people. – inscription on statue in his Potteries birthplace

A further five offences are punishable by an indirect free kick:

- dangerous play, such as raising a foot to the goalkeeper
- charging fairly but when the ball is not within playing distance
- obstructing an opponent
- charging the goalkeeper
- for the goalkeeper,

(a) taking more than four steps while holding or bouncing the ball,

(b) touching the ball with his hands after a deliberate back-pass by a team-mate

(c) time-wasting, including holding the ball for more than six seconds

Entering the field of play without permission, persistent infringement, dissent and ungentlemanly conduct incur a caution (yellow card) from the referee and, for the last three offences, an indirect free kick is awarded to the opposition.

Violent conduct, serious foul play, foul or abusive language or a second cautionable offence incurs a dismissal (red card). Fouling a player who has a clear goal-scoring opportunity is a sending-off offence, as is handling the ball so as to prevent a goal (the goalkeeper is obviously exempt from this last regulation).

Law 13: Free kick

A goal can be scored from a direct free kick but not, without being touched by another player, from an indirect free kick. Opponents must be 10 yards (9m) from the kick and, if it is in the de-fending side's penalty area, the ball must leave the area before another player can touch it.

The ball must be stationary at the start of the free kick, and the kicker can kick it only once before another player touches the ball.

Law 14: Penalty kick

A penalty kick is a direct free kick inside the penalty area. It is taken from the penalty spot, and all players save the goalkeeper and the penalty taker must be outside the area. Before it is taken, the goalkeeper can move along the goal-line but not forward of it. If time has been extended for a penalty to be taken, the match or half is over as soon as the kick is taken; in such an instance, time is not allowed for a shot from a rebound.

Law 15: Throw-in

A throw-in is taken to re-start the game after the ball has gone over the touch-line. The taker, who is of the opposing side to the player who put the ball out, faces the play and, with both feet on the ground, throws the ball with both hands from behind and over his head. Part of both of his feet must be behind or on the touchline.

Law 16: Goal kick

When the attacking team has put the ball out of play behind the goal-line, the game is restarted with a goal kick; this may be taken from any point inside the goal area by any defending player, including the goalkeeper.

Opposing players may not be in the area when the kick is taken, and the ball may not be played again until it has left the area.

Above: **Michel Platini takes a free kick for France against Spain.**

There was a 33rd team at World Cup 2002 – an international team of referees and assistants.

The composition or the 33rd team was as follows: Europe 14 referees and 14 assistants; Asia – 5 referees and 7 assistants; Africa – 5 referees and 5 assistants; North and Central America and the Caribbean – 5 refer-ees and 4 assistants; South America – 6 referees and 4 assistants; and Oceania – 1 referee and 2 assistants.

In any team there must be a balance between youth and experience, this was true of the 2002 FIFA World Cup referees. There were the ex-perienced referees such as Ali Bujsaim of the United Arab Emirates, Vitor Mello Pereira of Portugal, Gamal el Ghandour of Egypt, Kin Milton Nielson of Denmark, Italy's Pierluigi Collina and Scotland's Hugh Dallas.

The youngest referee was Mark Shield of Australia who impressed the FIFA Referee's Committee during the FIFA World Youth Championship in Argentina. Felipe Ramos of Mexico, Peter Prendergast of Jamaica, Carlos Simon of Brazil were all involved in the 2000 Sydney Olympic Games. So whatever their age all the referees were experi-enced at international level.

The assistant referees were also all carefully selected.

All the referees and assis-tants attended seminars and training prior to the tourna-ment. Special emphasis was placed on dealing with the increasing problem of simu-lation or, more accurately, cheating. Players are too often guilty of diving and it has become almost an art form – and very difficult for the referee to identify.

As part of FIFA's profes-sionalisation of refereeing, all underwent a specially pre-pared FIFA Referee Fitness Programme under Professor Werner Helsen of the Katholieke Universiteit Leuven in Belgium, a world expert in training programmes for referees.

The referees and assistants were the fittest and best prepared ever! ■

RECEIPTS The record receipts for a match, prior to the 1998 World Cup, was the £4.3M paid by spectators at the 1990 World Cup Final in Rome.

95

Right: **Weber scores and provides West Germany the life-line of extra time.**

World Cup Final, Wembley, 30 July 1966

They think it's all over – It is now!

England 4 (Hurst 3, Peters), **West Germany 2** (Haller, Weber)

When he took over as England manager in 1963, Alf Ramsey told a sceptical nation that England would win the World Cup in 1966 – and they did, but the hard way.

West Germany scored first, through Haller, after only 12 minutes, and then staved off defeat with the last kick of normal time when Weber levelled the game to 2–2. That should have given West Germany the psychological advantage, but Ramsey famously told his men before the start of extra time: 'You've beaten them once, now go on and beat them again.' West Ham team-mates Hurst and Peters had scored England's two goals; now Hurst made it 3–2 after 100 minutes of playing time with the most controversial goal in soccer history: did the ball bounce over the line or not after hitting the crossbar? No one will ever know, but the goal stood.

Hurst became the first player to score a hat-trick in a World Cup Final with the thunderbolt volley he delivered as the last kick of the game. The ordeal was over and England had won ∎

Mike Collett

The Ref Plays a Blinder

Following are two of the most notorious refereeing decisions. Both occurred during the 1980s, and both happened at World Cup finals, when the eyes of world turn as one to 'the beautiful game'.

In the 1986 World Cup finals Diego Maradona of Argentina clearly punched the ball into the net in the quarter-final against England. The Tunisian referee, Ali Ben Naceur, allowed the goal, the first of the game.

Argentina won 2–1 with Maradona later scoring a brilliant individual goal. They went on to win the trophy with Maradona claiming his controversial goal had been scored by 'the hand of God'.

With 57 minutes gone in the 1982 World Cup semi-final between France and Germany, Patrick Battiston ran onto a through ball that had beat the German defence. He pushed the ball past the onrushing goal-keeper, Schumacher, only to be brutally clubbed to the ground by a forearm smash.

Battiston lost two teeth and was knocked unconscious by the blow, and amazingly the referee took no action at all. Germany won 4–3, but went on to lose in the Final to Italy ∎

ALF RAMSEY At the beginning of extra-time in the 1966 World Cup final, the English coach was heard to say to his players, 'You've beaten them once, now go on and beat them again.'

The Most Bizarre Ending to a Game

In the 1978 World Cup finals match between Brazil and Sweden, Clive Thomas, from Wales, blew the final whistle as a corner, taken by Nelinho of Brazil, was in the air.

The ball was headed in by Zico but the goal, having been scored after the end of play, was disallowed. The game ended 1–1. Brazil still progressed to the second stage but Sweden failed to gain another point.

In the 1998 English FA Cup, a similar incident happened.

At the end of Wimbledon's match with Wrexham, Marcus Gayle's shot would have been the winner for Wimbledon if it hadn't been disallowed. The Dons managed to get their revenge – they won the replay ■

Glenn Moore

Above: **Swan before his disgraced exit from professional football.**

England 1964

The Soccer Conspiracy Case

As many as 60 players were proven to be involved, and 10 were sent to prison, including three of the best-known players of the time – Peter Swan, David 'Bronco' Layne and Tony Kay.

In December 1962 they were team-mates at Sheffield Wednesday, and they had bet a few pounds on their team losing at Ipswich. Wednesday did indeed lose the match, 2–0, but the £100 each player pocketed was to prove a very hollow prize. The story broke in the *Sunday People* in April 1964, when it was revealed that this was not a solitary example of a game being thrown: matches between Lincoln and Brentford and between York and Oldham had been fixed on the very same day. Swan and Kay, who had moved to Everton for a record £55,000, could have been part of the squad that won the World Cup for England. Instead, they became disgraced outcasts ■

Send off the Ref!

In 1997 Kurt Roethlisberger, a Swiss referee, was banned for life by UEFA for attempting to fix the result of a Champions League game between Grasshopper Zurich and Auxerre – but this wasn't his first bad performance.

Roethlisberger had officiated at the 1990 and 1994 World Cup finals but was sent home from the latter after a failing to award Belguim a penalty in a second round match which they lost 3–2 to Germany.

He was also suspended for three months in 1995 for misusing his position to win a seat in the Swiss parliament – he had posed in his referee's uniform with a political slogan over the FIFA badge in campaign literature.

In 1993 Eric Cantona of Manchester United was suspended for being sent off by Roethlisberger after a Champions' Cup match against Galatasaray. Cantona, who was banned for four months, later suggested that Roethlisberger had been 'bought'. He was further disciplined for this but may have been right ■

SWAN AND KAY Swan and Kay could have been part of the squad that won the World Cup for England. Instead they became disgraced outcasts . . .

97

CLUBS, SQUADS AND TEAMS

There is a direct line between the health and success of a nation's domestic leagues and success at international level. Clubs like Bayern Munich, Independiente and Manchester United have all shown the way on the world stage, and generally, the national side has followed. In this section we list the great clubs over the years, those that have had long periods of huge success and those that had only two or three years in the limelight. When it comes to the national sides, there are countries which have won the World Cup and there are those that have never progressed beyond the first round, but each has its own contribution to make. We finish this section with the great stadiums of the world, places which have become temples to the beautiful game.

Please note: Both the clubs and the nations are listed under the name used in their own country and the colours of all team strips are ordered shirt, shorts and socks.

A-Z of Countries

Algérie (Algeria)

Founded: 1962

Colours: Green; white; red

World Cup Appearances: 2
Best: 1st round 1982, 1986

Honours: African Nations Cup
winners 1990

Algeria has been one of Africa's most successful nations. The side won the African Nations Cup in 1990, having finished second in 1980 and reached the semi-finals in 1984 and 1988. Algeria came to international prominence by beating West Germany 2–1 in the 1982 World Cup Finals.

Argentina

Founded: 1893

Colours: Blue/white; black; white

World Cup Appearances: 13
Best: Winners 1978, 1986

Honours: Copa America Winners 1910, 1921, 1925, 1927, 1929, 1937, 1941, 1945, 1946, 1947, 1955, 1957, 1991, 1993; Confederations Cup 1993

Argentina are one of world football's superpowers. The side won the World Cup for the first time in 1978, achieved a second triumph in 1986, when led by the irrepressible Diego Maradona, and reached the 1990 final.
However, it is not only the side's recent history that is impressive: Argentina have been one of the most consistently successful footballing nations of the past 100 years. The game was taken to

Argentina by the British in the 1860s, initially being played only by British residents in Buenos Aires. By the turn of the century, however, Argentinian domestic football was thriving. In 1901, the national side took its place in the history books when it played neighbouring Uruguay in the first international match outside the UK. Professional football arrived in the country in 1931, following the success of the national team at the 1928 Olympic Games and the 1930 World Cup Finals; on both occasions, Argentina were runners-up to their great rivals Uruguay.

As so often happens, though, success also brought problems. Argentina's achievements did not go unnoticed in Europe, and many members of the side were lured away from the domestic league by the greater riches on offer in Italy. This had a knock-on effect on the national side: to avoid a repeat of that poaching, Argentina sent a third-rate side to the 1934 finals (in Italy, ironically) and did not

> **. . . it is not only the side's recent history that is impressive, Argentina have been one of the most consistently successful footballing nations**

make a serious challenge for football's greatest prize until some 40 years later.

Rejuvenation came in 1978, when Argentina took advantage of hosting the World Cup to finally win tournament. A team that contained only one overseas-based player (striker Mario Kempes, who became the star of

the competition) swept all before it, beating Holland 3–1 in a thrilling final. Again, many players defected to European clubs, but with the development of cheap air travel, the departures did not have the same debilitating effect on the national side, which continued to go from strength to strength.

By the time the 1986 World Cup Finals came around, Argentina was one of the favourites, largely because of Maradona. He inspired the side with some stunning performances, and although he was widely criticized for his 'Hand of God' goal against England in the quarter-finals (when he used his fist to 'score' a goal), it was fitting that, after a topsy-turvy final against West Germany, which Argentina won 3–2, he should lift the trophy.

Four years later, the same two sides met again in the World Cup

A-Z OF COUNTRIES

Above: The Australian national side for 1974.

Below: Bolivia v Germany in USA 94.

Final. This time, it was a bad-tempered game and largely devoid of skill. Argentina had two players sent off before being beaten by a penalty a few minutes from time.

Maradona was brought back into the fold for one final stab at glory in 1994, after serving a 15-month world-wide ban for drug abuse. His tournament ended in shame when he was sent home after testing positive for an illegal substance. With his expulsion went Argentina's hopes: they were sent tumbling by Romania. In 1997, Maradona was caught a third time for drug abuse, but the Argentine football association was already looking to the future, having retained the World Youth Championships in Malaysia that year.

Australia

Founded: 1961

Colours: Gold; green; white

World Cup Appearances: 1
Best: 1st round 1974

Soccer has always been a minor sport in Australia, being surpassed by cricket, rugby (both union and league) and Australian rules football.

The national side qualified for the 1974 World Cup Finals via the Asian group. Now, however, Oceania has its own qualifying groups. These do not offer automatic entry to the finals: to achieve their aim, Oceanic sides must follow a convoluted route. In 1994, for example, they had to beat first Canada, the CONCACAF runners-up, then Argentina to qualify, after winning the Oceanic group. Not surprisingly, this task proved too severe.

However, with success at youth level leading to many players, such as Mark Bosnich, being signed by European clubs, and former England coach Terry Venables appointed manager, Australian football appeared to be on the up, but suffered a blow by losing to Iran in a 1998 World Cup qualifying eliminator. Despite some financial problems, the domestic competition has been expanded to become truly national, while clubs have been forced to reduce links with their ethnic origins, which had alienated many Australians from the sport.

Belgique (Belgium)

Founded: 1895

Colours: Red; red; red

World Cup Appearances: 11
Best: 4th 1986

Belgium has the second oldest league outside the UK, but the Belgians' reluctance to embrace professionalism held them back for a long time. Belgium was one of only four European sides to take part in the first World Cup, but not until 1972, when professionalism was introduced to Belgian soccer, did the national team begin to improve.

Progress was so rapid between 1972 and 1984 that the Belgians reached the last eight of four successive European Championships. The team's best effort came

in 1980, when they finished runners-up to West Germany, and the mainstays of that side went on to serve the nation splendidly in further World Cups. Stars like goalkeeper Jean-Marie Pfaff and striker Jan Ceulemans were the cornerstones of an excellent team.

Belgium's finest World Cup moment came in 1986, when they reached the semi-finals, overcoming the Soviet Union 4–3 in a thrilling second-round match on the way.

Bolívia (Bolivia)

Founded: 1925

Colours: Green; white; green

World Cup Appearances: 3
Best: 1st round

Honours: South American Championship winners 1963

Bolivia are one of the best lesser teams in South America, most of their success being due to their record at home, where they play at high altitude. This is underlined by their winning the Copa America in 1963 and being runners-up in 1997, both times having hosted the tournament.

Brasil (Brazil)

Founded: 1914

Colours: Yellow; blue; white

World Cup Appearances: 17
Best: Winners 1958, 1962, 1970, 1994, 2002

Honours: South American Champions 1919, 1922, 1949, 1989, 1997, 1999; Confederations Cup 1997

The mere mention of Brazil conjures up images of great skill, stunning goals and beautiful free-flowing football. The greatest Brazilian player of all time, and arguably the best player ever to step on to a soccer pitch, Pelé,

described football as 'the beautiful game', and since he retired every Brazilian side has been attempting to live up to that description. Some of those teams have succeeded, some of them have failed, but at least all have attempted to play the game with flair and imagination. Perhaps this is why Brazil is the most widely respected and loved country in world soccer.

Domestic football in Brazil began towards the end of the 19th century, initiated by migrant British workers. Leagues were established in Rio de Janeiro and São Paulo by the turn of the century, but the national side was slower to get started, not making its international début until 1914, when it visited Buenos Aires to take on Argentina.

Brazil entered the South American Championship for the first time two years later, and in 1930 took part in the first World Cup Finals. On that tournament, the Brazilians have stamped an indelible mark. This is the only

Below: Brazil celebrate their victory over Italy in the 1994 World Cup final.

A-Z OF COUNTRIES

country to have played in every finals competition, and the only country to lift the trophy four times. It did take the Brazilians a while to get going – they crashed out in the first round in 1930 and 1934. In 1938, the team found their feet and reached the semi-finals.

The golden era of Brazilian football was between 1950 and 1970, during which period the side won the World Cup three times. They were runners-up when hosting the World Cup in 1950, reached the quarter-finals in 1954 and claimed the crown for the first time in 1958. With 17-year-old Pelé scoring twice, they hammered the host nation, Sweden, 5–2 in the final.

Four years later, in Chile, Brazil retained the trophy, but this time without the injured Pelé. He also missed much of the 1966 tournament in England after being brutally fouled – Brazil went out in the second round.

By 1970, the Brazilians had rebuilt, and the side that won the trophy in Mexico was widely regarded as the greatest football team ever. It played with a flair that has never been matched, and the 4–1 win over Italy in the final – especially the stunning fourth goal from Carlos Alberto – will never be forgotten. That victory meant Brazil kept the Jules Rimet Trophy, through having won it three times.

Not surprisingly, succeeding Brazilian sides have found it difficult to repeat past glories. They reached the semi-finals in 1974 and 1978, but failed in the next three tournaments. The balance of power was redressed somewhat in 1994, when Brazil took the trophy for the fourth time, although they needed a penalty shoot-out to beat Italy.

Brazil once again reached the final in 1998, but the team underperformed following Ronaldo's illness on the eve of the final, losing to host team France. Four years later he found redemption when he won the Golden Boot with 8 goals, scoring twice in the Final against Germany.

Right: Hristo Stoichkov celebrates scoring in USA 94.

Bulgaria

Founded: 1923

Colours: White; green; red

World Cup Appearances: 7
Best: 4th 1994

As with so many Eastern Bloc countries, Bulgaria made little impact in world football until the communists took over in 1944 and organized the domestic game. Alas, a rigid style of play was imposed on the national team, which discouraged individual flair and flexibility, so their performance was very predictable. Thus, although Bulgaria qualified for five of the seven World Cup Finals between 1962 and 1986, playing 16 matches, it failed to win one game. The team finally made the breakthrough in 1994. Under the leadership of Hristo Stoichkov, it reached the semi-finals, where it lost to Italy.

While the end of communism has improved the national side, the exodus of players to Western Europe has caused a decline in the domestic game.

Cameroun (Cameroon)

Founded: 1960

Colours: Green; red; yellow

World Cup Appearances: 5
Best: Quarter-finals 1990

Honours: African Nations Cup Winners 1984, 1988, 2000, 2002; Olympic Winners 2000

Cameroon put African football on the map with its exploits at the 1982 and 1990 World Cup Finals. The team made a bigger impact than any other African side had managed, and ensured that the Africans were allocated a third entry in the 1994 World Cup finals. Cameroon's greatest achievement came in 1990, when it reached the World Cup quarter-finals. Cameroon's most noted player was Roger Milla, delighting fans with his goals and his 'Milla Wiggle'.

Since Cameroon won the African Nations Cup in 1984 and 1988, the side can justifiably claim to have been Africa's best team in the

1980s, and although Nigeria took over that mantle for a while, they came back strongly in 2000 to win the African Nations Cup and the Olympics.

Canada

Founded: 1912

Colours: Red; red; red

World Cup Appearances: 1
Best: 1st round 1986

Honours: Olympic winners 1904 (Galt FC of Ontario)

Soccer in Canada has to compete with the major North American sports: baseball, gridiron, ice hockey and basketball. Because Canada is so large, there was no national league until 1987: one has to travel hundreds rather than tens of kilometres between fixtures, and sometimes it is thousands. So success at international level has been scarce for Canada, and the side has reached the World Cup Finals only once, in 1986.

Ceskoslovensko (Czech Republic/ Slovakia)

Founded: 1994

Colours: Red; white; blue

World Cup Appearances: 0 (8 as Czechoslovakia)
Best: Final 1934, 1962 (as Czechoslovakia)

Honours: European Championship winners 1976 (as Czechoslovakia), Olympic winners 1980 (as Czechoslovakia)

It was after the 1994 World Cup Finals that the Czech Republic was born. The former Czecho-slovakia split into the Czech Republic and Slovakia, and each formed its own association, league and national team. Of the two sides, the Republic's appears more capable of emulating the achieve-ments of the old Czechoslovakia, even though Slovakia finished ahead of them in their 1998 World Cup qualifying group. That Czech failure was a surprise after they finished runners-up to Germany in the 1996 European Championship.

The latter feat continued the success the old Czechoslovakia had regularly enjoyed since making its début in international football in 1908. The side was runner-up in the 1920 Olympics and finished second in the 1934 World Cup, losing in the final to Italy. The communist take-over after World War II led to a reorganization of the domestic league that initially hindered development. By the 1960s, however, Czechoslovakia had one of the best sides in world football

Below: European Championship winners in 1976, Czechoslovakia would build on this success by becoming Olympic champions in 1980.

– inspired by their most famous player, Josef Masopust. In 1960, he led the team to third place in the first European Cham-pionship, and in 1962 he boosted it to the World Cup final, which it

Cameroon put African football on the map with its exploits at the 1982 and 1990 World Cup finals. The team made a bigger impact than any other African side had managed

lost to Brazil. Olympic glory fol-lowed in 1964, but Czechoslo-vakia's greatest achievement came 12 years later: the side beat West Germany (on penalties) in the European Championship Final.

Left: Colombia's 1994 World Cup campaign was marked by turgid football and tragedy.

Chile

Founded: 1895

Colours: Red; blue; white

World Cup Appearances: 7
Best: 3rd 1962

The Chileans have often been the 'nearly' men of South American football. Until Colo Colo's 1991 Libertadores Cup win, no Chilean side had even won a major honour. Although Chile qualified for five of the 11 post-war World Cups, only once did the side progress beyond the first round – in 1962, when the finals were being played in Chile. The team reached the semi-finals before losing to Brazil, the eventual winners.

Twice Chile has finished as runner-up in the South American Championship (1979 and 1987), but it faces the same problems as other Latin American countries: European clubs continually raid its domestic league, poaching all the best talent.

China

Founded: 1924

Colours: Red; white; red

World Cup Appearances: 1

China took part in the first international on Asian soil – against the Philippines in February 1913 – but that is the country's only real claim to footballing fame. Despite a huge population, success has been hard to come by. They finished as runners-up in the 1984 Asian Cup. However they qualified for their first ever World Cup in 2002.

Below: China's greatest success was to finish runner-up in the 1984 Asian Cup.

Colombia

Founded: 1924

Colours: Red; blue; red/white/blue

World Cup Appearances: 4
Best: 2nd round 1990

Colombian football has suffered years of disputes and disruptions, the most notable occurring in the 1950s when a breakaway league, the DiMayor, was formed. The DiMayor was outside FIFA's jurisdiction, and Colombian sides began importing players from all over South America and from the UK, luring them by offering huge salaries. This league collapsed in 1954, and although Colombia was readmitted to FIFA, many clubs were left in desperate financial trouble. Since then, there has been progress, but not without some tortuous twists in the tale. A new breakaway federation was formed in 1965, and FIFA was forced to intervene, effectively taking over the running of Colombian football from that time until 1971, which was when the current administration came to power.

The present Colombian side is reckoned to be the nation's best ever, and it stars the likes of Carlos Valderrama and Faustino Asprilla. It was expected to perform well in the 1994 World Cup tournament, but the side crashed out in the first round. A few days after the team arrived home, defender Andres Escobar, who had scored an own goal in the match that ended in a 2–1 defeat by the USA, was shot dead as he left a restaurant in Medellin. It is thought that his execution had been ordered by drug barons. Colombia's well-known narcotics problem continues to cast a giant shadow over the game, with kidnappings, murders and corruption causing havoc in the nation's domestic football.

Costa Rica

Founded: 1921

Colours: Red; blue; white

World Cup Appearances: 2
Best: 2nd round 1990

Honours: CONCACAF winners 1941, 1946, 1948, 1953, 1955, 1960, 1961, 1963, 1969, 1989

Costa Rica is one of the best Central American teams, but has never made its mark on the world game. The side's finest achievements came in the 1990 World Cup, when it defeated Scotland and Sweden to reach the second round. Paulo Wanchope has brought the Costa Rican game to wider attention with his exploits for Derby County and Manchester City in England.

China appeared in their first ever World Cup this year, although they finished bottom of their group and failed to score a single point.

Croatia

Founded: 1991

Colours: Red; white; blue

World Cup Appearances: 2
Best: 3rd 1998

Football has provided the one bright spot amid the turmoil in modern Croatia. The Croatians have all pulled together behind their national football team, and that fervour, together with great technical ability, has made Croatia one of Europe's most respected sides. Such is the measure of its progress that, when it reached the finals of Euro 96, it was immediately reckoned one of the favourites, despite only forming its own association in 1991.

Croatia still has some of the finest footballers in Europe. Men like Davor Suker, Alen Boksic and Zvonimir Boban could walk into virtually any international side in the world, and the 1998 World Cup Finals, when Croatia came third in its first appearance, served to underline the country's considerable footballing potential.

Danmark (Denmark)

Founded: 1889

Colours: Red; white; red

World Cup Appearances: 3
Best: Quarter-finals 1998

Honours: Olympic winners 1906, European Championship winners 1992, Confederation Cup winners 1995/6

Denmark was close behind the UK in taking up football, and the country has some of the oldest clubs in the world. In the past 20 years, the national team has

Above: Denmark celebrate winning the 1992 European Championships against all expectations.

developed into one of the best in Europe. That wasn't always the case: the Danes' rigid rules regarding amateurism meant they were left behind when the rest of Europe began to turn professional. However, this did enable them to enjoy success at the Olympic Games, winning Gold in 1906, and Silver in 1908 and 1912.

Danish football went into decline during the inter-war years. Qualification for the 1948 and 1960 Olympics sparked hope of a revival, but the rules about amateurism put paid to that. Furthermore, foreign-based players were banned from the national side. Had that ruling not been lifted in the mid-1970s, Denmark would still be down among the also-rans. But, as a flood of players left Denmark for foreign fortunes, the Danish Association had no option but to end such prohibition. The Danes subsequently reached the semi-finals of the 1984 European Championship and the second round of the 1986 World Cup.

This was just a taster for what was to come in 1992. As a last-minute replacement for the expelled Yugoslavia, Denmark arrived in Sweden for the European Championship as a rank outsider. The side's response was to thrill everyone by taking the crown in the final against Germany. Players like Peter Schmeichel and the Laudrup brothers, Brian and Michael, have followed Allen Simonsen in becoming known world-wide.

Deutschland (Germany)

Founded: 1900

Colours: White; black; white

World Cup Appearances: 15
Best: Winners 1954, 1974, 1990

Honours: European Championship winners 1972, 1980, 1996; Olympic winners 1976 (East Germany)

Germany is the most consistent nation in world football. It might not always offer the best team, but one thing is certain: at the time of a major championship, the Germans will be a finely tuned outfit capable of beating any side in the world. Three World Cups and three European Championships between 1954 and 1996 are testimony to that.

It wasn't always so: Germany's pre-war record was relatively poor, third place at the 1934 World Cup being the best the team could manage. World War II resulted in the creation of two nations out of what had been one. East Germany formed its own association, league and national side, but never matched the West's achievements. When the East was readmitted to FIFA in 1950, having been banished four years earlier, West Germany, as by then that team was known, was flourishing.

West Germany won its first World Cup in 1954; what made the

Above: Germany's Gerd Muller prepares to shoot in the 1974 World Cup finals.

Opposite, right: Alan Shearer in action for England against Germany in the 1996 European Championship.

Opposite, left: Egypt has enjoyed a renaissance over the last decade building upon the success and influence of domestic club Zamalek.

achievement all the more remarkable was that the squad beat Hungary in the final. Not only had Hungary beaten Germany 8–3 in an earlier round of the tournament, but also this was only their second defeat in five years of international competition! This triumph was only the beginning of an astonishing period for West Germany. In the World Cup, the side reached the semi-finals in 1958, the quarter-finals in 1962, and the finals in 1966. And all that despite the fact that full-time professionalism was not introduced until 1963.

Within ten years of that change, the West Germans were unquestionably the dominant force at both club and international level. Bayern Munich won a hat-trick of European Cups in 1974, 1975 and 1976, and provided most of the West German national

team that won the European Championship in 1972 and 1980, and the World Cup (in Germany) in 1974. That particular World Cup side represents the greatest in German history. It was built around three true greats – goalkeeper Sepp Maier, defender Franz Beckenbauer (the world's first and best attacking sweeper) and striker Gerd Muller, who scored an astonishing 68 goals in 62 matches during his international career. The 1974 tournament also provided the East with their greatest success when they beat West Germany in a group game.

West Germany's success rate was slowed only briefly by the break-up of that great side. Led by stars like Karl-Heinz Rummenigge and veteran Paul Breitner, the team finished runners-up to Italy in the 1982 finals, and Argentina in 1986. Four years later, with Jurgen Klinsmann and Lothar Matthaus to the fore, the West Germans reached the final again and beat Argentina 1–0.

Unification, which brought with it players like Matthias Sammer, further strengthened the side. By beating the Czech Republic in the final of Euro 96, Germany proved again that they get it right for the big tournaments. Surprisingly they reached the final of WC 2002 losing to Brazil.

Egypte (Egypt)

Founded: 1921

Colours: Red; white; black

World Cup Appearances: 2
Best: 1st round 1934, 1990

Honours: African Nations Cup winners 1957, 1959, 1986, 1998

Egypt was the first African nation to join FIFA (1923), so it comes as no great surprise that the side won the first two African

Nations Cups and made an early World Cup appearance in 1934. Egyptian football then declined until the 1980s, when it hosted and won the African Nations Cup in 1986, and reached the 1990 World Cup Finals. Zamalek, its most powerful club side, have long been a force in African football.

El Salvador

Founded: 1935

Colours: Blue; blue; blue

World Cup Appearances: 2
Best: 1st round

Honours: CONCACAF winners 1943

El Salvador's claim to fame – or should that be claim to shame? – is the 1969 'Football War', which took place with Honduras. The countries met twice in a World Cup qualifying group, and both matches ended in riots. Eventually, there was a play-off – which El Salvador won – but shortly afterwards, the nation's army invaded Honduras, claiming that the move had been made to protect El Salvadoreans who were living there. The subsequent conflict cost 3,000 lives before eventually it was resolved.

England

Founded: 1863

Colours: White; navy blue; white

World Cup Appearances: 11
Best: Winners 1966

Honours: Olympic winners 1908, 1912 (as Great Britain)

England gave football to the world, and in 1996 it 'came home', according to the famous slogan for that year's European Championship (Euro '96), held in England. In the intervening period,

A-Z OF COUNTRIES

though, football was stolen and improved by other nations. England has just one international success to its credit – the 1966 World Cup.

Modern football began on the playing fields of English public schools in the 19th century, after spending centuries as a wild inter-village game often involving teams of hundreds kicking around a pig's bladder or some other suitable 'ball'. Similar games – albeit more peaceful – are often revived at festival occasions, but the game as we know it became organized in 1863, when the Football Association was formed.

The oldest cup competition in the world – the FA Cup – was launched in 1871, followed by the first international match between England and Scotland. In 1888, the Football League was formed by the professional clubs of the north and midlands, who had gradually usurped the southern amateur clubs based on old school links and the services. At the turn of the century was born the British Championship, played between England, Scotland, Ireland and Wales. In 1908 and 1912, England and Scotland combined as Great Britain to win the Olympic title and confirm the side's place at the head of world football.

The FA, which had joined FIFA in 1905, resented the expansion of the game as the rest of the world began to take to it, and withdrew from football's governing body in 1920 because it refused to play against wartime enemies. The FA later rejoined, only to resign again in 1928 in an argument over the definition of the word 'amateur'. It was 1950 before England first entered the World Cup. The side failed to get beyond the first round – losing, incredibly, to the USA – but the English still could not believe that the rest of the world had caught up with them.

All that changed in 1953, when Hungary thrashed England 6–3 at Wembley, England's first home defeat by a non-UK nation. Further failures at the 1954, 1958 and 1962 World Cup Finals forced the English

Above: Luis Enrique in action for Spain against Bulgaria in Euro 96.

to face the reality that other countries were passing them by. However, lifted by home advantage, they realized their potential by gaining the World Cup in 1966. Famously titled the 'Wingless Wonders', they operated under a system created by manager Alf Ramsey to make the best use of the players he had available. The thrilling 4–2 final victory over West Germany, when Geoff Hurst scored a hat-trick, justified Ramsey's much criticized system.

That triumph was the springboard for English clubs to enjoy an unparalleled spell of success on the European scene. Manchester United won the European Cup in

1968 and, after regular English success in the other competitions, were emulated by Liverpool, Nottingham Forest and Aston Villa in the late 1970s and early 1980s. However, the Heysel Stadium disaster in 1985, when Liverpool and Juventus fans clashed at the European Cup Final and 39 fans, who were, for the most part, Italian, lost their lives, led to a five-year ban, during which the domestic game stagnated, becoming obsessed with power rather than skill.

The national side, which had reached the World Cup quarterfinals in 1970, failed to qualify for the 1974 and 1978 tournaments, but appeared to overcome the European club exile by reaching the quarter-finals and semi-finals in 1986 and 1990 respectively. However, failure in the 1992 European Championship Finals, and missing out altogether in the 1994 World Cup, suggested that domestic sterility had filtered through to the national side.

Recently England were more successful: when they were hosts for Euro 1996, they lost on penalties to Germany in the semi-final; they reached the 2nd round in France 1998, losing to Argentina; and reached the quarter-finals in Japan and Korea losing out to the eventual winners Brazil.

España (Spain)

Founded: 1913

Colours: Red; dark blue; black

World Cup Appearances: 11
Best: Quarter-finals 1934, 1986, 1994, 2002

Honours: European Championship winners 1964, Olympic winners 1992

Spain's place at the forefront of European soccer has more to do with performances at club level than with the achievements of its national team. Clubs like Barcelona and Real Madrid continue to be a major force in international competitions; the national side merely enjoys a reasonable level of success on a consistent basis.

Football began in Spain in the 1890s – it was started by migrant British workers – and in 1913, the Spanish Football Federation was formed to bring together the various regional organizations. The national side played its first match in 1920 and enjoyed some early success, reaching the quarter-finals of both the 1928 Olympics and the 1934 World Cup. The Spanish Civil War and World War II halted Spain's international matches for almost ten years, but the domestic

Above: France, hosts and winners of the 1984 European Championships.

league thrived as, for political reasons, the rivalry grew between the two big clubs, Real Madrid and Barcelona. By the 1950s, when both clubs began importing foreign stars like Di Stefano, Puskas and Kubala, the Spanish League's best clubs were the strongest in Europe.

This was demonstrated by the Spaniards' stranglehold on European club competitions. Real Madrid won the first five European Cups (1956–60), while Barcelona won the Fairs Cup (later to become the UEFA Cup) in 1959, 1960 and 1966. Valencia, Real Zaragoza and Atletico Madrid likewise enjoyed European success during this period, and the national side won its first major honour – the 1964 European Championship. But, while the club sides have continued to fare well, the national team has disappointed – not least when Spain hosted the 1982 World Cup. Although they won the European Championships in 1964, and the Olympics in 1992 (both at home), simply reaching the 1994 and 2002 World Cup quarter-finals matched their best World Cup performance.

France

Founded: 1918

Colours: Blue; white; red

World Cup Appearances: 11
Best: Winners 1998

Honours: European Championships winners 1984, 2000; Olympic winners 1984

England may have invented football, but it was the French who organized it and gave the world the structure it has today. The French were the chief innovators of FIFA, UEFA, the World Cup, the European Championship and the European club cups. It was thus fitting that, in 1998, they hosted and won the last World Cup of the millennium.

Coached by Aime Jaquet and inspired by Zinedine Zidane of Juventus, they cruised impressively past a disrupted Brazilian side to win the Final 3–0 in Paris.

The subsequent celebrations showed the pent-up desire of the French for success after failing to

A-Z OF COUNTRIES

Above: The Ghanaian national squad.

Opposite: Switzerland attacking in Euro 96.

Below: Greece, who were knocked out of the USA 94 in the first round.

win the World Cup during the era of the great Michel Platini. Platini enjoyed a distinguished club career with Juventus in Italy and arguably has been the greatest player in the history of French football. However, not even his genius could see France over the final hurdle in the 1982 and 1986 World Cups – on both occasions, the French lost in the semi-finals to West Germany.

But there was no stopping Platini in the 1984 European Championship Finals, which they hosted. Platini scored nine goals in five games as France won the tournament with a style and panache that delighted everyone who watched the side play.

More success followed when France won the European Championship in 2000. However France, one of the bookmakers favorites to win World Cup 2002, missing Zinedine Zidane for the opening group matches, finished bottom of their group, failed to score a goal, gained just one point in a 0-0 draw with Uruguay and became the first champions to go out in such a manner since Brazil in 1996.

> **There was no stopping Platini in the 1984 European Championship finals, which they [France] hosted. Platini scored nine goals in five games as France won the tournament with a style and panache that delighted everyone who watched the side play.**

Ghana

Founded: 1957

Colours: White; white; white

World Cup Appearances: 0

Honours: African Nations Cup: 1963, 1965, 1978, 1982

So far, Ghana have not qualified for the World Cup finals, but their youth teams have been extremely impressive and have won the 1991 World Youth Championship. Known as the 'Black Stars', they have also won the African Nations Cup four times, and produced one of Africa's best players, Abedi Pele, who starred for Marseille in the 1980s.

Guatemala

Founded: 1926

Colours: White/blue; blue; white

World Cup Appearances: 0

Honours: CONCACAF winners 1967

Guatemala took an unwanted place in soccer history in October 1996, before the team's World Cup qualifier against Costa Rica, when – apparently because of ticket forgery and insufficient stadium control – 81 fans were crushed to death and another 147 were seriously injured.

Haiti

Founded: 1904

Colours: Red; black; red

World Cup Appearances: 1
Best: 1st round 1974

Honours: CONCACAF winners 1957, 1973

Haiti's moment of glory – and shame – came when its team reached the finals of the 1974

World Cup. A controversial qualifying tournament was followed by a trio of defeats in the finals, with 14 goals conceded. Ernst John-Joseph, the centre-half, failed a drug test, and the players were allegedly ill-treated upon their return home.

Hellàs (Greece)

Founded: 1926

Colours: White; blue; white

World Cup Record: 1
Best: 1st Round 1994

Honours: None

The Greeks invented the Olympic Games, an event in which athletes compete for glory rather than money. Because of this ideal, Greece had no national league until 1960, and no professionalism until 1979. The national side has suffered as a result. Greece has made it through to just two major tournaments: the 1980 European Championship and the 1994 World Cup.

Helvetia (Switzerland)

Founded: 1895

Colours: Red; white; red

World Cup Appearances: 7
Best: Quarter-finals 1934, 1938, 1954

Switzerland has always had a major part to play in world soccer – off the field at least, as both FIFA and UEFA are based there. The national team has been less influential, although they were strong between the wars, being World Cup quarter-finalists in 1934 and 1938, and Olympic runners-up in 1924. The Swiss continued to qualify for World Cups after World War II, and made the quarter-finals in 1954 as hosts. After 1966, how-

113

A–Z OF COUNTRIES

ever, the national side slid into decline, failing to qualify for six successive World Cups and seven European Championships. Under English coach Roy Hodgson, they finally made it to USA 94 and Euro 96. But since Hodgson left (for Internazionale, and then Blackburn Rovers), the Swiss have struggled.

As elsewhere, the British helped get the Swiss game started in the 1800s, and the nation's two top clubs both have English-language names: Grasshopper (Zurich) and Young Boys (Berne).

Above: Ray Houghton celebrates his match-winning goal against Italy in 1994.

Opposite: Mancini gets to the ball, belying the myth that the Italians are not good in the air.

Honduras

Founded: 1935

Colours: Blue; blue; blue

World Cup Appearances: 1
Best: 1st round 1982

Honours: CONCACAF winners 1981

Honduras has had serious internal political problems and some external ones: it was at full-scale war with El Salvador (q.v.) in

1969. The team has appeared in the World Cup Finals just once, in 1982, when it went out in the first round, despite drawing with the hosts, Spain.

For its first 30 years Italian football was in a mess. The league was formed in 1930. This was the boost the Italian game needed.

Iran

Founded: 1920

Colours: Green; white; red

World Cup Appearances: 2
Best: 1st round 1978, 1998

Honours: Asian Championship winners 1968, 1972, 1976

Iran was Asia's most powerful side in the 1970s, winning a hat-trick of Asian Championships, and every game it played in those tournaments. Iran also qualified for the 1978 World Cup Finals, holding Scotland to a 1–1 draw. In France 98 they beat the USA.

Ireland, Republic of

Founded: 1921

Colours: Green; white; green

World Cup Appearances: 3
Best: Quarter-finals 1990

While domestic football in Eire is weak, the national side has become one of the better teams in Europe. Eire played its first international against Bulgaria in 1924, but despite having gifted players like Johnny Giles, Liam Brady and Frank Stapleton, it was never quite able to qualify for the major tournaments. That situation changed in 1986, when Jack Charlton, a player in the England side that won the 1966 World Cup, was appointed as national team manager. Charlton utilized his players' strengths, manipulated the rules to plunder the English league for footballers who could claim distant Irish ancestry, played to a direct system and gave his team a huge self-belief.

The results were immediate: the Irish reached their first major finals at the 1988 European Championship. The side's reputation was further enhanced when it reached the quarter-finals of the 1990 World Cup, losing to the hosts, Italy, and it succeeded – where the UK nations failed – by reaching the 1994 World Cup Finals. In the 2002 World Cup Ireland, managed by Mick McCarthy, lost on penalties to Spain in the second round.

Israel

Founded: 1928

Colours: White; blue; white

World Cup Appearances: 1
Best: 1st round 1970

Honours: Asian Championship winners 1964

Israel's political problems have troubled the nation's international soccer, not to mention FIFA. The hostile Arab nations surrounding Israel refused to play the team, and in 1976 Israel was thrown out of the Asian Confederation. Bizarrely, the side was an associate member of Oceania until eventually it was accepted into UEFA in 1991.

Italia (Italy)

Founded: 1898

Colours: Blue; white; blue

World Cup Appearances: 12
Best: Winners 1934, 1938, 1982

Honours: European Championship winners 1968; Olympic winners 1936

Italy is among the world's most powerful football nations. It is one of only three countries (the others are Brazil and Germany) to have lifted the World Cup three times. The national team is always one of the most difficult to beat, and the Italian domestic league is now widely regarded as being the best in the world.

That was not always the case – indeed, more the converse. For its first 30 years, Italian football was in a mess, with various regional

A-Z OF COUNTRIES

leagues and the two main industrial cities of the north – Milan and Turin – dominating. The situation improved in 1929, when the Football Association settled in Rome; the league was formed in 1930. This was the boost the Italian game needed, and it led to a period of astonishing success for the national side. Under the guidance of the legendary coach Vittorio Pozzo, the Italians lost only seven games during the 1930s, winning the World Cup in 1934 and 1938, with the 1936 Olympic title thrown in for good measure.

World War II ended Italy's reign over world football, and further tragedy came soon after hostilities ended. Torino were the most significant club side in the immediate post-war period, winning four consecutive league titles and providing virtually the entire national team. On a return flight from Lisbon in 1949, Torino's plane crashed into the Superga Hill, outside Turin, killing ten international players.

Not surprisingly, this led to a decline in Italy's footballing fortunes, although many critics attributed part of the blame to the growing number of foreign imports coming into the Italian game. This led to the imposition of a ban on foreign transfers in 1964. While this hampered Italian club sides in Europe, it sparked a resurgence of the national team, as a new generation of indigenous young stars developed. The culmination was that Italy won the European Championship in 1968.

The side followed that by finishing as runner-up to Brazil in the 1970 World Cup Finals, but thereafter Italian football retreated into a dull and sterile defensive system – *catenaccio* – with the attitude that not losing was more important

Below: The war in the Balkans has weakened the Yugoslavian team, to the benefit of Croatia especially.

than winning. Neither club sides nor the national team flourished, although Italy did reach the semi-finals in the 1978 World Cup.

In 1980, the ban on foreign imports was lifted and a period of success for Italian clubs followed. Juventus dominated the European scene in the early 1980s, inspired by French ace Michel Platini, while AC Milan took over in the latter half of the decade, led by Dutch masters Ruud Gullit, Marco Van Basten and Frank Rijkaard. The national side also enjoyed arguably its finest hour when it won the 1982 World Cup in Spain, captained by the 40-year-old goal-keeper Dino Zoff and inspired by top scorer Paulo Rossi.

Italian clubs continue to dominate the European scene but the National side seems unable to develop a winning team. They disappointingly lost to South Korea in WC 2002.

Jugoslavija (Yugoslavia)

Founded: 1919

Colours: Blue; white; red

World Cup Appearances: 9
Best: 4th 1962

Honours: Olympic winners 1960

Yugoslavia returned to the international fold in 1994 after a two-year absence caused by the break-up of the former state. Bosnia, Croatia, Macedonia and Slovenia formed their own separate associations, leaving Yugoslavia to draw players from the four remaining

> By the early 1990s, Yugoslavia had developed the makings of an excellent side: Red Star Belgrade won the European Cup. . . . Then came the civil war and the country was banned from taking part.

regions: Montenegro, Vojvodina, Kosovo and Serbia.

The old Yugoslavia had been, perhaps, about to enter the most successful phase of its footballing history. That history began in 1919, only a year after the formation of the nation itself (although the first club, Hajduk Split, had been set up in Croatia in 1911), with the creation of an association; a national league got under way four years later. The standard was not particularly high, as was demonstrated in Yugoslavia's international début in 1920: Czechoslovakia won 7–0.

By the late 1920s, things had improved, and the Yugoslavs actually reached the semi-finals of the first World Cup in 1930 – although failure to qualify for the finals in both 1934 and 1938 suggests that this may have been a fluke. They did win the Olympic title and finish runners-up in the European Championship in 1960, but with their players scattered across Europe, playing for foreign clubs – Yugoslavia is the game's biggest exporter of players – it was becoming increasingly difficult to maintain a settled side.

By the early 1990s, Yugoslavia had developed the makings of an excellent side: Red Star Belgrade won the European Cup in 1991 – the first East European side to do so – and Yugoslavia was highly fancied to perform well at the 1992 European Championship Finals. Then came the civil war, and the country was banned from taking part in the European Championship. The talent remains, however, as a successful qualifying campaign for the 1998 World Cup Finals clearly illustrated.

Magyarorszàg (Hungary)

Founded: 1901

Colours: Red; white; green

World Cup Record: 9
Best: Runners-up 1938, 1954

Honours: Olympic winners 1952, 1964, 1968

Hungary will always have a special place in football history because of the 'Magical Magyars' side of the 1950s. This was unquestionably the greatest team of its era, as it proved by becoming the first foreign nation to beat England at home (in 1953), when it thrashed Walter Winterbottom's side 6–3 at Wembley. This was only one of the side's many achievements in a five-year golden spell, during which it lost only one game before, surprisingly, being defeated in the 1954 World Cup Final by Germany. That Hungarian side included Ferenc Puskas, who was one of the finest players of his generation, and one of the best of all time, who terrorized world soccer with his breathtaking skills.

The Hungarian uprising of 1956 broke up this exceptional side. However, the Hungarians enjoyed another successful period during the 1960s. The new stars were Florian Albert and Ferenc Bene, who inspired their side to Olympic Gold in 1964 and 1968.

However, Hungarian football has been in decline, and the team has failed to make any sort of mark on the world game. Hungary did not qualify for the 1970, 1974, 1990, 1994, 1998 or 2002 World Cup Finals; and

Hungary will always have a special place in history because of the 'Magical Magyars' side of the 1950s. This was unquestionably the greatest team of its era.

Above: South Korean fans.

As co-hosts of 2002 South Korea put Asian football on the map, losing to Germany in the semi-finals after a run of amazing results, beating Poland, Portugal, Italy and Spain.

South Korea

Founded: 1928

Colours: Red; red; red

World Cup Appearances: 6
Best: 4th 2002

Honours: Asian Championship winners 1956, 1960

South Korea has usually been the strongest nation in Asian soccer, but has done little at world level. Despite often reaching the World Cup Finals, it has not made the impact that North Korea did at the 1966 World Cup Finals: Pak Do Ik will be remembered forever as the man who scored the most famous goal in Asian football, the one that beat Italy in the first round. In an astonishing quarter-final, North Korea led Portugal 3–0 after 20 minutes before an amazing comeback saw the Portuguese through 5–3.

Liberia

Founded: 1936

Colours: Blue/white; white; blue/white

World Cup Appearances: 0

Liberia may not be a household name on the international circuit, but the nation's best footballer certainly is. George Weah, the 1997 World Player of the Year, is Africa's biggest footballing hero; he starred for AC Milan, in Italy. Sadly, he is never likely to play on bigger stages: his team-mates are not in his class and the national federation is so strapped for cash that Weah sometimes pays the team's accommodation and travel bills personally.

achieved little when it did get through, apart from thrashing El Salvador 10–1 in 1982.

Four years later, Russia trampled Hungary 6–0 to confirm how far the Magyars had fallen down football's league of excellence.

Mexico

Founded: 1927

Colours: Green; white; green

World Cup Appearances: 12
Best: Quarter-finals 1970, 1986

Honours: CONCACAF winners 1965, 1971, 1977, 1993, 1996, 1998; Confederations Cup 1999

Mexico is comfortably the best side in the Central American region, which has enabled it to be regular World Cup participants without improving its standards enough to make an impact. Mexico's federation was formed in 1927, and the nation has qualified for the finals in 11 of the 16 World Cup tournaments, despite being banned from the 1990 competition for having fielded over-age players in a youth tournament.

Mexico's best efforts in the finals were in 1970 and 1986. On both occasions, they were the hosts. The country was particularly unlucky in 1986 when an excellent side, led by Real Madrid's star striker Hugo Sanchez, was beaten on penalties in the quarter-finals by West Germany. Many commentators believe Mexico would benefit from joining the South American group; in 1993, when Mexico and the USA were

The breakthrough for Dutch football came in 1970 when Feyenoord won the European Cup. This victory was followed by a hat-trick of Champions' Club successes for Ajax.

invited to take part in the South American Championship, the national side reached the final (losing to Argentina).

Morocco

Founded: 1955

Colours: Red; green; red

World Cup Appearances: 4
Best: 2nd round 1986

Honours: African Nations Cup winners 1976

Morocco was the first African side to qualify for the World Cup Finals (in 1970) and has twice applied, unsuccessfully, to host the finals (for 1984 and 1998). Morocco qualified for the finals in 1986, 1994 and 1998, confirming the side as one of Africa's most powerful soccer teams.

Nederlands (Holland)

Founded: 1889

Colours: Orange; white; orange

World Cup Appearances: 7
Best: Runners-up 1974, 1978

Honours: European Championship winners 1988

The Dutch are masters of the art of free-flowing football. Unfortunately, they are also masters of pressing the self-destruct button. Too often in major tournaments, in-fighting within the squad has prevented it from making the progress it should have done. Despite producing some of Europe's greatest players – Johan Cruyff, Johan Neeskens, Ruud Gullit, Marco Van Basten and others – the Dutch have just one major triumph to their credit: the 1988 European Championship. Twice Holland has finished as runner-up in the World Cup (1974 and 1978), but for a

Opposite: In the 1978 World Cup finals Argentina outclassed Holland, who always struggled without Johan Cruyff.

country that has been able to choose from so many superb players, that record is not as good as it should be.

The Dutch were enthusiastic early followers of soccer, partly because the country is so close to England, and they assembled one of the leading amateur sides of the early 1900s. As professionalism took hold in other countries during the 1920s, Dutch soccer went into a decline, and this lasted until the 1960s. The country's worst period came after World War II: only one win in five years for the national side prompted a restructuring of the domestic game. In 1957, a national league was formed, and professionalism was introduced to reduce the flow of good players to foreign countries.

The breakthrough for Dutch football came in 1970, when Feyenoord won the European Cup. This victory was followed by a hat-trick of Champions' Cup successes for Ajax, who for a long time provided the backbone of the national team.

The Amsterdam club flourished again in the 1990s, but the national side remained unable to match their success, and consequently

Below: Hugo Sanchez, a star for Real Madrid and Mexico.

reduced their dependence on Ajax after Euro 96.

New Zealand

Founded: 1938

Colours: White; black; white

World Cup Appearances: 1
Best: 1st round 1982

As in Australia (q.v.), football in New Zealand faces stiff competition from other sports, notably rugby union, and the national side also suffers from the contorted World Cup qualifying system. It has reached the finals just once, in 1982, but was eliminated in the first round.

Nigeria

Founded: 1945

Colours: Green; white; green

World Cup Appearances: 3
Best: 2nd round 1994, 1998

Honours: African Nations Cup winners 1980, 1994
Olympic Winners 1996

Nigeria has taken over Cameroon's mantle as the leading footballing nation in Africa; perhaps that is only to be expected of a country that has over 500 registered clubs.

It took the 'Green Eagles' a long time to make their mark – they won the African Nations Cup for the first time as late as 1980 – but since then they have enjoyed plenty of success, most notably at youth level. In 1985, Nigeria became the first African country to win a FIFA world tournament at any level, when the Under-17s won the World Championship in China, a title they claimed again in 1993.

In 1994, Nigeria finally made the breakthrough at senior level, reaching the World Cup Finals for

Right: The New Zealand national side is often referred to as the 'All Whites' – it is a pity that they cannot emulate the national rugby team.

Opposite: The Norwegians are a formidable side, if only because of their defensive strength and counter-attacking speed.

Below: Football in Japan has taken on a much higher profile since the formation of the J-League.

the first time. It qualified for the knock-out stage, but exited narrowly to Italy. Since then, the Under-23 squad won Olympic Gold at Atlanta in 1996, while the senior side qualified for France 98 and Japan/Korea 2002. These successes provided some measure of compensation when the side was barred from the 1996 and 1998 African Nations Cup for political reasons.

Nippon (Japan)

Founded: 1921

Colours: Blue; white; blue

World Cup Appearances: 2
Best: 2nd round 2002

Honours: Asian Championship 1992

In 2002, history was made by Japan and South Korea when they became the first countries to co-host a World Cup.

The Japanese certainly have the technology and infrastructure to stage the event, but only recently have developed a football culture. The introduction of a professional league in 1993 has changed the face of the game. Backed by huge corporations, teams have been handed the financial muscle to compete for the best players in the world, albeit usually as they approach the end of their careers. Stars like

Gary Lineker, Zico and Pierre Littbarski were among the first to be persuaded to move to Japan, and the J-League is now thriving. As the league improves because of the foreign imports, so too will the national side, the indigenous players becoming accustomed to playing at a higher standard on a regular basis.

When co-hosting WC 2002 Japan did well to top their group before losing to Turkey in the second round.

Norge (Norway)

Founded: 1902

Colours: Red; white; blue/white

World Cup Appearances: 3
Best: 2nd round 1998

Norway are no longer regarded as minnows on the European football scene, but for a long time they lived in the shadows of Sweden and Denmark, having won the Scandinavian Championship only once, in 1929–30. Attitudes changed in 1994, when Norway qualified for the World Cup finals for the first time since 1938: the side topped its group, ahead of Holland, England and Poland, so this can hardly be dismissed as a fluke.

Playing to a direct style, manager Egil Olsen moulded his side into a team that was very difficult to beat rather than one that might necessarily win – much as Jack Charlton did with the Republic of Ireland. This policy earned Norway few friends, although the team had some excellent players: goalkeeper Erik Thorstvedt, mid-fielder Oyvind Leonhardsen and striker Jostein

Playing to a direct syle, manager Egil Olsen moulded his side into a team that was very difficult to beat rather than one that might necessarily win.

Flo, to name just three examples. Norway failed in the first phase in USA 94 and did not qualify for Euro 96, but with almost all the team playing in the English Premiership, emphatically qualified for France 98.

Northern Ireland

Founded: 1880

Colours: Green; white; green

World Cup Appearances: 3
Best: Quarter-finals 1958

Northern Ireland boasts the world's fourth oldest football association and its third oldest league. The Northern Irish have been playing international football, initially as United Ireland, since 1883. However, for a long time they played against only the British nations; and it was not until 1951 that they finally took on foreign opposition, when they tackled France in Belfast.

Above: The Peruvian national side.

Below: The Austrian player, Hans Krankel.

It didn't take the Northern Irish long to catch up with the rest of the world. In 1958, they reached the quarter-finals of the World Cup – doing better than both England and Scotland – with a side led by Tottenham's legendary captain Danny Blanchflower. Ulster has also produced one of the game's all-time greats, George Best; despite his presence in the national side, however, it failed to make an impact during the 1960s and 1970s, and Best never had the opportunity to test himself on the biggest stage.

The early 1980s, though, saw an upturn in Northern Ireland's fortunes, and, guided by Billy Bingham, the team enjoyed great adventures at the 1982 and 1986 World Cup Finals. In 1982, with Pat Jennings in goal and Norman Whiteside, at 17 years and 42 days, beating Pelé's record as the youngest World Cup finalist, they stunned the tournament by topping their first-round group – beating the hosts, Spain, 1–0 in the process – before bowing out in the second round. The side was less successful four years later; but today, the Northern Irish have several excellent young-sters coming along and are hopeful of qualifying again for a

World Cup Finals tournament and emulating the success achieved by the class of 1982.

Österreich (Austria)

Founded: 1904

Colours: White; black; black

World Cup Appearances: 7
Best: 3rd 1954

Austria's football history could have been so different had it not been for World War II. At the start of the 1930s, the Austrian Wunderteam looked to be virtually unbeatable: in 30 matches between Spring 1931 and Summer 1934, it scored 101 goals. It seemed no one would be able to stop the Austrians from winning the 1934 World Cup. However, the side was defeated by the hosts, Italy, in the semi-finals.

Austria's chances of making up for that disappointment in the 1938 World Cup were wiped out by the German occupation; indeed, from March 1938, 'Austrian' football, as such, ceased to exist. The side regrouped in the 1950s and it was assumed to have an excellent chance in the 1954 World Cup event – but the Germans beat them 6–1 in the semi-finals.

Above: Poland v England at Wembley in 1997.

little noticed until, tragically, it became a focus of world attention in 1964, when 300 fans died in a riot. The same morbid attention was attracted in 1988, when the entire Alianza team was killed in a plane crash.

The national side won the South American Championship twice on home soil, in 1939 and in 1975. The latter side is regarded as Peru's best, with Teofilo Cubillas and Hector Chumpitaz at its core. Apart from the triumph of 1975, it reached the quarter-finals of the 1970 World Cup, and the second round in 1978, losing – some claim by a suspiciously heavy 6–0 score-line – to hosts Argentina.

Polska (Poland)

Founded: 1919

Colours: White; red; white/red

World Cup Appearances: 5
Best: 3rd 1982

Honours: Olympic winners 1972

Poland has slipped into the second division of European football in recent times, but the national team had a period of great success in the 1970s and 1980s.

The Polish state did not come into existence until 1921, and football did not flourish until the post-war communist take-over.

The club side Gornik Zabryze was first to make an impact, reaching the 1969 European Cup Winners' Cup Final, then the national side found glory with great players like Kazimierz Deyna, Gregorz Lato and Wlodzimierz Lubanski. The Poles won Olympic Gold in Munich in 1972, finished third in the 1974 World Cup, having knocked out England in qualifying, and reached the Olympic final in 1976. With Zbigniew Boniek, a new side reached the semi-finals of the 1982 tournament. Internal strife, leading to the end of communism, saw a period of decline as many players sought their fortunes abroad.

Since then, Austria has slipped. The side hit an all-time low in 1991 when beaten 1–0 by the Faroe Islands. The islands were playing their first match in an international competition.

Paraguay

Founded: 1906

Colours: Red/white; blue; blue

World Cup Appearances: 6
Best: 2nd round 1994, 1998, 2002

Honours: South American Championship winners 1953, 1979

For such a small country, Paraguay has done remarkably well at international level. Twice winners of the South American Champion-

ship, they have also qualified for the finals of six World Cups, including 1998 and 2002 where they reached the second round losing to Germany.

Perù (Peru)

Founded: 1922

Colours: White/red; white; white

World Cup Appearances: 4
Best: Quarter-finals 1970

Honours: South American Championship winners 1939, 1975

The Peruvian FA was formed in Lima in 1922, and teams from the capital – Alianza, Universitario and Sporting Cristal – have always dominated. Peruvian football was

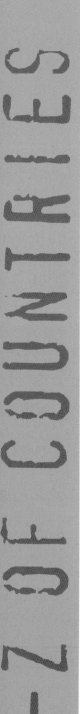

Above: Romania in 1996.

Portugal

Founded: 1914

Colours: Red; white; red

World Cup Appearances: 3
Best: 3rd 1966

Portugal's failures on the international scene are in stark contrast to the successes of its clubs. The national side finished third in the 1966 World Cup, when Benfica's Eusebio was arguably the player of the tournament (he scored nine goals in five games), but since then it has been almost non-stop disappointment. Portugal has qualified for only two World Cups since: in 1986 finishing bottom of its group, and in 2002 again failing to make the second round despite them being one of the favorites.

On the domestic circuit, Portugal's Big Three – Benfica, Sporting Lisbon and Porto – have dominated at home and have prospered abroad. On only one occasion has one of these three teams failed to gain the league title, Belenenses breaking their monopoly in 1948.

In Europe, Benfica have won the Champions' Cup twice (1961 and 1962) and have reached a further six European finals. Sporting Lisbon won the Cup-Winners' Cup in 1964, while FC Porto lifted the Champions' Cup in 1987.

Below: The Portuguese have always promised much, but never really delivered at a national level.

Românâ (Romania)

Founded: 1908

Colours: Yellow; blue; red

World Cup Appearances: 7
Best: Quarter-finals 1994

Romania was one of the first Balkan countries to take up football: the country's ruler, King Carol, a huge fan of the game, instigated the formation of a federation in 1908. When he returned to power in 1930, he insisted that Romania entered the first World Cup; the team made the long trip to Uruguay, one of only four European teams to do so. Further fruitless trips followed in 1934 and 1938. It was 32 years before Romania reappeared in the finals, and not until 1990 did they qualify for a second stage. That team lost on penalties to Ireland, but four years later their technical skills were evident as they knocked out Argentina, although again they lost on penalties, this time to Sweden.

At domestic level, the communist government had changed things in the 1940s, and two of the clubs formed in Bucharest – Steaua, the army team, and Dinamo, the police team – dominated. In 1986, Steaua became the first club from behind the Iron Curtain to win the European Cup, and this side, keenly sponsored by President Ceaucescu, formed the nucleus of the national team. Mid-fielder Gheorghe Hagi – 'the Maradona of the Carpathians' – Ilie Dumitrescu and Dan Petrescu were the key players in that team. Romania, like Bulgaria, have profited from their best players relocating to the West, but as elsewhere in Eastern Europe, for the time being the domestic game is in decline.

One of the best youth development structures in Europe has produced a regular flow of talented players and has provided success in the World Youth Cup in 1989 and 1991.

Russka (Russia)

Founded: 1922

Colours: White; blue; white

World Cup Appearances: 2
Best: 1st round 1994, 2002

Honours: European Championship winners 1960 (as Soviet Union), Olympic winners 1956, 1988 (as Soviet Union)

When the Soviet Union began to split up in 1991, Russian football was thrown into chaos. The Soviets had qualified for the 1992 European Championship Finals in Sweden, and they were allowed to enter under a flag

Portugal's failures on the international scene are in stark contrast to the successes of its clubs. The national side finished third in the 1966 World Cup, but since then it has been non-stop disappointment.

of convenience as the CIS (Commonwealth of Independent States), but soon afterwards even the CIS ceased to exist, and the 15 former Soviet republics began to operate independently.

Russia is still a big country with a big population, so it is easily the best equipped of the newly created states to succeed in football. It began by qualifying for the finals of the 1994 World Cup and of Euro 96,

Above: Russia playing Germany at Euro 96. The team did not get the results its talents and form deserved.

although on both occasions the performances were disappointing. However, with players like Andrei Kanchelskis – though Ukranian-born – in the ranks, surely one day the nation will repeat some of the

Above: The South African side which won the 1996 African Nations' Cup.

successes enjoyed by the old Soviet Union.

The Soviets, admittedly enjoyed a reputation for producing good sides rather then great ones. Their sole international triumph was achieved in 1960, when the USSR beat Yugoslavia 2–1 in the first European Championship Final. The side included the legendary goal-keeper Lev Yashin. The Soviets also finished in runner-up position in the European Championships of 1964 and 1972, and reached the World Cup quarter-finals in 1962 – and they made it into the semi-finals four years later.

The mid-1970s saw a period of decline, but in 1988, a team based on Dynamo Kiev (from the Ukraine) were again runners-up in the European Championship.

Scotland

Founded: 1873

Colours: Dark blue; white; red

World Cup Appearances: 8
Best: 1st round

For a country of its size, Scotland boasts an astonishing record at

Opposite: Sweden's Kennet Anderson fending off the opposition in Euro 96.

international level: when it missed out on the World Cup Finals in 1994, this was the first time it had failed to reach the final stages in six attempts, having qualified from 1974 to 1990. But, while reaching the finals has rarely been a prob-lem for the Scots, it's a different tale once they get there. The side has failed to get past the first round even once, and it has suf-fered embarrassing results against the likes of Peru, Iran and Costa Rica. Not even great players like Kenny Dalglish, Billy Bremner and Denis Law have been able to do anything about that record, and matters have been no different in the European Championship Finals. Scotland qualified for the final stages for the first time in Sweden in 1992, but once again fell at the first hurdle, and repeated this miserable performance in Euro 96.

Scotland hosted the world's first ever international match. It took place on November 30, 1872, and the visitors were England: the scoreline was 0–0. The rivalry between the two countries is as fervent now as it was then, and clashes between football's oldest enemies, as in Euro 96, are still eagerly anticipated on both sides of the border. The domestic game

has long been drained by players moving to England. Scottish mana-gers of English teams have had particular impact, including men like Sir Matt Busby, Bill Shankly, Alex Ferguson and Kenny Dalglish.

The domestic game has survived because of the power and rivalry between Celtic and Rangers, representing respectively the Catholic and Protestant factions of Glasgow. Although Ferguson's Aberdeen and Jim McLean's Dundee United briefly created a 'new firm' in the 1980s, the 'old firm' has dominated Scottish football: from 1964 to 1973, Celtic won nine championships in a row, a feat equalled by Rangers in 1997.

For a country of its size, Scotland has an astonishing record at international level: when it missed out on the World Cup finals in 1994, this was the first time it had failed to reach the final stages in six attempts . . .

South Africa

Founded: 1892

Colours: Gold; black; white

World Cup Appearances: 2
Best: 1st round 1998, 2002

Honours: African Nations Cup winners 1996

South Africa announced their return to the international football fold when they claimed the 1996 African Nations Cup. The nation's rugby players and cricketers have done magnificently on the international stage since the ending of apartheid; after readmission to FIFA in July 1992, South Africa's national soccer side has also responded, following the Nations Cup win by qualifying for the 1998 World Cup. It struggled initially as, unlike in cricket and rugby, there had been no 'rebel' tours of sanctions-busting sportsmen. This was largely because football is played predominantly by blacks, although whites were allowed to play alongside. Some, like Gary Bailey and Colin Viljohn, made careers in England and played for their adopted country. New stars, black and white, like Lucas Radebe and Mark Fish have also gone abroad, but now play for South Africa.

Sverige (Sweden)

Founded: 1904

Colours: Yellow; blue; yellow/blue

World Cup Appearances: 10
Best: Runners-up 1958

Honours: Olympic winners 1948

Sweden's record in terms of both club and national sides is remarkable when you consider that the Swedes still do not have a full-time professional football league. Many of Sweden's players are amateurs, and their top stars are almost all tempted abroad. Even

qualifying for the World Cup Finals is quite an achievement, yet as recently as 1994 they reached the semi-finals. Similarly, the Swedes have done well to compete with such distinction in the European club competitions, their greatest successes occurring in 1989 and 1992, when IFK Gothenburg won the UEFA Cup. Earlier – in 1979 – Malmö had reached the European Cup Final.

The country played its first international in 1908, and entered the first four Olympic tournaments – all with limited success, despite the presence of Sven Rydell, who scored 49 goals in 43 internationals. The Swedes' brightest decade came in the 1940s, when they won the 1948 Olympic title with a formidable forward line comprising Gunnar Gren, Gunnar Nordahl and Nils Liedholm, who became known as the 'Gre-No-Li' trio. The three were subsequently bought by Italian giants Milan, and consequently were banned from the national side because of the strictly amateur rules of the association. Sweden still finished third in the 1950 World Cup finals.

In 1958, with the import ban lifted, Sweden hosted the World Cup and finished as runner-up to Brazil. In 1992, playing host allowed Sweden to reach the European Championship for the first time. But although they continue to produce top-quality players like Tomas Brolin, Martin Dahlin and Jesper Blomqvist, the Swedes do not look as though they are capable of winning a major title.

Trinidad & Tobago

Founded: 1906

Colours: Red; black; red

World Cup Appearances: 0

Trinidad & Tobago may not have a great footballing tradition, but there are a few star names in the team now – none bigger than striker Dwight Yorke, probably the best-known player to come out of the Caribbean. However, his great friend, Shaka Hislop who now plays for Portsmouth, preferred to play for England, underlining Trinidad & Tobago's limited potential.

Tunisie (Tunisia)

Founded: 1956

Colours: Red; white; red

World Cup Appearances: 3
Best: 1st round 1978, 2002

Tunisia does not have a footballing past to shout about, but it holds a special place in the history of African football. It was the first African side to win a match in the World Cup Finals, defeating the mighty Mexico 3–1 in 1978. It also qualified for 1998 and 2002.

Türkiye (Turkey)

Founded: 1923

Colours: White; white; white/red

World Cup Appearances: 2
Best: 3rd 2002

Turkey has consistently struggled to make a mark on the international scene – which is surprising, since the country has a keen interest in football. Turkish fans are among the most fervent in the world, and the fiercely competitive domestic league boasts many talented players. Clubs like Galatasaray and Fenerbahce have started to make an impression in European club football, but the national side has qualified for only one World Cup, in 1954, and one European Championship, in 1996.

The 1996 success was ironic, as the squad was guided to the finals by Fatih Terim, a Turk: for many years, Turkey had relied on foreign managers to look after the national team, and had had little or no success. Nevertheless, once they made

it to Euro 96, they reverted to type, losing all three games in their first-round group and tumbling out without scoring a goal.

However, Turkey were one of the surprise teams of Japan and Korea 2002, finishing second in their group, behind Brazil. They then beat Japan and Senegal in the knock-out stages of the tourna-

> **The Turkish domestic league boasts many talented players, but before 2002 the national team had only qualified for one World Cup. In 2002 they did extremely well, coming third overall.**

Opposite: Nejib Gommidh playing for Tunisia v Poland in Argentina 78.

Below: Turkey in action during Euro 96.

ment before losing to Brazil in the semi-final.

Ukraine

Founded: 1992

Colours: Yellow; blue; yellow

World Cup Appearances: 0

Ukraine boasts the most successful Soviet club side in history, Dynamo Kiev, and should have a strong national team. Its biggest concern is that several of the nation's top stars, like Andrei Kanchelskis and Oleg Salenko, were allowed to play for Russia in the 1994 World Cup Finals and have elected to continue doing so.

sport that does not lend itself to advertising breaks remains.

Uruguay

Founded: 1900

Colours: Light blue; black; black

World Cup Appearances: 10
Best: Winners 1930, 1950

Honours: South American Championship winners 1916, 1917, 1920, 1923, 1924, 1926, 1935, 1942, 1956, 1959, 1967, 1983, 1987, 1995; Olympic winners 1924, 1928

Uruguay was, arguably, the first great team the world had seen. Before World War II, it was all-conquering, effectively winning three World Championships. When Uruguay claimed Olympic Golds in both 1924 and 1928, the side amazed Europe with its range of skills. Having proved its ability in the Olympics, it repeated the feat in the first World Cup finals. These were held in Uruguay, and it was no surprise that the host nation took the title, scoring 15 goals in its four games and conceding only three. Naturally, it had some of the best players in the world, men like captain José Nasazzi and the outstanding strikers Hector Castro, Pedro Cea and Hector Sarone.

Uruguay refused to defend the title in 1934, upset by Europe's lack of interest in the first tournament, and was also absent in 1938. However, when the World Cup returned in 1950, following World War II, the Uruguayan side was there and defeated hosts Brazil in the deciding match. Striker Juan Schiaffino, regarded as Uruguay's best-ever player, scored the first of the decisive goals.

Although Uruguay has continued to win occasional South American Championships, and still produces great players like Enzo Francescoli and Reuben Sosa, the side has disappointed on the world scene. It has also gained a reputation as being hard and ruthless.

United States of America

Founded: 1913

Colours: White; blue; red

World Cup Appearances: 7
Best: Semi-finals 1930

Honours: CONCACAF winners 1991

Numerous attempts to get the game up and running in the USA have been made and, so far,

Above: Some of Uruguay's fanatical fans.

Opposite: Peter Nicholas of Wales.

Below: Zambia *circa* 1988.

have failed. Although the sport is very popular, with many women and children playing regularly, sustaining a national league has been difficult. The closest the Americans came was in the 1970s, when major stars like Pelé, Franz Beckenbauer, Johan Cruyff and George Best were enticed to the country to play in the North American Soccer League, but that league folded in 1984.

However, the USA has a place in soccer history for providing one of the biggest upsets of any World Cup. This occurred in 1950, when a goal from Larry Gaetjens earned the side a memorable 1–0 victory over England. After that, however, the country failed to reach another finals until 1990, but four years later the Americans were back, and this time as hosts, FIFA attempting to raise football's profile in the eyes of the US public. A new league was formed on the back of this tournament – with rather less reliance placed on importing star names from overseas. However, the problem of attracting network television coverage to a

Wales

Founded: 1876

Colours: Red; red; red

World Cup Appearances: 1
Best: Quarter-finals 1958

The Welsh are the 'nearly' men of international football, certainly among the countries of the British Isles. While both Northern Ireland and Eire have reached major finals in the past 12 years, Wales has not done so for almost 40 years. The side reached the World Cup once, in 1958, when a team containing the legendary Ivor Allchurch and John Charles made it to the quarter-finals, losing 1–0 to Brazil. Not even the presence of talent such as Ian Rush, Mark Hughes, Neville Southall and Ryan Giggs could end the depressing sequence, and the country failed dismally to make any impact on the 1998 qualifying campaign.

But the Welsh FA is trying to do something about the situation. It started by forming a national league in 1992, with a place in the European Cup as an incentive for the winners. This was seen as a way of persuading those Welsh clubs playing in England – Cardiff, Swansea and Wrexham – to join the new league. As yet, that has not happened. Until it does, it seems that football will always play second fiddle to rugby in Wales.

Zambia

Founded: 1929

Colours: Green; white; black

World Cup Appearances: 0

Zambian football will always be remembered for the plane crash that, in April 1993, wiped out the entire national squad, aside from five overseas-based players who, fortunately, were not on the flight to Senegal. The Zambians managed to rebuild their side to reach the 1994 African Nations Cup Final, an astonishing achievement.

GAZETTE

Football and Art

The uncomfortable relationship between football and art is best illustrated by the US movie *Escape to Victory* (1981; also released as *Victory*), in which a diverse bunch of footballers, including Pelé, Bobby Moore, Ossie Ardiles and John Wark, 'acted' alongside Sylvester Stallone in a World War II prison-camp drama.

Above: **Colin Firth as an Arsenal fan in *Fever Pitch*.**

As with other football movies, like *Yesterday's Hero* (1979), loosely based on the career of George Best and starring Adam Faith and Ian McShane, and *When Saturday Comes* (1995), a fan-turns-player tale with Sean Bean, the problem concerned the actual football scenes.

Actors play football about as well as footballers act. Add in the belief that women dictate family cinema attendances and that, until recently, they were no more interested in soccer than the arts community in general, and you understand why there have been so few films based on the game. The *Arsenal Stadium Mystery* (1939), based on Leonard Gribble's novel, was a rare early attempt.

Fever Pitch

Arguably the best football movie so far is *Fever Pitch* (1997), based on the Nick Hornby novel. This solves the problem of the football scenes by being about not a player but a fan; its few clips are from televised matches. The best 'constructed' playing sequence is, however, that in *Kes* (1969), when Brian Glover acts as a PE teacher running a game for the benefit of his own ego.

Other branches of culture – in the English-speaking world at least – have likewise tended to ignore the game until quite recently. Tom Stoppard's stage play *Professional Foul* (1977) was an isolated example in the theatre until, prompted by the game's new popularity, there appeared two successful

Above: **Bobby Moore (third from left) and Pelé (centre) along with Michael Caine (third from right) in *Victory*.**

ART Cantona was so captivated by the painting 'The Art of the Game' by the Manchester artist Michael Browne that he bought it; . . . this depicts Cantona as Christ.

FACT FILE

HIGHEST INDIVIDUAL SCORE IN ONE EUROPEAN CLUB COMPETITION MATCH

6 – Lothar Emmerich (Borussia Dortmund v Floriana), European Cup-Winners' Cup, 1965

HIGHEST INDIVIDUAL FA CUP SCORE

13 – Jon Petrie, (Scottish FA Cup, Arbroath v Bon Accord), 1885

HIGHEST INDIVIDUAL SCORE IN ENGLAND

10 – Joe Payne (Luton v Bristol Rovers), 1936 Division 3 South

HIGHEST INDIVIDUAL SCORE IN TOP ENGLISH DIVISION

7 – James Ross (Preston North End v Stoke), 1888

7 – Ted Drake (Arsenal v Aston Villa), 1935

HIGHEST UK AGGREGATE

550 – Jimmy McGrory (1922–38: Celtic, Clydebank, Scotland)

HIGHEST ENGLISH AGGREGATE

464 – Arthur Rowley (1947–65: West Bromwich Albion, Fulham, Leicester, Shrewsbury)

FASTEST OWN GOAL

8 seconds: Pat Kruse (Torquay v Cambridge), 1977

renaissance painting, 'The Resurrection of Christ', this depicts Cantona as Christ, Alex Ferguson as Caesar and Nicky Butt, David Beckham and Gary and Phil Neville as Roman legionaries.

The soccer boom has led to an upsurge in other areas of football art, with London and Manchester hosting separate exhibitions in 1996. The former display included possibly the earliest use of football in art, a 1784 engraving featuring William Pitt and Charles Fox treating the contemporary issue of India as a political football. Also on show were Japanese woodblock prints from 1886 and 1897 and a 1952 French lithograph. Unavailable was one of the best-known football paintings of all, 'Going to the Match' by L.S. Lowry.

Perhaps the best visual football art has been photographic. Football pictures, for newspapers or otherwise, have moved beyond 'goal' snaps: originality is now the watchword and supporters and locations are as likely to be the subject of the photographer's lens as the players.

A Literary Footnote

Nick Hornby's novel *Fever Pitch* (1992) has inspired more than a play and a film: it has spawned dozens of imitators. While much of this genre is amateurish, there have been some fine pieces.

Actors play football about as well as footballers act. Add in the belief that women dictate family cinema attendances and that, until recently, they were (debatably) no more interested in soccer than the arts community in general, and you understand why there have been so few films based on the game.

Previously football had nothing like the literature of, say, cricket. A few good books had been written by journalists like Arthur Hopcraft,

theatrical presentations: *An Evening with Gary Lineker*, based on the 1990 World Cup, and *Fever Pitch*, the precursor of the movie.

Soccer Boom

The 1990s soccer boom has led to a proliferation of football advertisements, often produced for boot companies, in which players like Alessandro Del Piero, Matthias

Sammer, Ian Wright, David Platt and Eric Cantona have featured. Cantona went on to act in French cinema. He also wrote poetry, as did, rather more successfully, former Wales and Liverpool striker John Toshack. Cantona was so captivated by the painting 'The Art of the Game' by the Manchester artist Michael Browne that he bought it; based on a 15th-century

Above: **A scene from** *The Arsenal Stadium Mystery*.

BRIAN GLOVER The best 'constructed' playing sequence is that in Kes, when Brian Glover (runs) a game for the benefit of his own ego.

133

Above: **A Sheffield United fan in real life, Sean Bean played a local footballer who stars for The Blades in *When Saturday Comes*.**

FACT FILE

FACT: In February 1997 Italy became the first team to defeat England in a World Cup tie in England. Later that year England became the first team to avoid losing in a World Cup tie in Rome – Italy had won the previous 15 such matches.

FACT: The 2006 World Cup finals are to be held in Germany, while the 2010 will be held in one of the African countries.

Brian Glanville and John Moynihan, and there had been occasional references by authors like Julian Barnes and Irvine Welch. J.B. Priestley wrote about the game in *The Good Companions* (1929) and William Shakespeare, William Wordsworth, Rudyard Kipling and Arnold Bennett all made reference to the game.

An enterprising English company has taken to reproducing on a line of shirts various soccer-related comments by noted writers and philosophers; these include Albert Camus (who played as a goalkeeper in Algeria), William Shakespeare, Ludwig Wittgenstein and the philosopher Friedrich Nietzsche.

In time, perhaps, the line of t-shirts will include offerings from Attila the Stockbroker (punk poet and Brighton supporter) and Barnsley Football Club's poet-in-residence.

Chant Don't Sing

As well as the sublime there has been the ridiculous: the music. Football records, with a few exceptions – notably England's Italia 90 offering (New Order's 'World in Motion') and their Euro 96 song ('Three Lions' by David Baddiel, Frank Skinner and the Lightning Seeds) – are awful. Kevin Keegan, Glenn Hoddle, Chris Waddle and Jimmy Greaves have recorded individual efforts, but Peter Osgood should have the final word: he recorded the legendary 'Chirpy, Chirpy, Cheep, Cheep' ∎

Glenn Moore

ERIC CANTONA I have the impression if he cannot score a beautiful goal he would rather not score. – Michel Platini, manager of France

World Cup Semi-Final Mexico City, 17 June 1970

Extra time Brilliance

Italy 4 (Boninsegna, Burgnich, Riva, Rivera)
West Germany 3 (Muller 2, Schnellinger)

Arguably the most dramatic match in the history of the World Cup, this wasn't the greatest ever played – because from the seventh minute, when Boninsegna gave Italy the lead, until deep into injury time, when Schnellinger equalized for West Germany, nothing much happened.

It is remembered because of what happened in extra time: five goals were scored. The Germans, inspired by Franz Beckenbauer – playing with an injured arm in a sling – made it 2–1 after 95 minutes, Muller scoring. Burgnich made it 2–2 shortly after that, and two minutes before the interval Riva shot low into the far corner to make it Italy 3, West Germany 2. Seven minutes later Muller scored his tenth goal of the tournament to make it 3–3, but from the restart Rivera earned his country a place in the final for the first time since 1938, where they lost out to the inspired Brazilians ■

Mike Collett

Above: **Mortensen heads in Matthews' cross making it 3–2.**

FA Cup Final, Wembley, 2 May 1953

The Wizard of the Dribble

Blackpool 4 (Mortensen 3, Perry)
Bolton Wanderers 3 (Lofthouse, Moir, Bell)

In 1948 and 1951 Blackpool and Stanley Matthews had finished as losers in the FA Cup Final. In 1953 just about the whole of England – excepting Bolton and their supporters – was willing Matthews to get, at last, the winner's medal that had eluded him for over 20 years.

Matthews was 38: this was surely the last chance for the most famous player in the world to achieve his lifetime ambition. But, after 55 minutes, the 'Wizard of Dribble' had failed to perform, and Blackpool were trailing 3–1. Suddenly fate relented:

Matthews began to dazzle, and Blackpool staged the most astonishing fightback in FA Cup Final history. He crossed from the right so that Mortensen could score his second goal of the match, making it 2–3. With two

(Continued page 136, col. 4)

Above: **A tense moment in the Italian goalmouth.**

RIVERA Rivera earned his country a place in the final for the first time since 1938, where they lost out to the inspired Brazilians . . .

135

The Greatest Matches

West Germany, 1971

The Schalke Scandal

Above: **The Bundesliga was left shattered by the Schalke scandal.**

One of world soccer's biggest bribery scandals broke in 1971 when it was revealed that dozens of matches in the Bundesliga had been fixed throughout the previous season; at least half a million Deutschmarks had been paid in bribes.

The scandal focused initially on a match between Schalke and relegation-threatened Arminia Bielefeld on 17 April 1971; Schalke, odds-on favourites to win easily, surprisingly lost. When the scale of the scandal was realized it had a huge impact throughout West Germany. Attendances nose-dived and clubs began to get into serious financial difficulties; the finger of suspicion never stopped pointing. In all, over 50 players, coaches and officials were punished, the team Kickers Offenbach was banned from playing any matches for two years, and Arminia was demoted to the regional leagues. However, West Germany rebounded to take the 1974 World Cup with the impact magnified by their hosting of it ■

Football, Human Rights and Communism

The qualifying process for the 1974 World Cup required one European team to play-off against a South American side. In the event this pitted the communist Soviet Union against Chile, where a bloody military coup under General Pinochet had recently overthrown Salvador Allende's left-wing government. The Soviets were already uncomfortable with the situation.

The Soviet Union's main objection to playing Chile in Chile was that during the coup, many left-wing activists had been summararily executed in the national Stadium in Santiago.

After a goalless draw in Moscow the Soviets refused to play the second leg because it was scheduled to be played in the stadium where the massacre took place. FIFA duly commissioned an inquiry and concluded that a different Chilean venue be sought. Agreement was impossible. Bizarrely, Chile turned up and kicked off despite having no opponents (rather as Scotland did for their tie against Estonia in qualifying for the 1998 Finals – though this was because of a dispute over kick-off times in Estonia). The Soviet Union was expelled from the competition, while Chile were knocked out in the first round of the finals ■

(The Wizard of the Dribble continued . . .)

minutes to go and Blackpool still trailing, Mortensen thundered home a free kick from outside the penalty area to equalize and become the first man this century to score a hat-trick in the FA Cup Final.

It seemed the match was destined for extra time but, in the last minute, Matthews took the ball to the by-line and cut it back for Perry to crash home the winner. Mortensen scored the hat-trick, but the match has entered football folklore as the 'Matthews Final'. The best-loved player in England had finally achieved the medal all England – outside Bolton – wished him ■

HAT-TRICK Geoff Hurst is the only man to have scored a hat-trick in a World Cup Final – in 1966 at Wembley.

Italy, 1980

The Paolo Rossi Affair

Paolo Rossi was a national hero in 1982, having helped Italy win the World Cup, but just two years earlier he had been disgraced for his part in a match-rigging scandal. At the time, Rossi was on loan to Perugia from Vicenza; he accepted a bribe as part of a betting scam.

The details emerged when two gamblers revealed all because they regarded their winnings as insufficient. The scandal involved several Serie A teams, notably AC Milan and Lazio. On 23 March 1980, 11 players and the president of AC Milan, Felice Colombo, were arrested, and most were later banned for life. The inquiry centred on AC Milan's 2–1 win over Lazio, but many other games were involved. AC Milan, who finished third in 1980, and Lazio, 13th, were demoted to Serie B, and Rossi himself received a two-year ban, which ended just before the 1982 World Cup started. He was forgiven by the authorities and allowed to play ■

Mike Collett

Above: **Banned, reprieved and winner of the Golden Boot at the 1982 World Cup.**

Above: **Paolo Rossi, from villain to hero.**

Vicenza's Saviour

Paolo Rossi came to notice at the age of 21 when, having failed to progress at Juventus, he inspired unfashionable Vicenza to second place in Serie A.

Rossi topped the Serie A scoring chart with 24 goals as the newly promoted side from the Italian northeast pushed a Juventus side which included Gentile, Scirea, Bettega, Tardellia and Causio all the way for the 1977–8 league title.

After playing for Italy in the 1978 World Cup, Rossi scored 15 goals in the following season, but Vicenza were still relegated and he moved back to Juve for £1.3M.

He was then banned for his part in the match-fixing scandal, but was reprieved shortly before the 1982 World Cup. He won the top-scorer's golden boot and a winner's medal ■

Glenn Moore

ROSSI Paolo Rossi was a national hero in 1982, having helped Italy win the World Cup, but just two years earlier he had been disgraced . . .

137

A-Z of Clubs

Aberdeen (Scotland)

Honours: 4 League titles; 7 Scottish Cups; European Cup-Winners' Cup 1983; European Supercup 1983

Colours: Red; red; red

Founded in 1903, Aberdeen took some 75 years before being able to mount a full-scale challenge to the Scottish dominance of Glasgow's Rangers and Celtic. The leap forward occurred when Alex Ferguson was appointed as team manager in 1978; during his eight-year period in charge, Aberdeen became Scotland's most successful club, winning a total of three League titles and five Scottish Cups, with the finest moment occurring in 1983, when the side trounced Real Madrid in Gothenburg to win the European Cup-Winners' Cup tournament. Later that year, the side added the European Supercup to the tally, beating the European Cup holders Hamburg. After Alex Ferguson's departure for Manchester United in 1986, however, Aberdeen's fortunes fell into decline.

Below: Jim Leighton celebrating Aberdeen's 1983 European Cup - Winners' Cup success.

Ajax Amsterdam (Holland)

Honours: 28 League titles; 15 Dutch Cups; European Cup 1971, 1972, 1973, 1995; UEFA Cup 1992; European Cup-Winners' Cup 1987; European Supercup 1972, 1973, 1995; World Club Cup 1972, 1995

Colours: Red/white; white; red/white

Ajax is one of Europe's most successful sides, and also one of its greatest nurseries of talent. Twice it has enjoyed the fruits of

its advanced youth system, only for the continent's richest clubs to prise the relevant players away. Now that the club has moved (1996) into the 52,000-capacity Amsterdam ArenA Stadium, Ajax may have found a means of generating enough money to avoid the constant need to sell its most skilled players.

The move was not entirely popular with fans, but it was necessary as the club declined in the wake of the Bosman legal case (*see* page 22). Having beaten AC Milan to win the 1995 European Cup, and Gremio to win the World Club Cup, Ajax lost six top players and the 1996 European Cup Final. In the following year, it failed to win the Dutch League for the first time in four seasons, and manager Louis Van Gaal left for Spain to join Barcelona. The exodus of players saw the departure of Patrick

Kluivert – scorer of the goal that had beaten AC Milan in the 1995 European Cup Final – Nwankwo Kanu, Finidi George, Marc Overmars, Michael Reiziger, Winston Bogarde and Clarence Seedorf.

In previous years, great players like Dennis Bergkamp, Marco Van Basten and Frank Rijkaard had developed at the old De Meer Stadium, but Ajax's greatest talent was one of the earliest, Johan Cruyff, who led the side to three successive European Cup wins and two World Club Cup victories. In 1972, Ajax held five titles simultaneously, something not even the club's class of 1995 could match. The other great names of the 1970s line-up included the midfield pair of Johan Neeskens and Arie Haan, and the defender Rudi Krol. Those three, together with Cruyff, went on to play in the 1974 World Cup Final.

Above: Johan Cruyff and happy Ajax players after winning the 1987 European Cup-Winners' Cup.

After Johan Cruyff was sold to Barcelona in 1973, Ajax did not re-emerge as a force until the late 1980s. By then, the club had taken on Cruyff as its manager, and it won the 1987 European Cup-Winners' Cup with Van Basten, Rijkaard and Bergkamp playing under his command.

Ajax's UEFA Cup triumph in 1992 meant that it became only the second club, after Juventus, to have won all three European club competitions.

Ajax's greatest talent was Johan Cruyff, who led the side to three successive European Cup wins and two World Cup victories. In 1972, Ajax held five titles simultaneously.

Anderlecht (Belgium)

Honours: 25 League titles; 8 Belgian Cups; European Cup-Winners' Cup 1976, 1978; UEFA Cup 1983; European Supercup 1976, 1978

Colours: White/purple; white/purple; white

Belgium's most successful club did not establish itself until after World War II. Anderlecht sides won League titles in every decade from the 1940s to the 1990s, the club's most dominant spell being represented by no fewer than 12 championships between 1950 and 1968. The foundations for that success were laid by the coach Bill Gormlie, a former Blackburn goalkeeper.

Anderlecht lost the 1970 Fairs Cup Final, but made up for that by reaching the Cup-Winners' Cup Final in three consecutive years – 1976, 1977 and 1978 – winning in both 1976 and 1978. During this era, it imported some of Holland's finest players, including Arie Haan and Rob Rensenbrink. Anderlecht won the UEFA Cup in 1983, and was runner-up the following year.

In September 1997, Anderlecht admitted having bribed the referee to fix the second leg of its 1984 UEFA Cup semi-final against Nottingham Forest, and was banned from participating in European competition for a year.

Below: Anderlecht, banned from European competition in 1997.

Arsenal (England)

Honours: 12 League titles; 9 FA Cups; UEFA Cup 1970; European Cup-Winners' Cup 1994

Colours: Red/white; white; red/white

Arsenal was England's dominant club in the 1930s, when a team created by Herbert Chapman won three successive League titles and two FA Cups. Sporadic subsequent success gradually declined until there were 17 fallow years; then, in 1970, Arsenal won the Fairs Cup. A year later, Bertie Mee's team attained the League/Cup double. This was achieved in nail-biting fashion. The club won the League on the last day of the season with

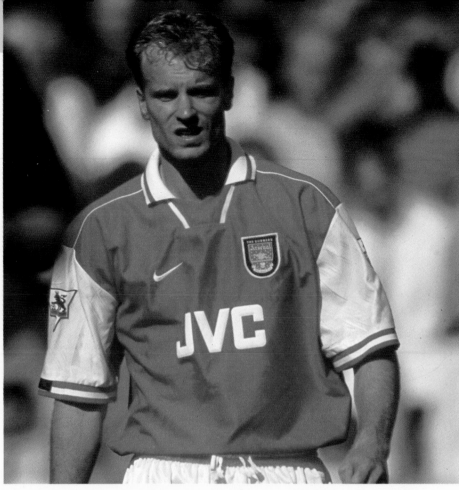

Bob Paisley, Ramsey is the second most successful club manager in the history of the game: he won 12 major trophies, including six FA Cups. Moreover, he sat in the Villa Park hot seat for an amazing 42 years.

Between 1910 and 1981, the First Division championship evaded the Villains, but in the latter year they brought it back to Villa Park, winning the 1982 European Cup as a bonus.

Arsenal gained the nickname 'Gunners' because the club was founded by workers from the Royal Arsenal at Woolwich, in south-east London.

Above: Dennis Bergkamp, a player who hit the form of his life when he moved to Arsenal in 1997.

a 1–0 win over local rivals Tottenham, only two days after having won the FA Cup in extra time against Liverpool.

Arsenal gained the nickname 'Gunners' because the club had been founded by workers from the Royal Arsenal in Woolwich, southeast London, in the late 19th century. It moved to north London, but won nothing until Chapman's appointment in 1925. His team featured strikers Ted Drake, who scored a League-record seven goals in one game, and Cliff 'Boy' Bastin who, with 178 goals, held the club's scoring record for 51 years until 1997, when it was broken by Ian Wright.

Arsenal's next title, after the 1971 double, came in 1989, and this gave English football its closest championship finish. In the last minute of the last game, the side won 2–0 at Liverpool to finish level on points and goal difference; the team clinched the title only through having scored more goals than Liverpool during the championship.

Since Arsene Wenger joined the Club as manager in 1996 he has guided them to two doubles (Premiership and FA Cup), in 1998 and 2002. Arsenal also became the first team in over 20 years to retain the FA Cup when they beat Southampton 1–0 in the 2003 final.

Aston Villa (England)

Honours: 7 League titles; 7 FA Cups; European Cup 1982

Colours: Claret/blue; white; claret/blue

Villa was formed in 1874 and was one of the founder members of the Football League. In 1897, under the guidance of George Ramsey, it became only the second club to do the League/Cup double – Preston North-End was the first (1889). After Liverpool's

Right: Gareth Southgate when he played for Aston Villa.

Atletico Madrid (Spain)

Honours: 9 League titles; 9 Spanish Cups; European Cup-Winners' Cup 1962; World Club Cup 1974

Colours: Red/white; blue; white

Atletico was formed in 1903 and has always had to live in the shadow of Real Madrid and Barcelona. Although wealthy now, the club has experienced hard times, notably after the Spanish Civil War, when it had to merge with the Air Force club to stay afloat.

Its first taste of European glory came in 1962, when it won the Cup-Winners' Cup; it lost in the final of the following year. In 1974, Atletico was one minute away from winning the European Cup when Bayern Munich equalized; Bayern won 4–0 in the replay. But, as Bayern was not prepared to take on Independiente in the World Club Cup, Atletico stepped in and won the competition.

Opposite: Barcelona are one of the only major clubs not to display a sponsor's name on their shirt. This is a matter of pride for both players and supporters alike.

Below: Atletico Madrid has always suffered in the shadow of Real Madrid and Barcelona.

During the late 1980s, Atletico was taken over by the controversial building tycoon Jesus Gil. Subsequently, he pumped millions into the club and brought in high-profile coaches, such as Ron Atkinson and Cesar Luis Menotti. That said, it was the lesser-known Yugoslav coach Raddy Antic who led Atletico to the League/Cup double in 1996.

Auxerre (France)

Honours: 1 League title; 2 French Cups

Colours: White; white; white

This club became a major force in French football thanks to Guy Roux. He became coach in 1961, when Auxerre was just a tiny amateur club; with him still in charge in 1996, the side took the French League/Cup double. Auxerre operates one of the best youth-development programmes in the game.

Barcelona (Spain)

Honours: 16 League titles; 24 Spanish Cups; UEFA Cup 1958, 1960, 1966; European Cup-Winners' Cup 1979, 1982, 1989, 1997; European Cup 1992; European Supercup 1992, 1998

Colours: Dark blue/red; dark blue/red; dark blue/red

More than just a club, Barcelona is a symbol of Catalonia, its rivalry with Real Madrid being affirmed during the Franco dictatorship and maintained to the present day. Established by a Swiss emigrant in 1899, the club was a founder member of the Spanish League, first winning it in 1929.

Barcelona used to play at the Les Corts Stadium, but are now based at the Nou Camp, a move financed in 1957 by the club's members: the stadium today can accommodate 115,000 and is part of a complex featuring many other sports. Pope John-Paul II is member No. 108,000.

Although Barcelona won the Fairs Cup (the old UEFA Cup) in 1958 and 1960, with star players Luis Suarez and Zoltan Czibor, its most successful period occurred during the early 1990s, under manager and one-time Barcelona player Johan Cruyff. It achieved four consecutive championship wins, 1991–4, and lifted the European Cup in 1992, in the process joining the elite group of clubs that have gained victory in all three of the European club competitions.

The 1992 team, which beat Sampdoria in extra time at Wembley, featured the Danish playmaker Michael Laudrup, the Bulgarian striker Hristo Stoichkov and the Dutch sweeper Ronald Koeman, who scored the game's only goal with a typical long-range free-kick. An indication of the club's pride came when, having had to play in their change strip, the players swapped to their traditional colours to receive the cup. Another example of this is that Barcelona is one of only a few major clubs whose players do not carry advertising on their shirts.

The 1992 European triumph followed defeats in the finals of 1961 and 1986, the second of these in a penalty shoot-out; English manager Terry Venables was the coach in the latter instance. In 1994, Barcelona lost in the final again, this time being beaten soundly 4–0 by AC Milan.

Three years later, Bobby Robson having replaced Cruyff as manager, Barcelona won the European Cup Winners' Cup and the Spanish Cup. Robson was replaced in 1997 by Louis Van Gaal. In the same year, Ronaldo, Barcelona's star of the season, joined Internazionale after a bitter transfer wrangle.

More than just a club, Barcelona is a symbol of Catalonia, its rivalry with Madrid dating back to the days of the Franco dictatorship.

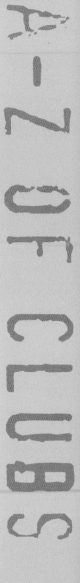

A-Z OF CLUBS

Bayern München (Germany)

Honours: 17 League titles; 10 German Cups; European Cup 1974, 1975, 1976, 2001; European Cup-Winners' Cup 1967; UEFA Cup 1996; World Club Cup 1976

Colours: Blue/red; blue/red; blue/red

Bayern Munich has come a long way since 1963, when the club's poor domestic record saw it omitted from the first national German championship (albeit only West Germany). In 1996, with a UEFA Cup triumph over Bordeaux, it became only the fourth club to win all three European club competitions. In the course of those 33 intervening years, Bayern rose to become Germany's most prestigious and successful club. The 1967 Cup-Winners' Cup victory over Glasgow Rangers, its first European success, provided the springboard for its domination of the European Cup, which it won each year between 1974 and 1976.

Bayern was the breeding ground for the German national team, producing world-class footballers like Franz Beckenbauer, Gerd Muller, Sepp Maier and Paul Breitner, who between them steered Germany to victory in the 1972 European Championship and 1974 World Cup. Then, in the late 1980s, Italian clubs started to poach Bayern's best players. Karl-Heinz Rummenigge and Lothar Matthaus went to Internazionale, while Jurgen Kohler and Stefan Reuter were bought by Juventus. After eight championships and two European Cup Final defeats between 1977 and 1995, Bayern won the UEFA Cup in 1996, inspired by Jurgen Klinsmann, in his first season back in Germany after six years abroad. He scored 15 goals in that European campaign, a new record,

Above: Bayern Munich win the European cup.

Above: Benfica is Portugal's most successful club.

then saw the club to the 1997 championship before returning to Italy and, after that, Tottenham.

Benfica (Portugal)

Honours: 30 League titles; 26 Portuguese Cups; European Cup 1961, 1962

Colours: Red; white; red

Founded in 1907, Benfica developed from a cycling-based sports club. It cemented its dominance with the creation of the 130,000-capacity Estadio de Luz in 1957. But Portugal's most successful football club has lived on memories for a long time. Financial and managerial disarray in the 1990s saw Benfica hand domestic supremacy to Porto, leaving it scrapping with city rivals Sporting for the honour of being not Portugal's, but merely Lisbon's best club. Between 1960 and 1977, Benfica won the Portuguese League in all but four years, and in the 1960s the club garnered two consecutive European Cups and became the runner-up in three other finals.

The inspiration for Bela Guttman's team of the 1960s was provided by Mozambique-born Eusebio and the indigenous José Aguas, the captain and centre-forward. The 1961 European Cup triumph, a 3–2 win over Barcelona, made Benfica the first Portuguese club to win a European trophy. A year later, Benfica retained it, beating the Real Madrid side of Alfredo Di Stefano and Ferenc Puskas 5–3 in Amsterdam, Eusebio scoring twice and Aguas once. The club has since lost five European Finals: the Champions' Cup in 1963, 1968, 1988 and 1990, and the 1983 UEFA Cup.

following year. Much later, the club won the South American Cup in 1977 and 1978, but the players' hard style of play – perfected by their manager Juan Carlos Lorenzo – never endeared them to opposition fans, and not one of them figured in the Argentinian national side that was assembled for the 1978 World Cup.

Boca reached its peak in beating West Germany's Borussia Mönchengladbach in the World Club Cup in 1977. After that, the team was built around Maradona. It declined after his departure, but came back strongly in 2000.

Left: Blackburn Rovers have levered themselves up into Premiership contention in the UK.

Below: Diego Maradona in the colours of Boca Juniors. The team declined when he left in 1981.

Bayern was the breeding ground for the German national team, producing world-class footballers like Franz Beckenbauer, Gerd Muller, Sepp Maier and Paul Breitner.

Blackburn Rovers (England)

Honours: 3 League titles; 6 FA Cups

Colours: Blue/white; white; blue/white

In 1995, revived by massive financial help from steel industrialist Jack Walker and managed by Kenny Dalglish, League founder members Blackburn achieved their first championship since 1914; goals from Alan Shearer helped pip Manchester United. A year later, Shearer was sold for a then world-record £15M.

Boca Juniors (Argentina)

Honours: 19 League titles; World Club Cup 1977, 2000; South American Club Cup 1977, 1978, 2000, 2001

Colours: Blue/gold; blue; blue/gold

Boca and River Plate are the two great football teams from the South American city of Buenos Aires. Boca won the last amateur championship in 1930 and the first professional tournament in the

Borussia Dortmund (Germany)

Honours: 6 League titles; 2 German Cups; European Cup-Winners' Cup 1966; European Cup 1997

Colours: Yellow/black; black; yellow/black

Borussia Dortmund sprang out of the shadow of Bayern Munich in the 1990s to stake its claim as Germany's other great football team. Formed in 1909, Borussia is one of Germany's best-supported clubs, but it achieved little before 1956. Then a championship triumph heralded a rich decade, with three titles, a domestic cup and the 1966 European Cup-Winners' Cup.

A domestic cup aside, 29 fallow years followed before an extraordinary blossoming under the managership of Ottmar Hitzfeld. Championships in 1995 and 1996 were followed by an unexpected 1997 European Cup victory over the Juventus 'dream team'.

Right: Borussia Dortmund play Manchester United en route to their 1997 European Cup triumph.

Below: Borussia Mönchengladbach at the 1975 UEFA Cup final, threatening Twente's goal with a header by Berti Vogts.

Borussia Mönchengladbach (Germany)

Honours: 5 League titles; 2 German Cups; UEFA Cup 1975, 1979

Colours: White; white; white

Mönchengladbach emerged from relative obscurity to rival Bayern Munich for the title of Germany's finest during the 1970s. Until then, the club's solitary major success had been in the West German Cup Final in 1960. Then coach Hannes Weisweiler developed a gifted side built around Berti Vogts, Gunter Netzer and Jupp Heynckes. Success on the European stage came soon. Victory over Twente in the 1975 UEFA Cup Final was followed, two years later, by an appearance against Liverpool in the European Cup Final. Borussia went down to Bob

Left: Cardiff often play in European competition, only to be outclassed by well-drilled and very talented European clubs.

Celtic (Scotland)

Honours: 37 League Titles; 31 Scottish Cups; European Cup 1967

Colours: Green/white; white; green/white

Founded in 1888 to raise funds for poor children, Celtic occupies the affections of the Catholic population of Glasgow, in contrast to Protestant-backed Rangers, although Celtic played Protestant players long before Rangers signed a high-profile Catholic. The club was a founder member of the Scottish League, and lifted its first title in 1893. Since then, it has vied for domestic supremacy with Rangers.

Celtic set a Scottish record by gaining nine consecutive League titles – from 1966 to 1974 – under their manager Jock Stein, a Protestant; to its fans' despair, the feat was equalled by Rangers in 1989–97. However, Celtic remains the only Scottish club to have won the European Cup, and was the first UK club to do so, beating favourites Internazionale 2–1 in 1967. Famously, this 'Lisbon Lions' side all came from within a 30-mile radius of Glasgow.

Since then, Celtic's teams have struggled to match that achievement, even though, lately, serious money has been spent in attempts to rebuild the side and ground – the results of this investment were initially mixed, but in 1998, under the Dutchman Wim Jansen, Celtic won the title again, preventing Rangers from gaining ten in a row. Jansen then left in acrimony.

Below: Kenny Dalglish in his Celtic days.

Paisley's marauding Liverpool side, but two years afterwards, it was back in the UEFA Cup Final – this time seeing off Red Star Belgrade.

Brondby (Denmark)

Honours: 8 League Titles; 3 Danish Cups

Colours: Yellow; blue; yellow

Brondby has nurtured some outstanding players who have then been bought by the bigger clubs of Europe, one such player being the brilliant Danish goalkeeper Peter Schmeichel. Several Brondby players were members of the Danish side that won the 1992 European Championship. Brondby itself enjoys a most respectable European record, and famously beat Real Madrid and Liverpool in the UEFA Cup during the 1990s.

Cardiff City (Wales)

Honours: 1 FA Cup

Colours: Blue; white; white

Cardiff remain the only club outside England to have lifted the FA Cup – in 1927, having beaten Arsenal 1–0 in the final. The hero of that team was the prolific scorer Len Davies, who gained 128 League goals for the club in the period between 1920 and 1931.

Since then, however, competition from rugby and local economics have forced the club into decline, although it has remained a regular entrant in European competition because of the weakness of the Welsh Cup.

Celtic remains the only Scottish club to have won the European Cup, and was the first UK club to do so.

147

Chelsea (England)

Honours: 1 League title; 3 FA Cups; European Cup-Winners' Cup 1971, 1998

Colours: Blue; blue; blue

Noted more for style than substance, Chelsea's 1997 FA Cup win against Middlesbrough ended 26 barren years. Italian international Roberto Di Matteo scored after only 47 seconds to set a new record for the fastest goal in the final. The victory meant that Dutch player-manager Ruud Gullit became the first foreign coach to win an English trophy. Gullit changed the face of the club by signing virtually a whole team of foreign imports, including Gianfranco Zola, another Italian, who was England's 1997 Footballer of the Year. Surprisingly, eight months later, Gullit was sacked. Gianluca Vialli then lead the team to European success.

Chelsea won its first League title in 1955 under Ted Drake, but had a long wait before further success.

The club then won the FA Cup in 1970 against Leeds; the Chelsea team starred English internationals Peter Osgood, Alan Hudson and Peter Bonetti. The side followed that by winning the 1971 Cup-Winners' Cup Final against Real Madrid.

Club Brugge (Belgium)

Honours: 11 League titles; 7 Belgian Cups

Colours: Black/blue; black; black

Bruges has had to be content with second place behind Anderlecht throughout the history of the Belgian League. Spells of superiority came when the club won the League/Cup double in 1977 and in 1996. However, it lost both the 1976 UEFA Cup Final and the 1978 European Cup Final to Liverpool, on each occasion by a one-goal margin.

Colo Colo (Chile)

Honours: 19 League titles; South American Club Cup 1991

Colours: White; black; black

Chile's most successful club gained its name from the local slang term for 'wildcat'. Founded in 1925, Colo Colo was the first South American club to tour Europe, visiting both Spain and Portugal in 1927; it established Chile's professional League in 1933. The Santiago-based club won the South American Club Cup in 1991, but lost in the World Club Cup Final against Red Star Belgrade in the same year.

Chelsea's 1997 FA Cup win made Dutch player-manager Ruud Gullit the first foreign coach to win an English trophy.

Below: A fan displays all the signs of 'Ruud'-mania – a condition rife among Chelsea supporters during the 1997–8 season when Gullit managed the club.

Dinamo Tbilisi (Georgia)

Honours: 10 League titles (2 Soviet and 8 Georgian); 9 Cups (2 Soviet and 7 Georgian); European Cup-Winners' Cup 1981

Colours: White/blue; white; white

Despite winning the Georgian League in each of its first eight years, 1990–97, since the break-up of the Soviet Union, Tbilisi has ceased to be the breeding ground that gave the outstanding Alexander Chivadze and David Kipiani to the USSR national side in the 1970s and early 1980s.

Two cups and a League championship between 1976 and 1979 saw the club briefly become a force in the USSR. Despite losing in the 1980 Cup Final, it entered the Cup-Winners' Cup the following year and, beating Carl Zeiss Jena of East Germany in the final, gained its only European trophy.

Dukla Prâha (Czech Republic)

Honours: 11 Czechoslovakian League titles; 8 Cups

Colours: Brown/yellow; yellow; red

Dukla's demise has been rapid. Once one of the most successful clubs in the former Czechoslovakia, largely due to its status as the Army Team, the side has become an also-ran since the fall of the Iron Curtain. In 1994, it was relegated from the first division of the new Czech Republic League, having achieved only one win all season.

Together with Sparta and Slavia, Dukla had formed part of the three-strong Prague football force that had dominated the Czechoslovakian game in the years after World War II. Inspired by its most famous player, the goalkeeper Ivo Viktor, the club won four consecutive championships between 1961 and 1964.

Crvena Zvezda Beograd (Yugoslavia)

Honours: 20 League titles; 15 Yugoslavian Cups; European Cup 1991; World Club Cup 1991

Colours: Red/white; red; red/white

Red Star Belgrade, or Crvena Zvezda Beograd, was one of Europe's biggest producers and nurturers of talent before the break-up of Yugoslavia during the early 1990s. The civil war resulted in the club's suspension from international and club competitions, while millions of pounds of transfer fees were frozen in banks throughout Europe.

Formed in 1945, Red Star had always been a 'selling club', and this explains why, for all the talent at its disposal, it achieved only a single victory in Europe. That occurred in 1991, when the side beat Marseille in an unexpectedly dull final, given their gifted group of players.

Above: Red Star Belgrade with the European cup which they won before going on to become World Club Champions as well.

Dundee United (Scotland)

Honours: 1 League title; 1 Scottish Cup

Colours: Tangerine; black; tangerine

In the mid-1980s, under manager Jim McLean, Dundee United was a force to be reckoned with in both Scotland and Europe. It won its first domestic championship in 1983, and a year later reached the European Cup semi-finals. In 1987, it was runner-up to IFK Gothenburg in the UEFA Cup Final. The club's Tannandice ground is a mere 400 yards (366m) from that of neighbours Dundee.

Dynamo Kyiv (Ukraine)

Honours: 13 Soviet titles, 5 Ukrainian titles; 9 Soviet cups, 2 Ukrainian cups; European Cup-Winners' Cup 1975, 1986; European Supercup 1975

Colours: Purple/white; purple; white

Kiev was dominant in the USSR between the late 1960s and the early 1990s, after which it became the main club in Ukrainian football. Founded in 1927, Dynamo had to wait until 1961 to land its first Soviet title, but then the club started an amazing run of success: the League/Cup double in 1967 was flanked by eight League titles, while another nine championships followed in 20 seasons. In 1975, Dynamo Kiev became the first Soviet team to win in Europe, beating Ferencvaros 3–0 in the Cup-Winners' Cup Final. Then, with Oleg Blokhin joined by Igor Belanov, the club repeated this success in 1986. Although Dynamo was briefly banned from competition in Europe during the mid-1990s following a bribes scandal, the side recovered to play a prominent part in the 1998 Champions League.

Eintracht Frankfurt (Germany)

Honours: 1 League title; 4 German Cups; UEFA Cup 1980

Colours: Red; black/red; black

Founder members of the Bundesliga in 1963, Eintracht Frankfurt is probably best remembered by many followers of the game for the 7–3 thrashing it received at the hands of Real Madrid in the 1960 European Cup Final (*see* Great Matches). The club won the UEFA Cup in 1980, beating compatriots Borussia Mönchengladbach. In 1996, it was relegated for the first time in its history and failed to gain instant promotion. Eintracht's last honour was the German Cup, which it lifted in 1988. That victory was the fourth success in the knock-out competition.

Estudiantes de La Plata (Argentina)

Honours: 5 League titles; South American Club Cup 1968, 1969, 1970; World Club Cup 1968

Colours: Red/white; white; red/white

Estudiantes, from the small town of La Plata near Beunos Aires, was briefly South America's best side, winning three consecutive club championships from 1968, and losing a fourth in 1971 only in the final. Yet the club's win-at-all-costs methods did little to enhance the image of South American football, especially after three violent World Club Championship matches against, respectively, Manchester United, AC Milan and Feyenoord from 1968 to 1970. In fact, three players were jailed after the AC Milan game.

Opposite: The mid-1980s Dynamo Kiev side which won the European Cup Winners's Cup went into decline, only become resurgent in the late 1990s.

Below: Daniel Amokachi and Barry Horne hold the FA Cup aloft as Everton proudly celebrate their 1995 triumph.

In 1975, Kiev became the first Soviet team to win in Europe, beating Ferencvaros 3–0 in the Cup-Winner's Cup final.

Everton (England)

Honours: 9 League titles; 5 FA Cups; European Cup-Winners' Cup 1985

Colours: Blue; white; blue

Everton started in 1878 as merely a church team, but no other club has spent as many seasons in the top flight as the Toffees – so-called because of Ye Ancient Toffee House, right next to the pub where the club was founded. The first ground was Anfield, which today is home to rivals Liverpool.

The club's record goal-scorer is 'Dixie' Dean, who registered 349 goals in 399 games between 1925 and 1937 – including a record 60 in the 1927–8 season. Dean helped Everton win the Second Division, First Division and FA Cup in consecutive seasons (1931–3). In 1936, Everton's game against Arsenal was the first to be shown on television. After a 1939 title, success eluded the side until the 1960s, when Harry Catterick built two teams that adhered to the club's 'school of science' reputation for good football. The 1969–70 championship mid-field combination of Alan Ball, Colin Harvey and Howard Kendall remains highly regarded.

Kendall returned to manage the club in the 1980s, winning two championships, an FA Cup and a European Cup-Winners' Cup with a team that included Neville Southall, Peter Reid, Kevin Ratcliffe and

Below: 'Fradi' is a leading club in Hungary, but since the fall of communism it has stuggled to make an impact in any of the European competitions.

Kevin Sheedy. Only an extra-time goal in the 1985 FA Cup Final denied Everton a unique League/FA Cup/ European Cup Winners' Cup treble.

Apart from the 1995 FA Cup, the last decade has seen an ongoing struggle against relegation.

Ferencvaros (Hungary)

Honours: 26 League titles; 17 Hungarian Cups; UEFA Cup 1965

Colours: Green/white; white; white

Easily Hungary's most successful club, Ferencvaros is nicknamed 'Fradi'. Based in Budapest, it has dominated the domestic game since its foundation in 1899, winning League Championships in every decade except the 1950s,

when it was weakened by political manoeuvering. A recovery in the 1960s was capped by success in the 1965 Fairs Cup. However, lack of money means that Fradi is now a power only at home.

Feyenoord (Holland)

Honours: 14 League titles; 10 Dutch Cups; World Club Cup 1970; European Cup 1970; UEFA Cup 1974, 2002

Colours: Red/white; black; red

Feyenoord of Rotterdam were founded by mining millionaire C. R. J. Kieboom in 1908, but success did not really arrive until the beginning of professionalism in Dutch football during the late

1950s. In that era, the club won the championship six times during 13 years, including League/Cup doubles in 1965 and 1969. In 1970, Feyenoord became the first Dutch club to win the European Cup, with a team that included outside-left Coen Moulijn, Swedish striker Ove Kindvall and Wim Van Hanegem. Ernst Happel was the influential coach at that time.

During the late 1970s and early 1980s, Feyenoord lost its grip on Dutch football and had to sell a lot of its most promising youngsters, including Ruud Gullit. Not until the return of former player Wim Jansen as manager did it revive, regaining the League title in 1993.

Everton's record goal-scorer is 'Dixie' Dean, who registered 349 goals in 399 games. His goals helped Everton win the Second Division, First Division and FA Cup in consecutive seasons.

Fiorentina (Italy)

Honours: 2 League titles; 5 Italian Cups; European Cup-Winners' Cup 1961

Colours: Purple; purple; purple

Fiorentina won its first League Championship in 1959, but the biggest moment in the club's history came when it was invited to play in the 1956–7 European Cup. In the final, it lost 2–0 to holders Real Madrid, the match being played in Madrid's stadium in front of 124,000 fans. Four years later, Fiorentina won the inaugural European Cup-Winners' Cup, beating Glasgow Rangers. In the following year, it reached the final, but lost to Atletico Madrid, in a replay staged four months after the first match.

Founded in 1923, the Florence-based club has never mounted a consistent challenge to Italy's big three – AC Milan, Internazionale and Juventus. It gained its second championship in 1969, and picked up the Italian Cup in 1975, but thereafter Fiorentina won nothing until the Italian Cup in 1996, when star Argentinian striker Gabriel Batistuta was influential. Earlier, in 1990, the club had reached the UEFA Cup Final with a team that starred Roberto Baggio, but lost to Juventus. The fans are among Italy's most passionate.

Above: Zico and Flamengo celebrate the 1981 World Club Cup.

Flamengo (Brazil)

Honours: 5 Championships; World Club Cup 1981; South American Club Cup 1981

Colours: Black/red; white; white

Brazil's most popular club plays its most important matches at the ageing 130,000-capacity Maracana Stadium and others

Above: Kevin Keegan in Hamburg's colours.

at the 20,000-capacity Gavea Stadium. It enjoyed its finest moment in 1981, when Zico, nicknamed 'the white Pelé', inspired it to World Club Cup and South American Club Cup victories; then he moved to Italy. The club has recently invested heavily in players such as Bebeto and Romario, although the latter soon returned to Spain.

Fluminense (Brazil)

Honours: 4 championships

Colours: Red; green/white; white

Right: Galatasaray's bright yellow strip has been the bane of English clubs in the European competition, not least because of the club's fanatical supporters.

Like Flamengo, Fluminense is an occasional Maracana resident whose status belies its lack of international success. Founded in 1902, Fluminense was the first

Brazilian club to go professional. In 1963, its derby with Flamengo drew an official crowd of 177,656, a world club record. Among its finest Brazilian players have been Didi, a 1958 World Cup winner, and Carlos Alberto, the 1970 World Cup winning captain.

Galatasaray (Turkey)

Honours: 14 League titles; 13 Turkish Cups; UEFA Cup 2002

Colours: Yellow; yellow; yellow

The most successful of the three Istanbul clubs – the others being Fenerbahce and Besiktas – that dominate Turkish football, Galatasaray overcame Manchester United in the 1993–4 European Cup to reach the last eight. The club made its biggest signings ever when it bought the Romanian Gheorghe Hagi in 1996 and, a year later, his compatriot Gica Popescu.

Hamburger SV (Germany)

Honours: 6 League titles; 3 German Cups; European Cup 1983; European Cup-Winners' Cup 1977

Colours: White; red; red

Founded in 1887, this is one of Germany's oldest clubs; it won two League titles during the interbellum. In 1983, under manager Ernst Happel, it beat Juventus to become the second German team, after Bayern Munich, to win the European Cup. That was its fourth European Final in six years, but over the course of the following 14, it won only the German Cup. Uwe Seeler, Manny Kaltz, Felix Magath and Kevin Keegan are among the players who have starred for the side.

Honved (Hungary)

Honours: 13 League titles; 5 Hungarian Cups

Colours: Red/black; black; black

Originally known as Kispest, after a district in Budapest, Honved was founded in 1909 and had a fairly anonymous record before World War II, winning only one Cup and finishing once as League runner-up. Then, with the post-war communist take-over in Hungary, the club was chosen to represent the new 'people's army' both at home and abroad, the idea being that this would promote national pride among soldiers. Renamed Honved, the side could recruit promising players from other clubs by simply conscripting them! This presaged an era of domestic dominance for Honved, inspired by the great striker Ferenc Puskas, who was awarded the honorary rank of major. During the following year, 1950, Honved picked up two League titles, one of them in the spring and the other in the autumn. The club made its European Cup début in 1956, but it lost in the first round; Puskas fled the country that same year to join Real Madrid after the Soviet Union crushed the attempted uprising in Hungary. Honved then went into decline; not until 1980 did the club win another League title. Thereafter, it enjoyed a measure of domestic success. The changing nature of Hungarian society after the demise of the Iron Curtain was underlined when the club eventually renamed itself Kispest-Honved.

Below: Hamburg beating Juventus in the 1983 European Cup Final.

IFK Göteborg (Sweden)

Honours: 18 League titles; 4 Swedish Cups; UEFA Cup 1982, 1987

Colours: Blue/white; blue; blue

IFK became the first Scandinavian side to win a European club honour when it beat Hamburg in the 1982 UEFA Cup Final. Five years later, and with half the 1982 side intact, IFK won it again, beating Dundee United. Since then, the club has continued to dominate the game at home in Sweden, but has failed to repeat these European triumphs.

With the post-war communist take-over, Honved was chosen to represent the new 'people's army'.

Independiente (Argentina)

Honours: 11 League titles; World Club Cup 1973, 1984; Copa Libertadores 1964, 1965, 1972, 1973, 1974, 1975, 1984

Colours: Red/blue; blue; black

South America's leading team in the early 1970s, Independiente, was just that, a team – so much so that the 1978 Argentinian World Cup winners had only one Independiente player, Daniel Berloni, in the starting line-up (although four were actually in the squad). Berloni was the third Independiente striker to make an impact on the international football scene, his predecessors being Raimundo Orsi – an Olympic runner-up in 1928 for Argentina and a World Cup medal winner in 1934 for Italy – and the Paraguayan international Arsenio Erico.

Of the two World Club Cup titles, the most notable came in 1973, when the team defeated Juventus in a one-off match in Italy. Eleven years later, they defeated Liverpool in Tokyo with Jorge Burruchaya in the line-up. Burruchaya was to go on to score the winning goal in the 1986 World Cup Final.

These successes followed two failures against Internazionale, whose defensive *catenaccio* style had frustrated the red devils from Avellaneda during the 1960s.

Founded by students in 1897, Juventus's name means 'youth', but the club is nicknamed the 'Old Lady'.

Internazionale 'Inter Milan' (Italy)

Honours: 13 League titles; 3 Italian Cups; European Cup 1964, 1965; UEFA Cup 1991, 1994, 1998; World Club Cup 1964, 1965

Colours: Black/blue; black; black

Italy's outstanding football club during the 1960s, Internazionale failed to perpetuate its successful traditions. During the following decades, the club was outshone both domestically and in Europe by its rivals AC Milan and Juventus. In recent years, it has spent heavily in an attempt to restore its position, the club president, Massimo Moratti, breaking the world transfer record in the summer of 1997 by paying Barcelona in excess of £19M for the renowned Brazilian striker Ronaldo.

The club attained its peak during the mid-1960s, when it achieved consecutive European Cup wins. First came the 3–1 victory over Real Madrid in 1964. However, the win that epitomized Inter's hard-fought, defensive style came a year later, against Benfica, as the side prevailed 1–0 to retain the trophy in front of its own fans in the San Siro Stadium.

Now Inter could realistically call itself the best team in the world, as it cemented its European Cup triumphs with World Club Cup wins over Independiente in both 1964 and 1965. Inter's coach, the Argentinian Helenio Herrera, masterminded these triumphs, using star mid-fielder Sandro Mazzola and striker Luis Suarez in front of the mean *catenaccio* defence. Defeat in the 1967 European Cup Final against Glasgow Celtic signalled the end of an era; thereafter, Inter won only a single championship in the 1970s, and just two in the 1980s.

In the 1990s, Inter invested heavily in multi-national talent, buying players like Lothar Matthaus, Jurgen Klinsmann, Dennis Bergkamp, Paul Ince and Youri Djorkaeff. During this period, the club did win three UEFA Cups, but league success eluded them, despite this investment.

Ipswich (England)

Honours: 1 League title; 1 FA Cup; UEFA Cup 1981

Colours: Blue; white; blue

Ipswich has given the English national side two managers. Sir Alf Ramsey left after steering Ipswich to Second and First Division titles in 1961 and 1962. Then, after building a team based on a strong youth policy, Bobby Robson went to the national side in 1982. His Ipswich team featured Terry Butcher, Mick Mills, Eric Gates and Paul Mariner. After winning the 1978 FA Cup, they were joined by Dutchmen Arnold Muhren and Frans Thijssen who, with 14-goal John Wark, helped Ipswich lift the 1981 UEFA Cup. In the 1990s, they were relegated and have returned to their roots, ex-player George Burley concentrating on youth.

Opposite: Ronaldo playing for Internazionale.

Below: Ipswich triumph in the 1978 FA Cup Final.

Juventus (Italy)

Honours: 27 League titles; 9 Italian Cups: European Cup 1985, 1996; UEFA Cup 1977, 1990, 1993; European Cup-Winners' Cup 1984; European Supercup 1984, 1997; World Club Cup 1985, 1996

Colours: Black/white; white; black/white

Founded by students in 1897, the club has a name that means 'youth', but is nicknamed the 'Old Lady'. Its centenary celebrations were dented at the end of the 1996–7 season when, having extended its record of Serie A League titles to 24, and lifted the World Club Cup and European Supercup, it unexpectedly lost the European Cup Final to Borussia Dortmund.

Although this Turin-based club has long dominated its domestic championship, helped since World

War I by funding from the Fiat motor company, European success eluded it until 1977 – even though during the 1950s, the much-loved and revered Welsh striker Jack Charles wore the club's famous black-and-white strip. Those colours derive from a turn-of-the-century gift of shirts by the English club Notts County.

It was in the 1970s and 1980s, during Giovanni Trappatoni's time as manager, that Juventus established itself as one of the world's greatest clubs. Between 1977 and 1985, it won all three European club competitions, the first team ever to achieve this. Juventus line-ups featured some of Italy's most renowned players, such as Dino

Below: Juventus against Ajax Amsterdam.

Zoff, Gaetano Scirea, Marco Tardelli and Paulo Rossi, who between them formed the backbone of Italy's 1982 World Cup-winning side. Juventus also bought exceptional foreign players, like Michel Platini and Zbigniew Boniek, the two most influential members of the club's 1985 European Cup-winning side.

Having won the league title in 1986, Juve waited nine years until its next Serie A success, being restored to primacy by Marcello Lippi. It achieved the League/Cup double in 1995, his first season in charge, and a year later won the European Cup with a team that featured Gianluca Vialli and Fabrizio Ravanelli. Both were promptly

sold, but Juventus reached the final again in the following two years, suffering defeats to Dortmund and Real Madrid.

Lazio (Italy)

Honours: 2 League titles; 3 Italian Cups; European Cup Winners Cup 1999

Colours: Blue; white; white

Lazio and Roma are Rome's two major clubs. Like rivals Roma, Lazio has spent heavily in the 1990s without much success. Founded in 1900, the club has, just after its 100th birthday, only one championship and one Italian

Cup to its name. Even its League success in 1974 was soured: the club was banned from playing in the European Cup because of its fans' behaviour in previous years.

In 1992 Lazio signed Paul Gascoigne, but he suffered an injury-plagued three years and did not inspire them to win any trophies. It was Sven-Goran Eriksson, who was appointed manager in 1997 that achieved this, inspiring them to the Scudetto – their long-held ambition.

A combination of tough and highly skilled players brought Leeds championship wins in 1969 and 1974.

Leeds United (England)

Honours: 3 League titles; 1 FA Cup; Fairs Cup 1968

Colours: White; white; white

In 1992, this club was the last winner of the Football League before the new Premier League supplanted it as the peak of the English game. Leeds achieved that success under manager Howard Wilkinson only two years after promotion from the Second Division. Wilkinson was sacked four years later, six months after taking Leeds to Wembley for the first time since 1973 – the year when Sunderland had, famously, defeated Don Revie's great, but unloved, Leeds team. A combination of tough and highly skilled players – like Allan

Above: Allan Clarke (centre) and Jack Charlton (rear) running out for Leeds United.

Clarke, Norman Hunter, John Giles, Billy Bremner and Terry Cooper – brought championship wins in 1969 and 1974, and runner-up slots from 1970 to 1972. In Europe, Leeds won the Fairs Cup following victory against Ferencvaros in 1968, and was an unlucky loser against Bayern Munich in the 1975 European Cup Final.

Liverpool (England)

Honours: 18 League titles; 6 FA Cups; European Cup 1977, 1978, 1981, 1984; UEFA Cup 1973, 1976, 2001; European Supercup 1977

Colours: Red; red; red

Fittingly for England's most successful club, Liverpool both instigated and finished a winning streak by English clubs of seven

European Cups in eight years. The Merseyside team won three of them under the aegis of Bob Paisley and, after Paisley's retirement, another under Joe Fagan. Liverpool ruled the English League for even longer than that, winning the title on a total of 13 occasions between 1964 and 1990.

All the triumphs were overshadowed, however, by two tragedies. The first occurred in 1985 at the Heysel Stadium, Brussels, when 39 fans, mainly Italian, died because of crowd trouble before Liverpool's European Cup Final against Juventus. Liverpool lost the subsequent, irrelevant, game 1–0. Four years later, the club was again touched by tragedy as 96 Liverpool fans died in the crush to get into Sheffield's Hillsborough stadium for

an FA Cup semi-final against Nottingham Forest.

Formed by Everton's ex-landlord after the other Merseyside club had left Anfield following a rent dispute, Liverpool gained various trophies, but had slipped into the Second Division by the time Bill Shankly took over as manager in 1959. Within seven years, the Scot had taken the club to promotion, to the League title, to FA Cup success and to the European Cup-Winners' Cup Final with a team featuring Ian St John, Roger Hunt and Tommy Smith. Later, in 1973, Liverpool sent out the first signals that it intended to dominate Europe by beating Mönchengladbach to win the UEFA Cup. Shankly retired a year later, and Paisley took over. In 2001,

Liverpool pulled off a treble, by winning the League Cup, FA Cup and the UEFA Cup.

Malmö (Sweden)

Honours: 14 League titles; 13 Swedish Cups

Colours: Sky-blue; white; white

Malmö was undoubtedly the Swedish team of the 1970s, winning five League Championships. In 1979, coached by Englishman Bob Houghton, it became the first Swedish side to reach the European Cup Final, losing to Nottingham Forest. But then fortune deserted the club: the 1980s and 1990s were barren times.

Below: Graeme Souness, Alan Hansen and Michael Robinson of Liverpool.

Left: Tony Book holds the 1969 FA Cup aloft for Manchester City.

players died (*see* page 73). Ten years later, with a team that starred Bobby Charlton (who survived the crash), George Best and Nobby Stiles (Denis Law had been injured), United beat Benfica at Wembley to become the first English club to take home the European Cup.

In 1974, however, Busby having retired and Best having walked out, United were relegated to the Second Division. The club came straight back, but not until 1993, under the guidance of Alex Ferguson, did it end a 26-year wait by taking the League title.

Ferguson patiently created a successful side around former England captain Bryan Robson. Further inspiration came from the Frenchman Eric Cantona, bought in late 1992. With him, United won League/Cup doubles in 1994 and 1996, and even greater success followed in 1999 when United achieved the treble of league, FA Cup and European Champions' League. Since then three more Premierships have been won (including 2003), although it remains to be seen how United will fare without star player David Beckham next season.

Below: Bryan Robson, the man crucial to the development of Alex Ferguson's Manchester United.

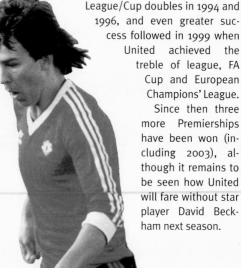

Manchester City (England)

Honours: 2 League titles; 4 FA Cups; European Cup-Winners' Cup 1970

Colours: Light blue; light blue; light blue

Traditionally, City is the Manchester team with the most local support, but this has brought it little success compared to rival United. The club won the European Cup-Winners' Cup in 1970 with a team managed by Joe Mercer and Malcolm Allison. City went through a succession of managers in the 1990s and 2000s, yo-yoing between relegation from and promotion to the Premier League.

In 1952, United won the league again, Busby by now having created the young team nicknamed the 'Busby's Babes'.

Manchester United (England)

Honours: 15 League titles; 10 FA Cups; European Cup: 1968, 1999; European Cup-Winners Cup 1991; European Supercup 1991

Colours: Red; white; black

Aside from a successful spell before World War II, United was just an ordinary club until Matt Busby arrived in 1945. Within three years, the former Scottish international had taken United to victory in the FA Cup, the club's first trophy since the 1911 League.

In 1952, United won the League again, Busby by now having created the young team nicknamed the 'Busby Babes'. After yet another League victory in 1956, United became the first English club to play in the European Cup (against the FA's wishes): the side reached the semi-finals in 1957, and repeated the feat in 1958, although its hopes were destroyed by the Munich air disaster, in consequence of which eight United

Marseille (France)

Honours: 8 League titles (1993 title revoked); 10 French Cups; European Cup 1993 (revoked)

Colours: White; white; white

Above: Raymond Goethals, Marseille's manager, with the 1993 European Cup.

Marseille was formed in 1898 and won its first League title in 1929. After World War II, Marseille won the 1948 championship, but despite huge sums spent on foreign stars, further success did not follow. By the time millionaire businessman Bernard Tapie took over in 1985, Marseille was in the Second Division.

Immediately thereafter, the club gained promotion and, with the attacking flair of Enzo Francescoli, Jean-Pierre Papin and Chris Waddle, swept to four League titles in a row. Marseille suffered the agony of defeat in the 1991 European Cup

Final, being beaten on penalties by Red Star Belgrade in Bari, but two years later the club defeated AC Milan 1–0 in Munich, the scorer being Basile Boli.

Later it emerged that three Valenciennes players had been offered cash to throw a League game the week before the final, a revelation that uncovered massive match-fixing (see page 190). Marseille's League and European Cup titles were revoked, the club was relegated, and eventually Tapie was jailed.

Arrigo Sacchi took AC Milan to almost unprecedented heights of success, leading the club to trophy after trophy.

Milan (Italy)

Honours: 16 League titles; 4 Italian Cups; European Cup 1963, 1969, 1989, 1990, 1994, 2003; European Cup-Winners' Cup 1968, 1973; European Supercup 1989, 1990, 1995; World Club Cup 1969, 1989, 1990

Colours: Red/black; white; white

Founded as Milan Cricket and Football Club by English expatriates in 1899, AC quickly discovered that football was its *pièce de resistance*. It won its first League title in 1901, repeating the feat a further six times before reaching its first European Cup Final in 1963. There the side beat holders Benfica 2–1; included in the line-up were Cesare Maldini (appointed Italy's national coach in late 1996), Giovanni Trapattoni (later Juventus' outstanding coach), and the great goal-scorer Gigi Rivera. AC's inspiration for both the 1963 win and its later triumph (1969) over Ajax was the coach Nereo Rocco, who had the side playing a rigid sweeper system.

The 1970s proved a lean decade, with only the 1973 European Cup-Winners' Cup to the club's name. Following relegation to Serie B after a bribes scandal in the early 1980s, AC was taken over by the media magnate Silvio Berlusconi. He injected vast amounts of capital into the club and appointed Arrigo Sacchi as manager. Sacchi took the club to almost unprecedented heights of success. He bought in the Dutch trio of Marco Van Basten, Ruud Gullit and Frank Rijkaard, and in combination with a defence featuring Franco Baresi and Paolo Maldini, they brought back trophy after trophy to Milan. Probably the peak came in 1989, when the side demolished Steaua Bucharest 4–0 in the European Cup Final.

Sacchi left to manage Italy in 1991. He was replaced by former AC Milan player Fabio Capello, who took the club to four League titles between 1992 and 1996. That team, minus the Dutchmen, re-visited earlier glories by destroying Barcelona, again 4–0, in the 1994 European Cup Final.

Below: The outstanding Milan side that played in the mid-1990s.

Millonarios (Colombia)

Honours: 13 League titles

Colours: Blue; white; white

The Bogotá club gained its name, meaning 'millionaires', in the 1930s when, with amateur players and then called Deportivo Munici-pal, it campaigned for a profes-sional League. During the 1950s, the club grew in stature, recruiting Argentina's finest players, who were on strike; these included Alfredo Di Stefano.

Monaco (France)

Honours: 7 League titles; 5 French Cups

Colours: Red/white; red; white

The Royal house of Monaco, the Grimaldi family, has provided funds to enable Monaco to sign players like Jurgen Klinsmann, Glenn Hoddle and Sonny Andersson, despite the club's very low gates. The side was the most consistent team in the French League between title wins in 1988 and 1997, when Monaco never finished outside the top ten. The club reached the European Cup-Winners' Cup Final in 1992.

Moskva Dynamo (Russia)

Honours: 11 Soviet League titles; 6 Soviet Cups; 1 Russian Cup

Colours: Blue; blue; white

Dynamo was the first Soviet club to travel outside the Iron Curtain when, in late 1945, it embarked on a friendly tour of England, Scotland and Wales. It drew with Chelsea and Glasgow Rangers, destroyed Cardiff 10–1 and beat Arsenal 4–3. Dynamo's most famous player was the goalkeeper Lev Yashin, who became well-known for playing in an all-black strip. He was the first keeper to be voted European Footballer of the Year, receiving that accolade in 1963.

The club had its origins in the 1880s, being founded by British cotton-mill owners. It was put on a formal footing in 1923, but did not win its first League title until 1936, gaining a League/Cup double a year later.

Despite championship wins, Dynamo did not play in European international competition until the 1971–2 season, when it finished as runner-up to Glasgow Rangers in the European Cup-Winners' Cup; this was the first time that any Soviet side had played in a European final.

Below: Nacional Montevideo v Nottingham Forest in the World Club Cup tournament of 1980.

A–Z OF CLUBS

Rival Moscow teams pressured Dynamo for honours, and the club won only one more championship, in 1976, before the dissolution of the Soviet Union. It has fared badly in the nascent Russian championship, having gained only a single Cup during the first nine years.

Nacional Montevideo (Uruguay)

Honours: 35 League titles; South American Club Cup 1971, 1980, 1988; World Club Cup 1971, 1980, 1988

Colours: White; blue; white

Uruguay's best club has regularly proved that it can compete outside Uruguay's borders – unlike the national team, which has not done so since the 1950s. On the back of the side's first South American Club Cup, in 1971, it won the World Club Cup. Nacional made it two in 1980, beating Nottingham Forest, and three in 1988, disposing of PSV Eindhoven in a penalty shoot-out.

Nantes (France)

Honours: 7 League titles; 3 French Cups

Colours: Green/yellow; yellow; yellow

Nantes has enjoyed brief success since World War II, but has never dominated French football. The club won the League twice in the mid-1960s, and formed the backbone of the French national side for the 1966 World Cup. In the late 1980s, the club's youth policy again saw players graduate to the national side, among them Marcel Desailly, Christian Karembeu and Patrice Loko. The latter two guided Nantes to the 1996 championship before, like so many players, moving on to wealthier clubs.

Above: Careca in action for Napoli.

Napoli (Italy)

Honours: 2 League titles; 3 Italian Cups; UEFA Cup 1989

Colours: Blue; white; blue

Napoli was briefly the best team in Italy after signing Diego Maradona from Barcelona, in 1984, for a then world-record transfer fee of £5M. Three years later, Maradona inspired the side to the League/ Cup double; this was its first Scudetto and only its third Cup success. Then Napoli won its first European honour, lifting the 1989 UEFA Cup against Stuttgart; the club's inspirations now included the Brazilians Alemao and Careca. In 1990, the side won the League again, ahead of European Cup-holders AC Milan.

In 1991, Maradona failed a dope test. As a result, he was banned and his career in Italy came to an end. The episode also signalled the end of Napoli's pre-eminence. Soon after, huge debts forced the Italian club to sell its best players and it was finally relegated to Serie B in 1998.

Newcastle United (England)

Honours: 4 League titles; 6 FA Cups; Fairs Cup 1969

Colours: Black/white; black; black

Newcastle United, a power in England during the 1950s, only just avoided dropping into the old English Third Division in 1992, before former Liverpool and England striker Kevin Keegan was hired as manager. A year later, Newcastle was back in the top division, thanks largely to the scoring of Andy Cole. In 1995, Cole was sold to Manchester United for a club-record £6.25M; a year later, Keegan paid a world-record £15M for Alan Shearer, who became the latest in a long line of famous Newcastle No. 9s, running from Hughie Gallacher and Jackie Milburn to Malcolm MacDonald.

Despite Alan Shearer, Newcastle failed to win their first trophy since the 1969 Fairs cup. Keegan resigned in 1997 and was replaced by Kenny Dalglish, then Ruud Gullit and finally Bobby Robson.

Nottingham Forest (England)

Honours: 1 League title; 2 FA Cups; European Cup 1979, 1980

Colours: Red; white; red

Formed in 1865, Forest is one of the oldest clubs in the world. The first refereeing whistle was tried out in a game between Forest and Sheffield Norfolk in 1878.

Forest played at six venues – it had a two-year spell at Trent Bridge cricket ground – before settling on the City Ground in 1898, the year of its first FA Cup triumph. Real glory came in the late 1970s when, under the guidance of Brian Clough and his assistant Peter Taylor, the club briefly stood at the top of European football. In 1978, the newly promoted club snatched

the League and went on to collect the European Cup for the following two seasons. The club also picked up the League Cup in 1978 and 1979. Then it had to wait until 1989 and 1990, again in the League Cup, for more trophies, before twice being relegated from the Premier League.

Notts County (England)

Honours: 1 FA Cup

Colours: Black/white; white; black

Notts County is the world's oldest surviving professional football club, and was one of the founder members of the Football League. Juventus, too, wears black-and-white stripes: the Italian club's first shirts were donations from the English club. Notts County became the first Second Division team to garner the FA Cup (in 1894), but the side's only claim to fame since has been the then-record signing of England centre-forward Tommy Lawton from Chelsea for £20,000, in 1947.

Panathinaikos (Greece)

Honours: 18 League titles; 16 Greek Cups

Colours: Green; green; green

Panathinaikos has long fought with Olympiakos for domination of Greek football, but Pana has outstripped its rival from Athens in European terms. In 1971, trained by Ferenc Puskas, it became the first Greek team to reach the European Cup Final, losing to Ajax. The Dutch prevailed again when the two sides met in the 1996 European Cup semi-finals.

Opposite: Kevin Keegan in his playing spell at Newcastle.

Below: Trevor Francis scores the goal that won Nottingham Forest the 1980 European Cup.

Paris St Germain (France)

Honours: 2 League titles; 5 French Cups; European Cup-Winners' Cup 1996

Colours: Blue/red; blue; blue

The *nouveau riche* of French football by comparison with Marseille and St Étienne, St Germain was founded in 1973 as a Third Division side to bring professional football to the capital. Two years later, it was in the First Division. It made no real impact, though, until in 1982 it won the French Cup, and it did the same in the following year. It gained its first French championship in 1986 and its second in 1994, this time with a team that starred, among others, former World Footballer of the Year George Weah, former Brazilian captain Rai and international winger David Ginola. In 1996, the

A-Z OF CLUBS

club won the European Cup-Winners' Cup. That victory, under coach Luis Fernandez, made St Germain only the second French team to win a European club cup after Marseille; the latter's 1993 European Cup was later revoked in the wake of a scandal (see page 190), so PSG was really the first.

Parma (Italy)

Honours: 1 Italian Cup; European Cup-Winners' Cup 1993; UEFA Cup 1995; European Supercup 1993

Colours: White/yellow; white/yellow; white

The Parma club, from northern Italy, was founded in 1968, and by 1992 was an established Serie A side; in that year, the club won the Italian Cup, its first domestic honour. The funds have been provided by the Parmalat food company, and the brains by managers Arrigo

Above: Parmalat sponsor the Parma side which has made great strides since its foundation in 1968.

Sacchi and then Nevio Scala. Under the latter, Parma won the 1993 European Cup-Winners' Cup and began to attract world-class talents like Gianfranco Zola and Faustino Asprilla. The club lost the 1994 European Cup-Winners' Cup Final, but in 1995 beat Juventus to win the UEFA Cup.

Penarol (Uruguay)

Honours: 40 League titles; World Club Cup 1961, 1966, 1982; South American Club Cup 1960, 1961, 1966, 1983, 1987

Colours: Black/yellow; black; black

Founded as the Central Uruguayan Cricket club in 1891, changing its name to Penarol as the British influence waned, this was the first team to win the World Club Cup three times, and is often described as South America's answer to Real Madrid, who beat them in the

inaugural World Club Cup. The club has been the dominant force in Uruguayan football from the start, providing a number of outstanding players for the country's 1930 and 1950 World Cup-winning teams. Penarol has since won five South American Club Cups and three World Club Cups, defeating Benfica, Real Madrid and Aston Villa in the process.

The most famous Penarol side was that which supplied the Uruguayan national team with no less than six players for the 1950 World Cup tournament, including the legendary Juan Schiaffino, who scored six goals in the finals to become top scorer. The goalkeeper from that 1950 national side, Roque Maspoli, was also a Penarol player, and he would become the manager of the club during the 1960s. With players like William Martinez and Albert Spencer, Mascoli fashioned a second great Penarol side, one whose achievements in the 1960s were emulated in the early 1980s by the side that included acknowledged Uruguayan great, Fernando Morena.

The most famous Penarol side was that which supplied their national team with six players for the 1950 World Cup.

Porto (Portugal)

Honours: 19 League titles; 13 Portuguese Cups; World Club Cup 1987; European Cup 1987, UEFA Cup 2003

Colours: Blue/white; blue; white

Porto was always considered the third team in Portugal until it picked up the European Cup in 1987, beating Bayern Munich in

Below: Porto in action.

Vienna. Impressive results and trophy wins since then have ensured that the 'Big Two', Sporting Lisbon and Benfica, has now become the 'Big Three'.

Porto was formed in 1893 in Oporto – the anglicized name reflects its origins. They pioneered the modern transfer system when – in the 1930s – the club bought two Yugoslav players; that far-sighted attitude was rewarded by championship successes in 1938 and 1939.

Preston North End (England)

Honours: 2 League titles; 2 FA Cups

Colours: White/navy; navy; navy

In 1888, Preston North End became a founder member of the English Football League and won every League game they played. The 'Invincibles' also hoisted the FA Cup. A year later, Preston retained the League title. The club was League runner-up for the next three seasons, but did not win the Cup again until 1938. England striker Tom Finney helped a relegated Preston back into the First Division after World War II, but with the lifting of the players' minimum wage, Preston declined.

PSV Eindhoven (Holland)

Honours: 15 League titles; 8 Dutch Cups; UEFA Cup 1978; European Cup 1988

Colours: Red/white; black; black

The team owned by Dutch electrical giants Philips has traditionally vied with Feyenoord to be recognized as Holland's best side after Ajax. Despite its ownership, Philips took little interest in serious investment until the 1980s. Nevertheless, PSV was able to tempt Ruud Gullit away from Feyenoord in 1985, and his goals won the club the 1987 Dutch championship. His subsequent sale – to AC Milan for a then world-record £5.7M fee – did not much affect PSV: in 1988, ten years after winning the UEFA Cup, the Dutch team collected the European Cup by beating Benfica on penalties. That victory capped a magnificent season, in which PSV gained the domestic League/Cup double as well.

In the 1990s, PSV signed Brazilian strikers Romario and Ronaldo, who followed in Gullit's footsteps by top-scoring in the League before leaving for bigger clubs. In 1997, PSV ended Ajax's stranglehold on the championship, and repeated the feat in 2001.

Queen's Park (Scotland)

Honours: 10 Scottish Cups

Colours: White/black; white; white/black

Queen's Park is one of the curiosities of the UK game. The Glaswegians have retained their amateur status long after all other Scottish clubs have turned pro or semi-pro. Also, despite average attendances in the hundreds rather than thousands, it plays its football at Hampden Park, Scotland's national stadium, which once held nearly 150,000 for an international.

Furthermore, Queen's Park is the only Scottish club ever to have contested the English FA Cup Final, finishing as runner-up in 1884 – when the club also won the Scottish Cup – and 1885. After ten Scottish Cups in 20 seasons to 1893, the club has failed to win a major honour.

Rangers (Scotland)

Honours: 49 League titles; 30 Scottish Cups: European Cup-Winners' Cup 1972

Colours: Blue; blue; blue

Rangers has consistently failed to translate its domestic supremacy into the dream of winning the European Cup. In 1997, the club equalled the record nine consecutive championships established in 1966–74 by its Glaswegian rival, Celtic, but yet again manager Walter Smith failed to take the side beyond the group stage of the European Cup. Between March 1993 and December 1996, Rangers won only one game in continental Europe. Possibly because of this, in 1997 Smith

Opposite: Only recently have PSV Eindhoven broken Ajax's stranglehold on the Dutch league.

announced that he would retire from the club at the end of the 1997–8 season, to be replaced by Dutchman Dick Advocaat.

The club did succeed in Europe in 1972, though, when it lifted the Cup-Winners' Cup by beating Dynamo Moscow. However, it was banned from defending the honour in the following year because its fans had rioted in Barcelona to celebrate the success. That victory came only a year after the Ibrox disaster, when 66 Rangers fans died in a stairway crush after a game against Celtic.

The start of Rangers' modern era of success came in 1985, when Graeme Souness was brought in as player-manager. He revolutionized the club by importing 18 English players and even breaking the Protestants-only rule by buying a Catholic, Mo Johnston; he also brought in black players like Mark Walters and Basile Boli. This season Rangers completed the treble in Scotland, winning the league, FA cup and CIS cup.

Rapid-Wien (Austria)

Honours: 30 League titles; 14 Austrian Cups

Colours: Green/white; white; white

Austria's leading side between 1912 and 1968, winning 25 titles, Rapid Vienna had to wait until 1982 before gaining its next title, under the inspiration of the striker Hans Krankel. In Europe, Rapid reached the Cup-Winners' Cup Finals of 1985 and 1996. Other moments of glory were experienced in 1938 and 1941, when the club took the German Cup and championship respectively, Austria having been temporarily absorbed into Greater Germany. Rapid was originally known as the First Workers Football Club, and its stadium, the Honappi, is named after Gerhard Honappi, a former player and the architect who designed it.

A–Z OF CLUBS

Real Madrid (Spain)

Honours: 28 League titles; 17 Spanish Cups; European Cup 1956, 1957, 1958, 1959, 1960, 1966, 1998, 2000, 2002; UEFA Cup 1985, 1986; World Club Cup 1960

Colours: White; white; white

Founded in 1902 as Madrid FC, this club gained the 'Real' ('Royal') prefix only when granted recognition by King Alfonso XIII in 1920. Although a founder member of the Spanish League, Real had to wait until 1932 for its first championship victory. In 1943, former player and coach Don Santiago Bernabeu took over as president and, under him, Real rose to greatness, building the 110,000-capacity stadium that bears his name. Real's heyday was the 1950s, with a side that included Alfredo Di Stefano, Ferenc Puskas and Raymond Kopa. This, arguably the first all-star European team, won the inaugural European Cup in 1956. Real retained it for the next four years, climaxing with the memorable 1960 final 7–3 (page 68) win over Eintracht Frankfurt.

Victory in 1966 brought a sixth European Cup, but Real's subsequent teams struggled to live up to the daunting legacy, only briefly recalling past European glories in UEFA Cup wins in 1985 and 1986. Successive domestic titles between 1986 and 1990 saw the forwards Hugo Sanchez and Emilio Butragueno hailed as heroes.

In the early 1990s, debts of over £60M saw Real miss out on Europe's best players, but in 1996 Fabio Capello was hired from AC Milan and inspired the club to a 27th championship. He returned to Italy in 1997, leaving an impressive team that went on to win three Champions' League titles in five years (1998, 2000 and 2002).

Many of the world's best players were in the 2003 team, including World Cup winners Ronaldo and Roberto Carlos. They will be joined next season by David Beckham.

River Plate (Argentina)

Honours: 24 League titles; World Club Cup 1986; South American Cup 1986

Colours: White/red; black; white/black/red

One of the two giants of Argentinian football, River Plate has produced some wonderfully talented players over the years: Alfredo Di Stefano, Omar Sivori, Ubaldo Fillol, Daniel Passarella, Leopoldo Luque and Mario Kempes. The club succeeded in winning the South American Cup and the World Club Cup in 1986, the same year that Argentina achieved World Cup victory in Mexico.

Traditionally regarded as the team for the wealthier faction of Buenos Aires, they are known as the 'Millionaires' Club'. Their rivalry with Boca Juniors is one of the most enduring contests in the Argentine league. Boca's win at Monumential, River Plate's ground, left River trailing 59–54 in 160 meetings since the professional game began in 1930. The club itself dates back further, to 1901, and the only surprise, given their pedigree, is that it took until 1986 for them to win the Copa Libertadores, defeating Ameica of Columbia. Previously, they had lost in the finals of 1966 to Penarol, and in 1976 to Cruzeiro. Having finally won in South America, they conquered the world by beating Steaua Bucharest in the 1986 World Club Cup final in Tokyo.

Opposite: Real Madrid has been dogged by huge debt, despite which the club has remained at the forefront of Spanish football.

Below: River Plate – the mid-1980s side which won the World Club cup.

Roma (Italy)

Honours: 3 League titles; 8 Italian Cups; UEFA Cup 1961

Colours: Red/yellow; red/yellow; red/yellow

Although one of the two major clubs in the Italian capital, Roma has only rarely given its fans much excuse to fill its 80,000-capacity Olympic Stadium beyond derby games with Lazio. It hit its peak in the early 1980s, winning the Italian Cup in 1980 and 1981, and two years later gaining its first post-war championship with a team trained by the Swede Nils Liedholm. The star was the Brazilian mid-fielder Falcao, and with him Roma reached the 1984 European Cup Final, held in the club's

A-Z OF CLUBS

St Étienne (France)

Honours: 10 League titles; 6 French Cups

Colours: Green; white; green

Once the greatest side in French club football, St Étienne is now only a pale shadow of the team that once captivated Europe with its wonderful style of football. The club reached the European Cup Final in 1975, losing to the all-conquering Bayern Munich. Great St Étienne players have included Dominique Rocheteau and Michel Platini.

Sampdoria (Italy)

Honours: 1 League title; 4 Italian Cups; European Cup-Winners' Cup 1990

Colours: Blue; white; blue

During 1988–92, this Genovese club was AC Milan's rival for the title of Italy's outstanding side. Inspired by striker Gianluca Vialli and Roberto Mancini, it won consecutive Italian Cups in 1988

own stadium. There the side lost on penalties to Liverpool – the first European Cup Final to be decided by a shoot-out.

Above: St Étienne reached the European Cup Final in 1975, but lost to Bayern Munich.

Opposite: Pelé in Santos colours.

Rosenborg (Norway)

Honours: 15 League titles; 8 Norwegian Cups

Colours: White; black; black

Rosenborg, of Trondheim, is one of Europe's most respected nursery clubs, producing players

Right: Sampdoria were AC Milan's main rivals between 1988 and 1992.

who have prospered in the Premiership and elsewhere. But, despite regularly selling its stars, it still produces fine shows in Europe. The highlight of its Continental experience was a 2–1 victory over AC Milan at the San Siro in the 1996–7 Champions' League, which put Rosenborg into the quarter-finals. The club was founded originally by 17-year-olds in 1917 as Sportsklubben Odd.

and 1989, and reached consecutive Cup-Winners' Cup Finals in 1989 and 1990, winning the latter. In 1991, it won its first League Championship, and a year later reached the European Cup Final, losing to Barcelona in extra time.

During the mid-1950s, Santos reorganized its youth system – and discovered Pelé, then aged only 15.

Santos (Brazil)

Honours: 15 São Paulo League titles; 5 national League titles; World Club Cup 1962, 1963; South American Club Cup 1962, 1963

Colours: White; white; white

Santos was founded in 1912 by three members of the Americanos club. In 1933, it became only the second Brazilian club to embrace professionalism. In the mid-1950s, it reorganized its youth system – and discovered Pelé, then aged only 15. The club surrounded the prodigy with fine players, like goalkeeper Gilmar, centre-back Mauro, wing-half Zito and centre-forward Coutinho. Santos scaled the competitive heights of international football during the early 1960s, when the side won both the South American Club Cup and the World Club Cup twice. Santos went on touring and raking in cash, using Pelé's name to attract the crowds wherever the club played.

São Paulo (Brazil)

Honours: 17 São Paulo League titles; 4 Brazil League titles; World Club Cup 1992, 1993; South American Club Cup 1992, 1993

Colours: White/red/black; white; white

The club was founded in 1935; most of the other big teams in South America were already well

established by then. Within a decade, however, São Paulo had become the strongest team in Brazil, winning the state title on a total of five occasions during the 1940s. In the 1960s, the club was overshadowed somewhat by Pelé's Santos and, apart from a brief flurry in the mid-1970s, it was not until the late 1980s – under the guidance of former national manager Tele Santana – that it revived. Bizarrely, however, the team was relegated in 1990 in its regional league, only to be reinstated through a change in the league structure. São Paulo went on to win two World Club Cups – against Barcelona in 1992 and Milan in the following year.

Sheffield (England)

Honours: none

Colours: Red; black; black

Now a lowly part-time side in England's Northern Counties (East) League, Sheffield was formed in 1855 and is the oldest football club in the world. It plays at the Don Valley Stadium, former home to the World Student Games, and won the Amateur Cup in 1904. It last reached the first round of the FA Cup in 1887.

Sporting Lisbon (Portugal)

Honours: 17 League titles; 16 Portuguese Cups; European Cup-Winners' Cup 1964

Colours: Green/white; white; white

Sporting Lisbon is a team that is desperate to relive its days of European glory. Winner of the Cup-Winners' Cup in 1964, it was neck-and-neck with Benfica in terms of Portuguese domination during that decade; the two clubs are only a mile apart, and the rivalry is intense. The late 1980s and early 1990s represented the worst period

in Sporting's history, so in 1992 its president, José Sousa Cintra, brought in the English manager Bobby Robson in an attempt to turn the club's fortunes around. In the end, Robson was given only 18 months to do the job, for after Sporting suffered a surprise UEFA Cup defeat, he was sacked. However, he moved north to steer Porto to twin titles, while Sporting continued to fail, despite, or perhaps because of, regular changes in manager.

Stade de Reims (France)

Honours: 6 League titles; 2 French Cups

Colours: Red/white; white; white

The club from the Champagne country reached the first-ever European Cup Final, in 1956, where it was beaten by Real Madrid 4–3 in a classic match. Reims suffered a repeat of that fate in 1959, this time losing 2–0, despite having Juste Fontaine in the side, the striker who, a year earlier, had been top scorer in the World Cup. The French club has long since faded from prominence.

Steaua Bucharest (Romania)

Honours: 19 League titles; 19 Romanian Cups; European Cup 1986; European Supercup 1986

Colours: Red/blue; red/blue; red/blue

Steaua first rose to prominence when backed by the Romanian dictator Nicolae Ceausescu, but has continued to dominate its country since the communist collapse in 1989. Steaua had the pick of the country's players, and in 1986 became the first East European team to win the European Cup, beating Barcelona – on Spanish

Opposite: São Paulo celebrate their World Club success in Tokyo in 1992 against Barcelona.

territory – in a penalty shoot-out. Three years, later the club reached the final again, but was thrashed 4–0 by AC Milan. The club has not enjoyed international success since the revolution.

Sunderland (England)

Honours: 6 League titles; 2 FA Cups

Colours: Red/white; black; red

The 'Bank of England' club was a dominant force in football during the 1890s, when it won three of its six championships and was runner-up twice. Sunderland faded somewhat after that, although famously gained the 1973 FA Cup by defeating Leeds United, then the best football team in the country. The club has recently moved into the new 49,000-seat Stadium of Light.

Torino (Italy)

Honours: 8 League titles; 5 Italian Cups

Colours: Red; red; red

Torino is traditionally the Turin team that enjoys the most local support, as opposed to Juventus (which shares the same Stadio Delle Alpi stadium), who receive support from all over Italy. Torino once possessed one of Europe's finest teams, but that side was wiped out in the 1949 Superga air disaster (see page 187). The club was relegated from Serie A in 1996.

In 1986, Steaua Bucharest became the first East European team to win the European Cup, beating Barcelona – on Spanish territory – in a penalty shoot-out.

Tottenham Hotspur (England)

Honours: 2 League titles; 8 FA Cups; European Cup-Winners' Cup 1963; UEFA Cup 1972, 1984

Colours: White; blue; white

To quote one of the club's most famous former players, Danny Blanchflower, Spurs has always been about 'the glory game'. That phrase outlined the club's tradition of not just winning, but winning with style, a tradition with which successive managers have found it difficult to cope.

After first gaining the FA Cup as a non-League team in 1901, Tottenham Hotspur suffered a near-barren half-century until the push-and-run team of Arthur Rowe took the League title in 1950. Eight years later, Bill Nicholson took over as manager, and this heralded the club's greatest era. Under the Scot, it won the League/Cup double in 1961, becoming the first club to do so in the 20th century, and was the first English club to win in Europe, lifting the Cup-Winners' Cup in 1963. An ill-judged venture into the merchandising of leisure clothing sent the club towards bankruptcy during the early 1990s, but then it was rescued by a partnership formed between electronics tycoon Alan Sugar and manager Terry Venables. Later, however, the pair fell out spectacularly.

Great Spurs players aside from Blanchflower have included Ossie Ardiles, Mike England, Paul Gascoigne, Jimmy Greaves, Glenn Hoddle, Pat Jennings, Gary Lineker, Dave Mackay, Alf Ramsey, Chris Waddle and John White.

Wimbledon is the Cinderella of English football, its achievements being nothing short of remarkable.

Opposite: Paul Gascoigne early in his career while playing for Spurs.

Left: Bobby Moore in West Ham strip.

when West Ham won the European Cup-Winners' Cup at Wembley, beating Munich. In the following decade, the Hammers lost the 1976 Cup-Winners' Cup Final 4–2 against Anderlecht.

Wimbledon (England)

Honours: 1 FA Cup

Colours: Dark blue; dark blue; dark blue

Wimbledon is the Cinderella of English football, the club's achievements being nothing short of remarkable. Having gained promotion from the part-time Southern League to the 92-club professional Football League only in 1977, it reached the First Division within a decade and maintained its place in the top flight for over ten years, despite continually selling its best players. In 1988, it beat Liverpool in the FA Cup Final.

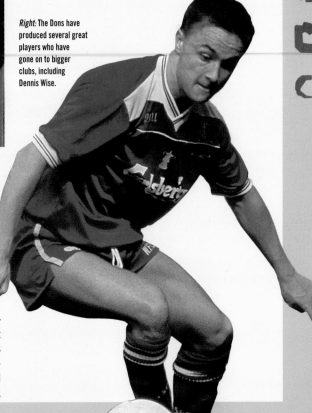

Right: The Dons have produced several great players who have gone on to bigger clubs, including Dennis Wise.

The Wanderers (England)

Honours: 5 FA Cups

Colours: Purple/black/pink; white; white/black

This side earned its place in English footballing history by becoming the first winners of the FA Cup, in 1872. Its early dominance led to it being awarded the Cup outright in 1878. The club disbanded in 1882.

West Ham United (England)

Honours: 3 FA Cups; European Cup-Winners' Cup 1965

Colours: Claret/blue; white; claret

The east London club provided – in Bobby Moore, Geoff Hurst and Martin Peters – three members of England's 1966 World Cup-winning squad. Those three had also starred in the previous year,

GAZETTE

Above: Newcastle fans in supporter uniform (replica shirts) at St James's Park, some going as far as wearing Alan Shearer masks.

Fan Culture

Who are the most important people in football? The players? The managers? The chairmen? The administrators? No, the most important are the fans, because without them there would be no such thing as professional football.

Television may, in some countries, now provide the game with a greater income than supporters do through the turnstiles, but without their contribution to the spectacle, the cameras would not be so interested. Besides, it is the fans whose demand to watch matches, both in the flesh and on the screen, has created the televised football boom in Europe and beyond.

Despite the fierce rivalries between clubs and countries fans are united by their love for the game. That is what brings them together – and what sets them apart.

Rival fans can easily be identified by their wearing of colours, of scarves depicting their heroes, and so forth.

ALAN SHEARER *A person you'd be delighted to have as your son.*
– Kenny Dalglish, his manager at Blackburn and Newcastle

This sort of practice, so long unique to football, is now being adopted by other sports; even cricket and tennis fans arrive at matches

With the advent of all-seater stadia and an increased demand for hospitality packages, the game begun to drift away from its working-class roots in some countries, but that is how it started and that is how it will remain in the eyes of many true football fans.

FACT FILE

UK

1st £1000:	Alf Common	(Sunderland to Middlesbrough, 1905)
1st £100,000:	Denis Law	(Manchester City to Torino, 1961)
1st £1M:	Trevor Francis	(Manchester City to Nottingham Forest, 1979)
1st £15M:	Alan Shearer	(Blackburn Rovers to Newcastle United, 1996)

World

1st £1M:	Giuseppe Savoldi	(Bologna to Napoli, 1975)
1st £10M:	Jean-Pierre Papin	(Marseille to Milan, 1992)
1st £20M:	Denilson	(São Paulo to Real Betis, 1998)

with their faces painted, sing football-style chants and perform the famous Mexican Wave.

David & Goliath

What makes fans follow their teams to all corners of their country, especially if they're followers of a team that gets constantly beaten? It is all very well for devotees of Manchester United, AC Milan and Real Madrid, but what about the poor souls who spend their lives rooting for the little fish? Well, this is where football differs so beautifully from many other sports in the world: it is the unpredictability of it all that makes it so fascinating. The fans have the chance to see their David flatten a Goliath – as happens far too regularly for the big clubs' liking. No wonder some fans will follow a minnow for years: there might be that one snatched moment of glory.

It does not matter how any corporate packages a club sells for a match; such 'fans' will never have the devotion or depth of feeling of the lifelong supporter. In

Above: **Italian fans giving it plenty.**

FRANCO BARESI   I need more players like Franco, who are on first-name terms with the ball. – Azeglio Vicini, manager of Italy

Above: **The Tartan Army of Scottish fans in full cry.**

song proved so popular that the eventual winners, Germany, adopted it. It was another example of world-wide supporters following an English lead, largely due to the amount of televised English football. Even if the 1980s habit of taking inflatables to games did not spread far, chants such as 'You'll never walk alone' and 'when the saints/reds/blues go marching in' are common around Europe. With more exposure to foreign matches the reverse is now true, with 'Champione' and 'Ole, Ole, Ole' being heard in Britain.

Hooliganism

A less pleasant export was hooliganism. While there had been incidents of fan violence in Britain and abroad for decades, the rise of 'Casuals' in the 1960s, committing premeditated acts of hooliganism, was a new development. This gradually spread overseas with the rise of Ultra groups in Spain and Italy while the Dutch took matters a step further with home-made bombs being used as weapons.

The authorities finally recognized the scale of the problem, although not before Liverpool and Juventus fans had rioted at the 1985 European Cup Final, with the result that 39 fans, mostly Italian, died. The world was appalled. The two best club sides in Europe were due to meet in what should have been a showpiece match, showing all of football's best qualities. Instead, the pictures flashed around the world showed only the ugly side of football – certainly of English football – and the result of the game became a secondary news item. The outcome of the sickening

recent years, with the advent of all-seater stadia and an increased demand for hospitality packages, the game begun to drift away from its working-class roots in some countries, but that is how it started and that is how it will remain in the eyes of many comitted football fans.

Mind you, no one with any sense is suggesting that we should return to the days when thousands of fans packed on to inadequate and unsafe terraces.

The Hillsborough tragedy of 1989 – when 96 Liverpool fans lost their lives during crushing at the Leppings Lane End before an

FA Cup Semi-Final against Nottingham Forest – changed the face of football for ever, certainly in the UK.

Having languished behind much of Western Europe, British clubs were now forced by law to update their grounds. Many clubs took the chance to do more than the minimum leaving Britain with one of the best collections of modern stadia anywhere in the world. Although there was some initial opposition to compulsory all-seater stadia, fans now agree that, while they would still like the option to stand, the changes have mostly been for the better.

Fan Culture

Besides, this is football. Whether fans stand or sit, they retain their sense of humour. The Brazilians offer perhaps the best example of this: a thronging tribe dressed in gold and green, dancing the samba wherever they go. But they are not alone. The Danish Roligans, the Dutch oom-pah bands, the firework-crazy Italian *tifosi* and the partying Irish all have their own distinctive styles in victory, defeat and draw. Even England got in on the act during Euro 96, when the whole nation was caught up in the idea that 'football was coming home'. That

PENALTIES Highest score in a penalty shootout: Argentinos Juniors 20, Racing Club 19, Argentina 1988.

violence was that English clubs were banned from Europe indefinitely.

That ban was lifted after five years during which government and football authorities had grappled with the problems with limited suc-

The real fans will always want to experience the unique atmosphere inside a football ground. It is a great sensory experience, the one-liners, the sights, the passion, even the smells are part of it.

cess. Eventually close-circuit television, greater police intelligence networks, and a new mood among supporters – partly due to the increase in football's middle-class popularity – combined to reduce hooliganism in the UK. It remains a problem, but is now more common elsewhere.

The same applies to racist abuse, which, because of all the improvements, is in decline in Britain, but still a problem in large parts of mainland Europe.

The Future's So Bright

The future does look brighter. Across the globe standards of stadia and play are improving with a consequent benefit for fans. As the world shrinks one danger is that there will be greater homogenity among fans, but at present that seems unlikely. Instead, fans enjoy more contrasts, with the supporters of South Africa, with their chants of 'Feesh' and 'Shoes' for Mark Fish and John Moshoeu, the latest to receive a wider recognition at France 1998.

The Real Thing

There are also fears over the prospect of fans being able to buy 'armchair season tickets' to have satellite television stations beam all their club's games into their living room. Some wonder how this will affect attendances. Judging by England and France, where crowds continue to rise despite greater

FACT FILE

FACT: In 1996 Bayern Munich became the fourth club to have won all three European competitions. The first three were Juventus, Ajax and Barcelona.

FACT: The first match to be decided by the 'golden goal' rule (the team to score the first goal in extra time is the winner) was a 1996 Auto Windscreens Trophy tie, in England, Iain Dunn scoring the winner for Huddersfield against Lincoln after 107 minutes. The rule was then adopted for Euro 96; Germany's Oliver Bierhoff won the competition through it with a 95th-minute goal in the final against the Czech Republic.

FACT: Highest score in a penalty shootout: Argentinos Juniors 20, Racing Club 19, Argentina 1988.

television exposure and rising admission prices, this will not happen. The real fans will always want to experience the unique atmosphere inside a football ground. It is a great sensory experience, the one-liners, the sights, the passion, even the smells are part of it, as well as the feeling that by being there in the flesh, you are doing your bit for the team.

Without the fans even the television viewer would be bereft. That is why fans remain the most important people in football ■

Above: Before France 98, Brazilian fans were referring to the tournament as 'Pente' – or Brazil's fifth title!

Ian Cruise

PENALTIES The first penalty was scored by John Heath, for Wolves against Accrington Stanley, in September 1891.

183

The Women's Game

Women's football dates back almost as far as the men's game but, largely due to the disapproving attitude of the sport's male administrators, it has been slow to develop.

Organized women's football in England was recorded as early as 1895, when a northern representative team beat a southern side 7–1 in London. Matches were also played in Scotland. In 1902, however, the Football Association banned its clubs from playing 'lady teams'. This injunction was briefly lifted during World War I with a mixed English team competing against a mixed Canadian one in 1917 – the men played with their hands tied behind their backs. Because of the war, the status of women in society rose, and accordingly their involvement in football increased.

The most famous team was the Dick Kerr Ladies, formed in 1917 by a group of female munitions workers at Kerr's Engineering Works, Preston. Their early games were played on waste ground outside the factory gates but, as their fame grew, they found themselves playing in front of large crowds at Football League grounds. One match in Ireland attracted 38,000 fans; another, against St Helen's Ladies at Everton's Goodison Park on Boxing Day 1920, was watched by 53,000 – with a reported 10,000-plus locked out! The Dick Kerr Ladies also played teams from France but, in 1921, the side was barred – along with all other ladies' teams – from playing on Football League grounds.

Above: **Wendy Toms, the first female referee's assistant in the English Premier League.**

The FA council edict read: 'The council feel impelled to express their strong opinion that the game of football is quite unsuitable for females and ought not be encouraged.' The Dick Kerr side continued to play for a while, raising an estimated £70,000 for charity, but women's football steadily declined in the UK. Elsewhere in Europe there was greater progress and, by the 1960s, there were instances of UK players moving to Italy as professionals, unsurprising in the domestic climate.

Mundialito

In 1969, in the wake of England's (male) 1966 World Cup win, the Women's FA was formed, with 44 clubs. Two years later the FA recognized the organization and lifted the ban on women playing on members' grounds. This followed the first, unofficial, Women's World Cup (1970), held in Italy. Chiltern Valley represented England then and in Mexico in 1971.

Since few schools catered for girls' football, and to this day some actively prohibit it, the female game was still very much a minority sport. In 1983, though, FIFA instructed the national governing bodies to take greater responsibility for the women's game. The following year women footballers were allowed to play at Wembley.

Confidential Progress

Attitudes in countries other than England were more progressive, as was evident when the English team reached the final of the first UEFA women's championship (1984). The first leg was shown live in Sweden

Above: **The Swedish Women's national team are renowned for their ball-skills.**

Euro 96. Most estimates suggest that in England, as in Spain and Germany, female fans make up 10–15% of the gate. However, few men – or women, for that matter – watch women's football.

England won the first Mundialito ('little World Cup') in Italy in 1988 but, though Wembley also staged a women's international that year, other countries were developing faster.

Football Management

There has, however, been an influx of women into football administration and the media in the UK and elsewhere. Julie Welch was the forerunner in England, reporting games for the *Observer* through the 1970s – her experiences were later made into a TV movie, *The Glory, Glory Game* – and her successors now work in print, radio and television. Birmingham City and Blackpool both have female managing directors, Karren Brady and Gill Bridge, respectively, with Blackpool having also a chairwoman, Vicky Oyston. On the pitch Wendy Toms, a qualified referee, became the first female referee's assistant in the Premiership in 1997.

Ancient History

The infamous comment by Ron Atkinson, the former Manchester United manager, that 'women should be in the kitchen, the boutique and the disco but not in football' increasingly seems a part of the game's ancient history ■

Charlotte Nicol

and the second, at Luton, attracted a Swedish TV crew and 36 journalists, including representatives from Scandinavia, the USA, France, the Netherlands and West Germany. In both cases there was barely a mention in the UK press. Again, English players moved to Italy so that they could play professionally.

By 1991, when the WFA launched a national league, there were 9,000 registered English women players (the number had risen to 14,000 by 1997), compared to 700,000 in West Germany. That year the USA beat Norway in front of a 63,000-strong crowd in the final of the first FIFA Women's World Cup, held in China. Four years later Norway beat hosts Germany 2–0. In 1996 76,000 fans watched the USA beat China in the Olympic Final, so emphasizing the status of the women's game in the USA. In that country soccer, as a non-contact sport (which American Football obviously is not), is seen by many as a 'female' game.

Watching the Boys

Women have become more interested in the game as a spectator sport in England following the improvement in facilities in the wake of the Hillsborough disaster (see page 186) – in which nine of the fans who died were female – 'Gazza's tears' in the 1990 World Cup, and

Above: **English women playing internationals still have to contend with sexism.**

WINNING The youngest player to win a World Cup winner's medal has been the 17-year-old Pelé in Sweden in 1958.

185

The Tragedies

In an arena which celebrates and tests the physical and mental stamina of some very gifted individuals, it seems all the more horrifying that disasters happen – but they do, and all football can do is to learn from them and not repeat the mistakes.

Stadium Disasters

The stampede in Ghana which killed 120 in May 2001 was the latest in a long line of stadium tragedies to plunge the world's favourite game into mourning. Most have been caused by poor stadium facilities or bad organization, but a significant number have been provoked by crowd violence.

In the Guatemala tragedy of October 1996, 81 people were crushed to death and another 147 seriously injured following a staircase stampede before the team's World Cup qualifier against Costa Rica. It is believed the 45,000 capacity stadium was full an hour before the kick-off, but then further arrivals, having bought forged tickets, were allowed in. About 60,000 people were inside when worried fans decided to leave, and this sparked a general panic.

Lenin Stadium

The world's worst sporting disaster occurred in October 1982, although official figures were not released until seven years later: 340 fans perished in the Lenin Stadium at a UEFA Cup tie between Spartak Moscow and Haarlem as departing spectators were lured back into the ground by a last-minute goal. This surpassed even the toll recorded at a 1964 Olympic qualifying match between Peru and Argentina: 318 died and 500 were injured when the crowd rioted at the National Stadium in Lima.

Hillsborough

The UK's worst sporting disaster occurred at the Hillsborough Stadium, home of Sheffield Wednesday, on April 15, 1989: 95 Liverpool supporters died at the scene of the FA Cup Semi-Final with Nottingham Forest. Late arrivals caused an alarming build-up of supporters outside the Leppings Lane end. This, in tandem with poor police management, precipitated a terrifying crush. Lives were lost in the tunnel between the gate (through which many latecomers poured in) and the terracing. However, most fatalities occurred where fans were trapped inside the perimeter fence. The toll rose four years later to 96 with the death of Tony Bland, who had spent the interim in a coma.

Above: **Tragedy at the Heysel Stadium Brussels, 1985.**

HOOLIGAN-RELATED TRAGEDIES

CONTINENTAL EUROPE

44 killed following a 1974 riot in Turkey

24 killed in a 1981 crush in Greece

15 killed in France in 1992 when a temporary stand collapsed

SOUTH AMERICA

74 killed in Argentina in 1968 when panicking spectators were crushed against locked gates after opposition fans threw lighted torches on them from above

24 killed in Colombia in 1982 when fleeing from hurled fireworks

ELSEWHERE

70+ killed in Nepal in 1988 when a sudden electric storm provoked a stampede towards locked exits

40 killed in 1991 in South Africa when fans were crushed to death trying to escape an outburst of fighting

JOCK STEIN UK football was stunned by the death of Scotland manager Jock Stein in September 1985 at the end of a Wales–Scotland World Cup qualifier.

Overdue Legislation

In the wake of Hillsborough fences were torn down. Lord Justice Taylor carried out an official inquiry, and as a result all-seater stadiums became compulsory for senior clubs. This legislation had been long overdue: a number of tragedies had previously scarred UK football, but nothing had been done to change the culture of neglect in stadiums. These disasters included the 1946 Burnden Park horror, with 33 lives lost and 500 people injured when a wall collapsed at Bolton, and two tragedies at Ibrox, Glasgow: in 1902 25 fans died during a Scotland–England international, and in 1971 66 people were trampled to death just before the end of a Rangers v Celtic New Year fixture. The latter disaster led to the 1975 Safety of Sports Grounds Act, but this did nothing to prevent the Hillsborough tragedy or the Bradford fire of 1985, in which 56 people died when litter beneath the main stand caught light.

The Bradford incident was followed, just three weeks later, by the Heysel Stadium disaster. Before the European Cup Final in Brussels between Liverpool and Juventus 39 fans, mostly Italian, died when a wall collapsed as they tried to flee from rampaging English fans.

There have been stadium tragedies in other parts of the world, and the statistics make grim reading.

Most football matches are now safe, but stadium problems do remain. In April 1997 five fans died in Nigeria because too few exit gates had been opened after a World Cup qualifier ∎

Trevor Haylett

Air Accidents

Football has been touched by tragedy as teams have travelled by air to games.

In 1949 Italian champions Torino lost their entire team, eight of them internationals, plus reserve players, manager, trainer and coach in a total toll of 28 following the crash at Supergra, near Turin, of a plane bringing them all home from a match against Benfica.

The 1958 Munich air disaster was a pivotal event in the history of Manchester United. Eight leading players, three officials and eight newspaper representatives were among the 23 who perished as a consequence of the aircraft – on its way home following United's winning European Cup tie in Belgrade – crashing on take-off after refuelling at Munich.

In 1961 the entire Green Cross team perished in an air crash in Chile. Bolivian fans mourn the 19 players from 'The Strongest Club' who lost their lives in the Andes in 1969. In December 1987 the 18-strong squad of Alianza Lima, one of Peru's top clubs, was wiped out when a military aircraft crashed into the sea off Ventillana. Two years later, in 1989, came the accident that killed 15 Surinamese players connected with clubs in the Netherlands. In 1993 18 members of the Zambian national squad died in an air crash into the Atlantic soon after take-off from Gabon.

Above: **Sir Matt Busby's statue stands in front of Old Trafford's Munich memorial.**

The Personal Tragedies

UK football was stunned by the death of Scotland manager Jock Stein (see page 87): he suffered a fatal heart-attack minutes after the end of the Wales–Scotland World Cup qualifier at Cardiff in September 1985. Tottenham's Scottish international Jim White was killed by lightning as he sheltered underneath a tree at a London golf course in 1964. And, in an 'Old Firm' clash in September 1931, the Celtic and Scotland goalkeeper John Thomson sustained a fractured skull when diving at an opponent's feet; he died later that evening.

Car accidents have been responsible for the deaths of two outstanding international players, Italy's Gaetano Scirea and Poland's Kazimierz Deyna. Scirea skippered the Juventus side that played Liverpool in the 1985 European Cup Final at Heysel. Deyna had won an Olympic Gold with Poland in 1972 and later went to play abroad – to Manchester City and then to the USA, where his fatal car crash occurred.

The 1994 World Cup Finals brought tragedy for the Colombian defender Andres Escobar, who was gunned down in the street shortly after his team's return home after their first round elimination. Escobar had scored the own goal which contributed to his side's defeat against the USA, and was shot after a late-night argument about the goal. There have been many more who have met untimely ends, they are too numerous to mention here.

Left: **Chelsea fans' tributes to the club's Managing Director Matthew Harding.**

VIOLENCE Chile v Uruguay, 1967: the game as abandoned following a mass brawl in which nine Uruguayans and 10 Chileans were sent off.

187

World Cup Semi-Final, Seville, 8 July 1982

Shoot-out!

West Germany 3 (Littbarski, Rummenigge, Fischer), **France 3** (Platini (penalty), Tresor, Giresse)
(West Germany won 5–4 in penalty shootout after extra time; score at 90 minutes: 1–1)

Six goals, the first penalty shootout in World Cup history, West Germany's incredible fightback when they appeared to be dead and buried, and Schumacher's blatant, unpunished foul on Battiston – these were the ingredients of a pulsating World Cup Semi-Final.

Littbarski put the Germans ahead after 17 minutes, only for Platini to equalize from the spot nine minutes later. The turning points involved two of the substitutes: France's Battiston was elbowed in the face by Schumacher after 62 minutes for a foul that put the Frenchman in hospital for two days, and Rummenigge came on after 96 minutes to revitalize the Germans after they had fallen 3–1 behind to goals from Tresor and Giresse early in extra time. Rummenigge pulled one back six minutes after his appearance and Fischer equalized six minutes after that. Finally, after more than two-and-a-half hours of unbearable tension, Hrubesch cracked home the decisive penalty in the shoot-out to give the Germans victory. But would the Germans have won if, as should have happened, Schumacher had been sent off? ■

Mike Collett

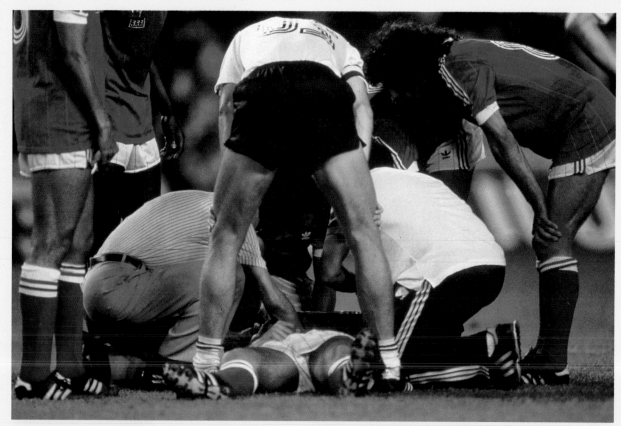

Above: **French players and medical staff attend the stricken Patrick Battiston.**

JOHN BARNES He should be playing for us, he reminds me of a Brazilian player.
– Carlos Perreira, manager of Brazil

Left: **France on the attack in Marseilles.**

European Championship Semi-Final, Marseilles, 23 June 1984

With 64 Seconds Remaining...

France 3 (Domergue 2, Platini) **Portugal 2** (Jordao 2)
(after extra time; score at 90 minutes: 1–1)

Two years after their shattering disappointment at Seville (see previous page), the French experienced a glorious victory. This semi-final was a far more memorable game than the final, against Spain, which France won 2–0 four days later.

The only incident of note in a poor first half came after 25 minutes, when Domergue, celebrating his 27th birthday, scored from a free kick to put France ahead. A Jordao header after 74 minutes was the only other goal in normal time. And so into extra time. Both teams were full of skill, attacking power and inventive mid-fields, but one man stood head and shoulders above the rest: Platini. He rescued France when all seemed lost – as it did when Jordao scored again after 98 minutes to put Portugal 2–1 ahead. With six minutes to go, France might have given up hope, but then Domergue equalized in the 115th minute and Platini, appearing to move in slow motion, created time and space for himself in the penalty box to lash home the winner. Only 64 seconds remained on the stadium clock. ∎

Mike Collett

PENALTY SHOOT-OUT The 1994 World Cup Final between Italy and Brazil was the first to go to a penalty shootout.

France, 1993

Stripped, Barred and Demoted

When Jacques Glassmann of Valenciennes revealed that Marseille had bribed his team to lose a French First Division match in April 1993, the £30,000 dug up from the garden of a team-mate's mother-in-law proved to be the tip of an iceberg. This was to be scandal which rock the French footballing establishment.

Marseille had been paying for fixed matches since 1987. During that time they had won the French title five times in a row, and in 1993 they became the first French club to win the European Cup. Punishment was severe. The club was stripped of its European title, barred from the competition the following year, and demoted to the Second Division. Two players from Marseille and two from Valenciennes were banned for life, while Bernard Tapie, Marseille's former owner, served time in prison. The club soon revived, but Tapie's political career was over ■

Above: **Standard Liège players offered their match bonuses to Waterschei.**

Belgium, 1982

A BELGIAN FIX

Standard Liège needed to win the last game of the 1981–2 season to become Belgian champions for the first time in 11 years. Their last match was against mid-table Waterschei, the Belgian Cup winners and a difficult team to beat.

So Standard's players, allegedly urged by their coach Raymond Goethals, offered Waterschei their winning bonuses if Waterschei would throw the match. The main conspirator was Standard's captain, Eric Gerets, who set up the scam with Waterschei's Roland Janssen. Needless to say, Standard won.

Thirteen players were suspended for between six months and three years and the club were fined £75,000; Standard's chairman Roger Petit and coach Goethals were banned from Belgian football for life. Gerets, who had by now transferred to AC Milan, was forced to quit the Italian club and serve his suspension.

When the punishments were handed out in late 1983, Belgium lost several key players from the national squad for the 1984 European Championship, including Walter Meeuws, although he later became Belgium's national coach. Goethals later managed Marseille under Bernard Tapie ■

SCANDAL The £30,000 dug up from the garden of a team-mate's mother-in-law proved to be the tip of the iceberg.

World Cup Group Match, Guadalajara, 7 June 1970

The Real Final

Brazil 1 (Jairzinho), **England 0**

Most matches are remembered for their goals, this one is recalled for a save. It was not the occasion, a World Cup group match which made it special, but the protagonists.

The teams were the World Cup holders, England, and the tournament favourites, Brazil. The save was by Gordon Banks, widely regarded as the best goalkeeper of his era, and the thwarted striker was Pelé, the world's greatest player.

It was ten minutes into the match, played in 98-degree noon heat for the benefit of European television viewers, when Jairzinho beat Terry Cooper on the English left flank and crossed deep to the far post. Pelé rose to produce a textbook downward header but Banks, who had been covering his near post, somehow got across and down to push the ball over the bar as Pelé wheeled away to start his celebrations. This set the tone for a fascinating contest in which Alan Mullery man-marked Pelé, Brian Labone watched Tostao, and Bobby Moore, in one of his finest games, marshalled the English defence. In midfield the contest pitted three of the 1966 winners, Bobby Charlton, Alan Ball and Martin Peters, against the likes of Clodoaldo and Roberto Rivelino while Geoff Hurst, another 1966 hero, led the

England attack. Francis Lee and Hurst both missed chances as England ended the first half even but, 14 minutes into the second period, Brazil finally beat Banks. Paulo Cesar found Tostao who drifted past three defenders before passing to Pelé. He, though quickly surrounded, laid a perfectly weighted pass to the arriving Jairzinho who rifled a shot past Banks with his right foot.

England, having been denied sleep by chanting fans surrounding the team's hotel the previous night – a legacy of their poor public relations and Brazil's excellent ones, might have been expected to wilt in the heat. But, while each player lost at least four kilograms in weight due to fluid loss in the game, they now demonstrated why they had been regarded as a stronger side than the one which won the World Cup four years earlier.

With Brazilian goalkeeper Felix Meilli showing customary vulnerability in the air, Alf Ramsey brought on Jeff Astle and asked his team to rain in crosses. This led to several chances but Alan Ball miskicked from one and Astle himself missed a glorious opportunity

Above: **With lightning reactions, Gordon Banks stops Pelé's header.**

when he shot over from 12 yards (10m) with just the goalkeeper to beat. With just ten minutes left, Ball shot against the crossbar and England's hopes were gone. The teams' mutual respect remained as both sides swapped shirts and mentally thought 'see you in the final'.

It was not to be. While both sides still progressed to the quarter-finals Brazil had earned the relatively com-

fortable task of disposing of Peru while England were faced by West Germany in a repeat of the 1966 final. With Banks absent with food poisoning they let slip a 2–0 lead to lose 3–2. It was to be 12 years before England appeared in another World Cup. Brazil went on to win the trophy with Jairzinho scoring in every game ∎

Glenn Moore

GORDON BANKS The save was by Gordon Banks, widely regarded as the best goalkeeper of his era, and the thwarted striker was Pelé, the world's greatest player.

191

A-Z of Grounds

Amsterdam ArenA
Amsterdam, Holland

Opened: 1996

Venue for: European Cup Final 1998

Record attendance: 52,000

Current capacity: 52,000

Ajax's new stadium, all steel and glass with an imposing roof, is a stadium fit for the 21st

Opposite (left): An empty Anfield does the stadium no credit – it is the fans (*right*) which make this club's ground one of the most impressive in the world.

Below: Ajax Stadium at night.

century. Opened in 1996 and built at a cost of £80M, it represents a stark contrast to the old De Meer Stadium; this opened in 1934, always retained a homely feel, and never held more than 24,000 people. It was the De Meer which saw the Ajax managed by Johan Cruyff dominate European football in the early 1970s, but for most of the last 40 years of its existence it was too

small and too cramped for a club of Ajax's stature. Finally, after an extended period of planning, Ajax left De Meer for their new home.

There have been problems with the Ajax Stadium, notably the fact that the roof keeps out the sunlight and affects the grass below, but there is a grand functionalism about the place and it makes a fitting home for Holland's most successful club.

Anfield
Liverpool, England

Opened: 1884

Record attendance: 61,905
(Liverpool v Wolves, 1952)

Current capacity: 52,364

Anfield has never been a great stadium in the sense that Old Trafford, Wembley and Munich are. When the Spion Kop was still standing, Anfield was impressive enough, but it wasn't the physical look of the place that took your breath away, rather the atmosphere inside it. In short, Anfield is one of the world's great football grounds because of the team that plays there, Liverpool, and that team's supporters, and partly also because of the history surrounding the stadium.

It is hard to imagine now, but Anfield started life as the home of Liverpool's modern arch-rivals Everton, who moved out in 1892 because of a row with the ground's owner over the rent. He was left with a stadium but no team – so he formed one. Liverpool Football Club has been based at Anfield ever since.

It was at Anfield, in the mid-1960s, that modern football supporters first became identifiable as a distinctive tribe, with fans chanting their own words to Beatles songs and bequeathing 'You'll Never Walk Alone' as an anthem for succeeding generations. The Spion Kop has been replaced by an all-seater stand; the Anfield Road Stand is another 1990s construction. In 1989, after the Hillsborough disaster, the Anfield pitch all but disappeared under a carpet of flowers laid by grieving fans. The brass carving over the Shankly Gates at the entrance to the stadium is inscribed with the words: 'You'll Never Walk Alone.' At Anfield, no one ever does.

Celtic Park

Glasgow, Scotland

Opened: 1892

Record attendance: 92,000 (Celtic v Rangers, 1938)

Current capacity: 60,506

Glasgow Rangers fans, of course, would not agree, but the new Celtic Park has a theatrical sweep and grandeur which Ibrox somehow lacks. True, Ibrox's superb redbrick South Stand is a listed building, and the sleek lines and well balanced look inside the stadium are fine enough, but Celtic Park is more imposing. The ground, nicknamed 'Paradise' by the Celtic faithful, has been totally rebuilt on the site during the past few years; all traces of the way it looked in the 1960s and 1970s have been totally obliterated. Celtic have played on this site for over a century, bringing back the title trophy 35 times and the Scottish Cup 30 times, not to mention the European Cup in 1967. With redevelopment now complete, the crowning glory for the new Celtic Park was to see the title restored here for the first time since 1988.

Above: Celtic Park, nicknamed 'Paradise' by the fans.

Crvena Zvezda Stadium

Belgrade (Beograd), Yugoslavia

Opened: 1945

Venue for: European Cup Final 1973

Record attendance: 96,070 (Red Star Belgrade v Ferencvaros, European Cup Winners' Cup Semi-Final 1975)

Current capacity: 97,000

Nicknamed the 'Marakana', Red Star Belgrade's home ground is in far better shape than the real Maracana in Rio de Janeiro. It has seen a number of matches of significance in Yugoslavian and Eastern European soccer history. It staged the first European Cup Final to be held in eastern Europe, Ajax beating Juventus 1–0 in 1973, and the east's first European Championship Final, Czechoslovakia defeating West Germany in 1976 in a penalty shootout. Yugoslavia beat England 5–0 here in 1958, and Partizan Belgrade beat Manchester United 2–0 in the first leg of their 1966 European Cup Semi-Final. Today Red Star – now more commonly called Crvena Zvezda –

dominate the Yugoslav League from this imposing fortress much as they did before the breakup of the old Yugoslavia. An imposing museum houses much of the silverware collected by the football club and by the 16 other sports affiliated to the organization.

El Monumental

Buenos Aires, Argentina

Opened: 1942 (rebuilt 1968, 1978)

Venue for: World Cup Final 1978, Copa America 1946, 1959, 1987

Record Attendance (rebuilt stadium): 77,000 (first set: West Germany v Poland 1978 WC)

Current Capacity: 77,000

One of the 15 25,000-plus grounds in Buenos Aires, this stadium will be remembered for the ticker-tape welcome it gave Argentina's 1978 World Cup side. The team went on to win the competition in El Monumental, beating Holland 3–1.

Officially called Estadio Anonio Liberti, the ground plays host to River Plate and the Argentine national side. Two-tiered and open-air, it also has four basketball courts, 12 tennis courts, two swim-

ming pools, a gym, a hotel and four training pitches in its complex.

Originally designed with a capacity of 150,000 and three tiers, it took two decades to complete in its original form. Much of it was changed in the build up to 1978 – including the grass which was inadvertantly killed by sea water irrigation during preparation.

Ernst Happel Stadium
Vienna, Austria

Opened: 1928

Venue for: European Cup Finals 1964, 1987, 1995

Record attendance: 90,593 (Austria v Spain, 1960)

Current capacity: 49,000

Better known as the Prater Stadium, the pride and joy of the Austrian Football Association was renamed after their old coach Ernst Happel, who died in 1992. In the same way that Munich is famous for its roof and Wembley changed character entirely after the roof was added in 1963, so the Prater Stadium, on the outskirts of Vienna, was, in 1985, transformed into one of Europe's great stadiums. Its incredible roof gave dignity to and uplifted the Prater.

However, although it is certainly a wonderful stadium, it lacks a heart – the very opposite of Anfield – and, great stadium though it might be, it lacks a great team. Still, it has had its moments; 275 of these came one night in 1944 thanks to pinpoint bombing by the Allies at a time when the stadium was being used by the Wehrmacht.

The Ernst Happel Stadium is in the middle of a huge park, and in 1960 a record crowd of 90,593 saw Austria play Spain. Alas, huge crowds no longer come here. UEFA occasionally stages a European final at it and Austria sometimes play an international, but overall this wonderful stadium is very much underused.

Above: Estadio Azteca, venue for two world cup finals.

Below: El Monumental during the build-up to the 1978 final.

Estadio Azteca
Mexico City, Mexico

Opened: May 29 1966 (rebuilt 1986)

Venue for: World Cup Finals 1970, 1986; Olympics 1968

Record Attendance: 114,580 (Mexico v Belgium, World Cup 1986. Also England v Argentina, Germany v Argentina, both also WC 86)

Current Capacity: 114,600

The only stadium to stage two world cup finals, one of which, the 1970 tie between Brazil and Italy (see page 69) has gone down in history. The other, Argentina's 3–2 win over Germany, followed Maradona's 'Hand of God' goal

against England at the Azteca in the quarter-finals. The city, over-populated, over-polluted, has problems but the stadium is possibly the best purpose-built football venue in the world. Built on an ancient lava plain to the south-east of the city, it has three levels of seating, 80 per cent covered, and good sightlines throughout, offering proximity and perspective. Good transport links enable it to escape the worst of the city's congestion. Constructed mainly of concrete it withstood the 1985 earthquake. Ameica, Necaxa and Cruz Azul use the ground between internationals and show-piece matches.

Below: Estadio da Luz or Stadium of Light.

Estadio da Luz
Lisbon, Portugal

Opened: 1954

Venue for: European Cup Final 1967

Record attendance: 120,000 (many times)

Current capacity: 85,000

In terms of size and expanse, the Stadium of Light is the largest football stadium in Europe, although, with the introduction of seating, its once huge capacity of 120,000 has been cut to about 80,000. Home of Benfica, the most successful club in Portugal with a membership of over 100,000, this is, like Barcelona's Nou Camp Stadium, at the centre of a sporting complex: the complex encompasses 21 other sports. A vast eagle and a statue of Eusebio embellish the main entrance.

Despite the fact that the trophy room contains no fewer than 15,000 pieces of silverware representing the success of the club in all sports, one of the most famous matches played here did not involve Benfica at all. Instead, it was between Glasgow Celtic and Internazionale in the 1967 European Cup Final (2–1) (see page 245). While the stadium does often bask

in sunshine, its evocative name – Estadio da Luz – derives not from the light (luz) but from the fact that it is in the Luz district of Lisbon.

Hampden Park
Glasgow, Scotland

Opened: 1903

Venue for: European Cup Final 1960, 2002

Record attendance: 149,415 (Scotland v england, 1937)

Current capacity: 52,000

There has been nowhere quite like the old Hampden Park to watch football. Mountainous terraces created vast expanses of swaying human masses, and the roar from over 100,000 well lubricated throats could inspire or intimidate the greatest of players. The finest match in soccer history graced Hampden in 1960, when Real Madrid defeated Eintracht Frankfurt in the European Cup Final in front of a 134,000-strong crowd (see page 68). That wasn't the biggest crowd ever to watch a match here, though, because, until the Maracana was opened in 1950, Hampden was the biggest ground in the world. Its record attendance came with the Scotland-England match of 1937. As relatively recently as April 1970, a crowd of 136,505 saw the European Cup Semi-Final between Celtic and Leeds United.

Above: Hampden Park, home to the national side and Queen's Park.

Below: The fans watching an away match on the big screen at Highbury

Hampden is the home ground of the Third Division amateurs Queen's Park, who play here in front of a few hundred people every other Saturday. The stadium has provided the perfect neutral territory for the Rangers-Celtic rivalry and has been a venue for international matches down the years. It has recently undergone a modernization and rebuilding programme and BT have agreed a 10-year sponsorship deal.

Highbury Stadium
London, England

Opened: 1913

Record attendance: 73,295 (Arsenal v Sunderland, 1935)

Current capacity: 38,500

Few stadiums anywhere blend the old and the new quite as successfully as Arsenal's Highbury Stadium. Once a monument to 1930s Art Deco, this is now also a statement of modern style and comfort. There are few stadiums in which stands are classified as buildings of special architectural merit, but this is the case with Highbury's twin East and West stands. These have remained virtually unchanged since their erection in the 1930s.

In the last few years, however, Highbury, like most English grounds, has changed beyond recognition. The atmospheric old North Stand has been replaced by a towering new all-seater stand, which faces the old Clock End. The clock is still there, but the open

Above: A fading hymn to football, the glorious Macarana is crumbling into disrepair.

terrace – where generations of away supporters were exposed to the elements – has been replaced by Arsenal's reluctant nod to commercialism, inside the ground at least: a South Stand with luxury boxes and balconies. Nonetheless, Arsenal plan to move to a new, purpose-built stadium, Ashburton Grove, with a capacity of 60,000 in the summer of 2005.

Below: Nou Camp, a focal point for Catalan pride in the football club.

won) is unlikely ever to be beaten (although Wembley may have surpassed it unofficially). But the stadium's glory-days are long gone. Much of it is now unusable and unsafe, and today crowds of under 10,000 are not unusual. Although the name retains an aura and the stadium is itself imposing, unless millions of pounds are spent on modernization Maracana's name and place in the record books will be all it has left.

Nou Camp
Barcelona, Spain

Opened: 1957

Venue for: European Cup Final 1989

Record attendance: 120,000 (many times)

Current capacity: 118,000

Nou Camp is not just a football stadium but a focal point of Catalan pride and nationalism and

Maracana Stadium
Rio de Janeiro, Brazil

Opened: 1950

Venue for: World Cup Final 1950

Record attendance: 199,854 (Uruguay v Brazil, World Cup Final, 1950)

Current capacity: 80,000

The Maracana Stadium is the biggest football stadium on earth, and its official world-record attendance of 199,854 for the 1950 World Cup Final (which Uruguay

the centrepiece of a vast sporting empire of which Barcelona FC is just one part. But what a part. With 115,000 members, Barcelona is the biggest football club in the world, and it regularly attracts crowds of 100,000-plus for League matches. The stadium is like a sporting canyon, with the pitch actually some 25 feet (8m) below street-level and the tiers of seats seemingly rising to the heavens. Like the Santiago Bernabeu, Nou Camp was modernized for the 1982 World Cup; it staged the opening game between Belgium and Argentina (1–0). Curiously, the memorable second-round match between Italy and Brazil (3–2) was instead held at Espanol's much smaller Sarria Stadium; however, Italy qualified here on their way to gaining a 2–0 win over Poland in the semi-finals. Only one European Cup Final has been staged here, AC

Milan's 4–0 win over Steaua Bucharest in 1989.

Old Trafford

Manchester, England

Opened: 1910

Record attendance: 76,962 (Wolverhampton Wanderers v Grimsby, FA Cup Semi-Final, 1939)

Current capacity: 68,936

Few grounds in the world have the aura and atmosphere of Old Trafford, which has been transformed over the years into not so much the 'Theatre of Dreams' which Manchester United like to call it but a 'Wrap-Around Pressure Cooker of Anticipation'. From 1910, when it was built, until 1961 Old Trafford hardly changed at all – apart,

Below: A pressure cooker atmosphere makes Old Trafford a very uncomfortable venue for visiting teams.

that is, from the night of 11 March 1941, when the main stand was destroyed and much of the rest of the ground badly damaged by a German bomb.

United played at Maine Road after World War II, returning home only at the start of the 1949–50 season. Three World Cup matches were played here in 1966; other set pieces have been the 1915 FA Cup Final and the final replays of 1911 and 1970. The new North Stand towers above the other three sides of the ground; not only the biggest stand in the UK, this also boasts the world's largest spanning cantilevered roof. After he died in 1994 a statue of Sir Matt Busby, father of the modern Manchester United, was erected just in front of the plaque which commemorates the players, officials and journalists who perished in the 1958 Munich air disaster. Truly a place of footballing history and myth.

A-Z OF GROUNDS

Olympic Stadium
Munich, Germany

Opened: 1972

Venue for: Olympic Games 1972; World Cup Final 1974; European Cup Finals 1979, 1993, 1997; European Soccer Championships 1988

Record attendance: 78,000

Current capacity: 69,256

Above: Built for the Olympics in 1972, the stadium is now home to TSV Munich 1860 and Bayern Munich.

Built on the site of the airfield from which in 1938 the British Prime Minister Neville Chamberlain flew back to his country with 'a piece of paper' in his pocket, the Olympic Stadium has been inspiring dreamers of quite another kind since it was created for the 1972 Olympic Games. Although still used for some athletics meetings, it is now the home of TSV Munich 1860 and Bayern Munich. Bayern's rise to prominence in the 1970s went hand-in-hand with their moving to the stadium; TSV Munich 1860, by contrast, have never really settled here, and so keep their main offices at their old Grünwalder Strasse ground. West Germany won the World Cup here in 1974 and Holland the European Championship in 1988, while Nottingham Forest (1979), Marseille (1993) and Borussia Dortmund (1997) have all been crowned European champions here. The crowning glory of the stadium is of course its breathtaking spiderweb roof, which even after 25 years can still intrigue and fascinate if the action on the pitch fails to catch your eye.

Olympic Stadium
Rome, Italy

Opened: 1953

Venue for: Olympic Games 1960; European Championship Finals 1968, 1980; European Cup Finals 1977, 1984, 1996; World Cup Final 1990

Record attendance: 82,000 (many times)

Current capacity: 82,000

Situated at the foot of Monte Mario, Rome's Olympic Stadium has an elegant symmetry, enhanced by the addition of a roof before the 1990 World Cup Finals. This roof has made the atmosphere inside the stadium on big-match days even more heated and volatile than before. Some truly dramatic matches have unfolded in Rome, like Liverpool's European Cup wins over Borussia Mönchengladbach (1977; 3–1) and over Roma themselves (1984; on penalties). The stadium was also, in 1990, the venue for the worst World Cup Final ever played: West Germany defeated Argentina 1–0 in a drab game. Both Lazio and Roma play their home matches here.

Below: The Olympic Stadium in Rome venue for the 1990 World Cup final.

San Siro
Milan, Italy

Opened: 1925 (present rebuilt stadium: 1989)

Venue for: European Cup Finals 1965, 1970

Current capacity: 85,500

Home to both Internazionale and AC Milan, the San Siro has ever risen in importance since its construction in 1925. From 1979 its official name has been the Giuseppe Meazza Stadium, in honour of the great Internazionale international

star of the 1920s and 1930s. The main feature of the stadium is the ingenious system of ramps running around its outside; these were retained when the ground was basically rebuilt, with a third tier being added, for the 1990 World Cup Finals. Exterior towers help support the roof, another addition

Above: The San Siro is another pressure cooker, this time powered by the inimitable *tifosi*.

for the World Cup. The whole effect is distinctive, dazzling and utterly unique. The only problem is that the roof covers most of the pitch, and so millions of pounds have had to be spent on improving the surface.

The San Siro staged the opening match of the 1990 World Cup, in which Cameroon beat the world

champions, Argentina, 1–0. Other games played here included the second-round match between West Germany and Holland (2–1) and the quarter-final between West Germany and Czechoslovakia (1–0). Internazionale themselves won the European Cup here in 1965, defeating Benfica 1–0.

Santiago Bernabeu
Madrid, Spain

Opened: 1947

Venue for: World Cup Final 1982; European Cup Finals 1957, 1969, 1980

Record attendance: 124,000 (Real Madrid v Fiorentina, 1957 European Cup Final)

Current capacity: 74,300

This was the home of the great Real Madrid side of the 1950s – of Alfredo Di Stefano, Ferenc Puskas and the rest – and their sterling deeds still seem to linger in the atmosphere. Despite its modern roof, added for the 1982 World Cup Finals, and the towering terraces, there is still something old-fashioned and tangibly nostalgic about the Santiago Bernabeu. The stadium is situated near the heart of Madrid. Two famous twin towers – which, unlike those at Wembley, comprise part of the interior of the stadium – are topped by neon signs carrying the club crest. In 1957–65 Real Madrid played 114 matches here without once losing, and during this period they also won the 1957 European Cup Final against Fiorentina (2–0) in front of a record 124,000 crowd. In 1982 it was Italy, not Spain, that enjoyed the greatest success any side can experience: they beat West Germany 3–1 in the World Cup Final.

Below: Santiago Bernabeu, venue for Italy's famous World Cup victory over West Germany in 1982

Sir Alfred McAlpine Stadium
Huddersfield, England

Opened: 1994

Record attendance: 23,678 (Huddersfield v Liverpool, FA Cup 3, 1999)

Current capacity: 24,554

If Huddersfield had a football team to match its stadium, the side would be challenging for the title again – something it last did in the 1920s, when manager Herbert Chapman laid the groundwork for three successive League Championships. The Sir

Alfred McAlpine Stadium – 'Alf', as the fans have dubbed it – is probably the most impressive and distinctive of all the new stadiums built in England during the 1990s. In 1995 it won the Royal Institute of British Architects Award as Building of the Year – the first soccer stadium to achieve this honour. The arched shape of the roofs of its stands are distinctive, and lift the spirits. To repeat, all this dazzling stadium now needs is a team to go with it.

Stadio Delle Alpi

Turin, Italy

Opened: 1990

Record attendance: 64,469

Current capacity: 69,041

This is a beautiful stadium, but ever since it opened it has been hated by the teams who have played there and the fans who

Above: The beautiful but unloved Stadio Delle Alpi during the 1990 World Cup.

have been forced to watch their football here. The Stadio Delle Alpi, currently the home to both Juventus and Torino, is an incredible blend of fantasy and pragmatic architecture – and seems destined to turn into a huge, unloved, forgotten white elephant. Built for the 1990 World Cup, it staged the dramatic semi-final penalty shoot-out between England and West Germany. It has also witnessed some of Juventus's glory-nights over the past few years. But fans do not like coming here, and Juventus played some of their Champions' League matches at other venues in the mid-1990s because the crowds at Stadio Delle Alpi were so small and uninspiring. The stadium's innovative architecture evokes the nearby Alps – hence the name – but it has never replaced the old Stadio Communale in the fans' affections . . . or the affections, it seems, of anyone associated with either Juventus or Torino. There are now plans for

both clubs to return to a rebuilt Stadio Communale. It is a wonder why the Stadio Delle Alpi was built in the first place, but, for afficionados of beautiful, stylistic stadia, it is a blessing that it was.

Wembley Stadium

London, England

Opened: 1923 (Rebuit 2006)

Venue for: Olympic Games 1948; World Cup Final 1966; European Cup Finals 1963, 1968, 1971, 1978, 1992; Euro 96 Final

Record attendance: 127,047 (unofficial estimate: 200,000) Bolton v West Ham, FA Cup Final 1923)

Current capacity: 0

The old Wembley was built, in only 300 working days, for the 1923 British Exhibition. The first match played there was on 26 April 1923: Bolton beat West Ham 2–0 in the FA Cup Final.

That match entered football folklore as the 'White Horse Final': PC George Scorey and his horse Billy helped clear the pitch of a crowd estimated to be about 200,000 (see page 248). Wembley, with its famous Twin Towers, is the footballing Mecca for players the world over. The most famous match played there was on 30 July 1966, when England defeated West Germany 4–2 in the World Cup Final. But this is far from the sole reason for Wembley's fame: each year the English Cup Final is held here and televised live around the world.

From 1923 until 1963, when its roof was added, Wembley hardly altered. The trouble has been that it hasn't altered much since 1963 either, the only change of note being that it became an all-seater ground, its capacity consequently being cut from 100,00 to 80,000. It was never home to a league team, although Leyton Orient played two home games there in the 1930s.

The New Wembley is due to be completed in early 2006 and will cost an estimated £757 million and will have a 90,000 capacity.

Below: Wembley, home to the FA Cup Final since 1923.

PLAYING FOR THE CUP

Cup competition ranges from the oldest domestic knock-out competition, the English FA Cup, to the World Cup Finals, when national sides play one another for the greatest prize in the footballing world. In this section we examine all the levels of knock-out competition from the UEFA Cup to the Copa Libertadores. And then there is a separate section on the World Cup itself, telling this great competition's story from its inception in 1930 to the festival of football in Japan and Korea 2002.

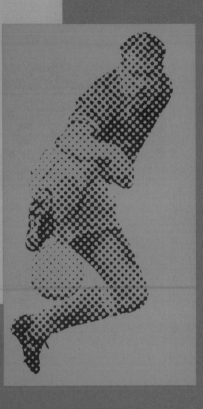

COMPETITIONS

The Competitions

INTERNATIONAL COMPETITIONS

Above: France rejoice after their 1994 triumph in the European Championship in Paris.

European Championship

Originally called the Nations' Cup, Europe's international competition has grown in size and stature. Held every four years, it dovetails neatly with the World Cup, so that every second year the finals of one of these tournaments take place. The 2000 European Cup saw for the first time two nations sharing host duties - Belgium and Holland.

Like the World Club Cup, this championship was the brainchild of the Frenchman Henri Delaunay, who was secretary of his country's

Right: Jurgen Klinsmann, captain of 1996 European champions Germany.

football federation in the 1950s. He died before the first competition was completed, but the trophy still bears his name. Delaunay's aim was to bring into a single competition three regional tournaments: the British Home Championship, the Nordic Cup and the Central European Championship. The first Nations' Cup began in 1958 with 17 countries. There were home and away matches, the finalists being determined on a knockout basis, and four teams contested the last stages. (Nowadays there are 16 finalists.)

The teams from the UK, Italy, West Germany and Holland all declined to take part. The Republic of Ireland was not so aloof; indeed, Dublin staged

the first Nations' tie when, on 5 April 1959, Ireland defeated Czechoslovakia 2–0, a scoreline which was overturned in the second leg. France, the USSR, Czechoslovakia and Yugoslavia disputed the inaugural final, which was hosted by France and won by the Soviet side.

The 1964 championships were held in Spain, and the Spanish national side succeeded in collecting its only major trophy to date before a 120,000-strong Madrid crowd. This time 29 countries had agreed to take part, though Scotland still declined to enter and England, in Alf Ramsey's

first match in charge, lost 5–2 to France in the qualifying rounds.

Four years later the qualifying tournament was expanded to eight groups, accommodating 31 entries, and thereafter the competition was known as the European Championship. West Germany and Scotland took part for the first time. England, then world champions, reached the semi-finals in Italy only to lose to Yugoslavia.

West Germany now began to dominate. The side won in Brussels in 1972, was beaten only in a penalty shootout by Czechoslovakia in Belgrade in 1976, and defeated Belgium in

Below: Denmark celebrate during their 1992 success in Sweden.

The 1964 championships were held in Spain, and the Spanish national side succeeded in collecting its only major trophy to date before a 120,000-strong Madrid crowd.

Rome in 1980. For that last competition the format was altered: the finals were enlarged to include eight teams, with the host nation an automatic qualifier.

The 1984 championship was a fantastic football festival. The flamboyant French, inspired by Michel Platini, proved unbeatable hosts. No British Isles nation qualified, but four years later, in 1988, the Republic of Ireland (for the first time in a major competition) and England made the finals. The Irish beat England, but neither qualified for the semi-finals; there Holland, the eventual winners, beat Germany. In 1992 Scotland reached the finals for the first time but, like England, progressed no further. The 1992 tournament saw Denmark as stars of one of the competition's most enchanting rags-to-riches stories. Having narrowly failed in the qualifying campaign, the Danes were summoned to Sweden when Yugoslavia was excluded because of the civil war. Denmark upset all predictions by winning through to the final, where the team beat Germany.

The expansion to accommodate 16 finalists in 1996, when England was the host nation, reflected not just the emergence of countries from Eastern Europe but also the strength and increasing popularity of Delaunay's dream. The Germans triumphed again, although their victory in the Wembley final, against the Czech Republic – the tournament's surprise packet – was not particularly convincing.

The 2004 tournament will be played in Portugal and may offer the host country their best chance of winning a major title.

Below: Bergkamp (right) in his international role for Holland.

Copy America

The South American Championship is the oldest international competition, predating its European equivalent by 50 years. Its roots lay in the regular fixture between Argentina and Uruguay for the Lipton Cup and the Newton Cup. In 1910 the Argentinians decided to take the challenge a step further, and invited Brazil and Chile to join in; Brazil in fact withdrew before the tournament began, and the final brought the two old adversaries together before 40,000 fans at the Gimnasia club in Buenos Aires. The game had then to be postponed until the

following day because fans burned down a stand; the rearranged fixture, at Racing Club's ground, saw Argentina beat Uruguay 4–1 in front of only 8000 supporters.

The tournament has continued to be dominated by Argentina and Uruguay; Brazil, surprisingly in view of their World Cup record, has struggled to make the same impact, finishing winners on just five occasions – only twice since 1950.

The Copa America has not always enjoyed the status it desires, to the extent that countries sometimes field weakened teams. Not until 1975 did all 10 nations of the Conmebol (the South American Confederation) take part.

Above: Celebrations at the end of another final in the Copa America.

Furthermore, the event has had its share of problems and changes. For seven years following 1967 it was not contested at all. In 1987, it settled down to be a regular two-yearly event staged in a single country. In 1993, in Ecuador, the tournament underwent another revamp and Mexico and the USA were invited to take part.

When Uruguay beat Brazil on penalties in the 1995 final it was the nation's 14th Copa America, putting them back on level pegging with Argentina. Brazil won against host nation Bolivia in 1997, and beat their old foes Uruguay in 1999. Columbia won in 2001.

Above: Nigeria's 1988 Olympic team in action in South Korea.

The Olympic Games

Even though football has never sat easily with the amateur ideals of the Olympic Games, it has formed part of the festival since 1908. By 1921 Baron Pierre de Coubertin, the founder of the modern Games, was voicing concern at the inclusion of team sports, believing they stirred unwanted nationalism. Football remained on the list, however, because the Games could not afford to continue without it. As an example, in Los Angeles in 1984 more fans (1,421,627) watched football than watched any other discipline, athletics included.

In 1908 at the London Games an England amateur team, including many of the country's best players, beat Denmark 2–0 in the final. In 1924 a South American nation appeared for the first time, Uruguay

Opposite: A South African fan enjoys the 1996 African Nations' Cup.

handing Europe a masterclass in skill and technique. Four years later Argentina competed alongside Uruguay, the two sides renewing their longstanding rivalry in the final. Ironically, the success of these matches, which undoubtedly contributed to the creation of the World Cup (see page 226), meant that after 1930 the Olympics were never particularly significant as a barometer of global football supremacy. Anyway, after 1950 the spread of professionalism meant that most countries were unable to send their best players; accordingly, the Eastern Europeans, who insisted their players were amateurs, dominated.

In 1980 FIFA changed its rules to bar from the Olympics European and South American players who had appeared in World Cup qualifiers. In Barcelona in 1992 this rule was further refined, so that only players

under the age of 23 were permitted. Naturally, while the IOC wanted full international teams to take part, FIFA preferred to protect the status of the World Cup.

At Atlanta in 1996, each country was allowed to use three over-age players. The United Kingdom continues to find itself out of step, however, fearing that a united team would lead to the four nations' demise as individual sides within FIFA. Whether or not this idea has any validity at all is open to debate

African countries have dominated the Olympic competition recently, Nigeria winning in 1996 and Cameroon in 2000. Surely it is only a question of time before an African country does well in a World Cup.

African Nations' Cup

Now that African countries are considered something more than makeweights at World Cups and Olympics, the African Nations Cup has developed as a competition of more than parochial interest. The first competition, staged in 1957 on the formation of the Confederation of African Football (CAF), involved only Egypt, Sudan and Ethiopia. South Africa was due to compete, but said it would do so only with either a white-only or a black-only team. CAF refused this expression of apartheid, so South Africa withdrew and remained a footballing outcast until 1992. Four years later the country staged the event and won it.

The tournament, held every two years, drew more entrants as it went along, and it now boasts 16 finalists. Ghana – twice winners, twice runners-up – was the team to beat in the 1960s. In 1982 Ghana triumphed again, despite losing to Libya in the opening game of the tournament; the two sides met again in the final, and this time Ghana triumphed thanks to a 7–6 penalty shootout.

In April 1993 an aircraft carrying Zambia home from a Nations Cup qualifying match in Mauritius crashed, killing all 18 players. However, the country's European-based players were not on board; rebuilding around them, Zambia qualified for the following year's finals. An emotional victory was denied them in the final by Nigeria, who thereby ended a run of three losing finals.

South Africa crowned their re-entry into the competition by winning in 1996. Egypt won in 1998. Cameroon, the dominant African nation at present, won in 2000 and 2002.

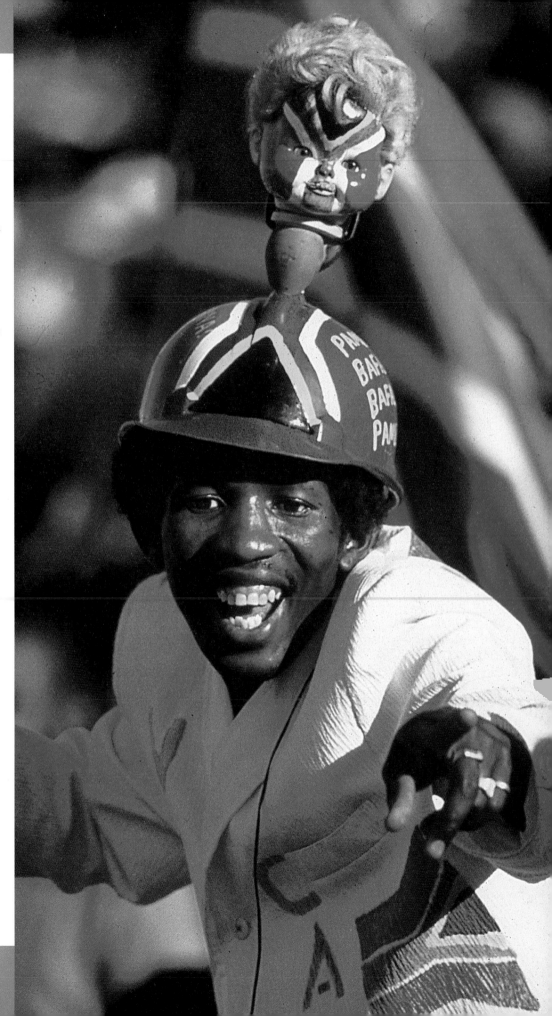

OTHER INTERNATIONAL COMPETITIONS

The Asian Cup, founded in 1956, quickly became superior to the football competition in the Asian Games, a localized version of the Olympics which began in 1951. The Asian Cup was dominated initially by South Korea and Iran, and more recently by the Arab states of Kuwait and Saudi Arabia.

Central America has its own championship, now known as the Concacaf Gold Cup, inaugurated in

Opposite: The World Club Cup has always been controversial, but winning it is cause for great celebration for players and managers alike.

Below: The Concacaf Gold Cup being awarded.

1941. Costa Rica's early dominance – eight victories between 1941 and 1963 – has diminished in recent times, especially since 1991 when the USA and Mexico joined in.

In 1995 the Intercontinental Cup (now Confederations Cup), between the winners of the various federation competitions, was started. The first contest was hosted by Saudi Arabia, and saw Denmark emerge as winner.

For younger players, FIFA stages championships at under-17 and under-20 levels, the latter competition being known as the World Youth Championship. The European Under-21 Competition now doubles as Europe's qualifying tournament for the Olympics. The South

American Youth Cup determines who goes through to compete in the World Youth Cup.

The first Women's World Cup was held in China in 1991, and was won by the USA. The beaten finalist, Norway, gained glory four years later, defeating Germany in the final.

The worst excesses began with Glasgow Celtic's visit to Argentina in 1967. The Celtic goalkeeper was struck by a missile before the start of the game with Racing Club.

CLUB COMPETITIONS

World Club Cup

The challenge to decide the world's finest club side ought to be a blue-ribbon event celebrating the game's finest individual and collective talents. Instead, it has often provided a stage for the game's worst excesses, erupting into gratuitous violence and creating an atmosphere such that Europe's finest have on occasion pulled out.

The idea originated in the late 1950s with Henri Delaunay, then UEFA's General Secretary. The cup is a two-team competition between winners of the European Champions Cup (some of whom have refused to enter) and the Copa Libertadores champions. Real Madrid was the first World Club champion, the maestros of 1960 – with legendary names like Puskas, Di Stefano and Gento – overcoming Penarol of Uruguay. In those early years the competition was organized over two legs, with points being decisive – a device which sometimes required a play-off.

The worst excesses began with Glasgow Celtic's visit to Argentina in 1967. The Celtic goalkeeper Ronnie Simpson was struck by a missile before the start of the game with Racing Club, and was unable to carry on. The deciding game, staged in Montevideo, degenerated into farce as Celtic had four players sent off and Racing two. The following year it was Manchester United's turn to suffer at the hands of Argentinians, this time hard man Estudiantes. United lost Bobby Charlton with a shin injury and had Nobby Stiles sent off for gesturing at a linesman. In the home game United saw George Best dismissed for fighting.

After many turbulent years, and many boycotts during the 1970s, the competition was revived in 1980 with a single-game decider – on neutral territory, in Japan, though controversy dogs this cup still.

Copa Libertadores

The club competition for South American sides has encountered similar problems to those that have blighted the World Club Cup and the Copa America: violence has proved an all-too-frequent spectre at the feast, while there have been regular, disruptive, changes to the rules.

The first tournament came as early as 1948, but because of financial problems it was put back on the shelf. The success of the European Cup, however, persuaded the South American authorities to try again. In 1962, after the second tournament, the organizers must have wondered why they had bothered. The second leg of the final between Penarol and Santos of Brazil had to be delayed by over an hour after the referee was knocked unconscious by a missile; then, on the resumption, a lines-

Below: São Paulo celebrate winning the Copa Libertadores.

man was struck by a stone. The game was promptly abandoned. Santos won the play-off.

In 1970, when Estudiantes met Penarol, their second leg ended in a free-for-all featuring not only both sets of players but the reserves as well. The indiscipline got worse the following season, when fighting between Boca Juniors and Peru's Sporting Cristal in Buenos Aires led to all the players being jailed. Thankfully the competition is now less of a nationalistic battleground.

Nevertheless, interest in the event rose to the extent that, as more and more countries entered, it became too big for its own good. The 1966 tournament – the first featuring two clubs from each of the 10 leading nations – comprised 95 games all told. Even now, after further alterations to the rules, the winners and runners-up must play a draining total of 14 matches.

The impetus for unification of the two competitions grew as the leading clubs from both blocs increasingly engaged in friendlies.

European Cup

The competition's original title, the Champion Clubs' Cup, would nowadays be a misnomer: demand from television and sponsors for an increased number of high-profile matches has resulted in teams finishing as low as fourth in their domestic leagues playing in the first round.

In the late 1920s the Mitropa Cup was held intermittently for clubs in Central Europe, while Italian, French, Spanish and Portu-guese sides contested in the Latin

Above: Liverpool after their 1984 European Cup success in Rome.

Cup. The impetus for unification of the two competitions grew as the leading clubs from both blocs increasingly engaged in friendlies. This cause was taken up by the French sports newspaper *L'Equipe*, which wanted to test English claims that Wolverhampton Wanderers was the cream of Europe because it had beaten Hungary's star-studded Honved. *L'Equipe* invited representatives of 20 leading clubs to Paris. FIFA gave support, and the newly formed UEFA took over the tournament's administration from 1955–6.

England was an absentee from that first contest: the Football League refused to let Chelsea join in. Hibernian, representing Scotland, reached the semi-finals. Real Madrid lifted the inaugural trophy, the first of five successive wins by that club.

In the second year, Matt Busby ordered his directors to ignore the League; Manchester United repaid his determination and foresight by progressing to the last four before losing to Real. The Busby Babes' development was, the following season, tragically interrupted by

the Munich air disaster (see page 187) as they returned from a quarter-final victory over Red Star Belgrade. While Busby, once he had recovered from his own serious injuries, rebuilt his team, Benfica and the Milanese clubs Internazionale and AC Milan held sway. By 1968, however, Manchester United had a team capable of bringing the trophy to England; Wembley was an appropriate venue for its extra-time victory over Benfica. The previous year Glasgow Celtic had led the Britain's re-emergence as serious contenders by beating Internazionale.

Above: John McGovern lifts the European Cup for Nottingham Forest.

Opposite: Alan Smith, the match winner in Arsenal's 1994 European Cup Winners' Cup success over Parma.

Internazionale regained the crown in 1969, but then the Latin countries were overtaken by more northerly clubs. Feyenoord of Rotterdam was the first Dutch winner, in 1970, and this preceded a run of three successive titles for Feyenoord's Amsterdam rival Ajax. Bayern Munich then performed a similar hat-trick, but from 1977 there was a sequence of six victories for English sides: Liverpool (1977, 1978, 1981), Nottingham Forest (1979, 1980) and Aston Villa (1982) between them made up for the country's disappointing showing on the world stage. Liverpool's fifth final, in 1985, brought the competition's worst day: 39 people, mostly Juve supporters, died when a wall collapsed as they fled rampaging Liverpool fans. This led to all English clubs being banned from European competition – a ban lifted in 1991.

In 1992, pressure from clubs hungry for the riches of a European Super League forced a significant change of the rules; teams were grouped on a league basis to produce two finalists. Since then the competition has expanded still further. At the beginning of the 2002–03 season a total of 15 teams qualified for entry into the group stages of the competition, with a further 58 participating in three qualifying rounds for entry into the competition proper.

In recent years Real Madrid has been the team to beat – winning three titles in five years (1998, 2000 and 2002). The Real Madrid team of 2003, who lost in the semi finals were a World Superstars XI, including Ronaldo, Luis Figo, Zinedine Zidane, Raul and Roberto Carlos.

European Cup-Winners' Cup

Because of the creation of this competition, many countries restarted old knockout trophies or initiated new ones. Just 10 teams contested the first Cup-Winners' Cup Final, in 1960, the only occasion a two-game final has been held. Although the Latin countries were again immediately successful, UK sides found this an easier competition than the European Cup. By 1965, with the entry now numbering 30, Tottenham Hotspur and West Ham had put their names on the trophy. Manchester City and Chelsea followed

Liverpool's fifth final in 1985 brought the competition's worst day; 39 people, mostly Juve supporters, died when a wall collapsed as they fled rampaging Liverpool supporters.

before in 1972 Glasgow Rangers, after having been runners-up twice, gained the prize – although the club's success was blighted by rioting fans and it was subsequently banned for a year.

Now generally accepted as the weakest international competition, the European Cup-Winners' Cup is the only one that has been won by teams from the former countries Czechoslovakia (Slovan Bratislava, 1969), East Germany (Madeburg, 1974) and the USSR (Dynamo Kiev, 1976 and 1986; Dinamo Tbilisi, 1981), and from France (Paris St Germain, 1996).

So far no club has successfully defended the Cup, although seven holders have been losing finalists the year after. The closest to retaining the cup have been Arsenal: having beaten Parma in the 1994 final, the side was defeated a year later by an extraordinary last-minute goal from Real Zaragoza.

The competition was dropped by UEFA after the 1999 Final – Lazio beat Real Mallorca 2–1.

UEFA Cup

For a long while this competition was seen as the slightest of the three European tournaments. Certainly it began inauspiciously (1955): it was just a sporting sideshow, known as the Inter-Cities Fairs Cup, at various trade fairs in different European cities. It has since superseded the European Cup-Winners' Cup in the strength of its entry. The UEFA Cup (the name-change came in 1971) is open to those clubs that finish behind their domestic champions, and teams from several of the

In winning the first title, Barcelona put a familiar Latin stamp on the new competition. An opening sequence of five Spanish victories was interrupted only by Roma in 1961. English clubs then reigned supreme for six years.

more powerful nations participate. More recently, in the 1990s, it has become the competition to which are also sent the champions from the smaller countries. Another qualifying route is via the Inter-Toto Cup, the long-established summer competition. Now the smaller nations partake in a qualifying round for the Champions' League, with the runners-up of that, plus the third placed teams after the first group stage of the Champions' League going into the UEFA Cup.

Fifty-eight teams were in the 1997–8 first round proper, a further 38 having been knocked out in the qualifying stage. The competition has come a long way since 1955, when 12 cities agreed to the suggestion of the Swiss Vice-President of FIFA, Ernst Thommen, that they should add a competitive element to their trade fairs. This first Fairs Cup was not a success. It took three years to produce a

winner, using a group system made more complex by the withdrawals of Cologne and Vienna. Nor was there uniformity among the remaining sides: London was represented by an amalgam of the capital's professional players and Birmingham by Birmingham City.

In winning the first title, Barcelona put a familiar Latin stamp on the new competition. An opening sequence of five Spanish victories was interrupted only by Roma in 1961. English clubs then reigned supreme for six years, a period which saw Newcastle collecting its only continental trophy (1969).

In 1971–2 the competition had its new name and England provided both finalists. Thereafter, West German and Dutch clubs came into their own. More recently, the Italians have come to dominate – in the seven finals up to 1995, three were all-Italian affairs. Entry is based on past performances by a nation's clubs in all European

Above: To the victor everything, to the loser nothing.

Opposite: Goal-mouth action – when Marseille played Red Star Belgrade in 1991, they lost.

Right: Ruud Gullit with the European Cup in his Milan days.

221

competition and Italy, Spain, Germany and England usually have four entrants. The final has been a single match since 1998.

African Cups

Africa has staged the Champion Clubs' Cup since 1964, with the league winners of each country and the defending champions competing on a home-and-away knockout basis. From the 1997–8 season a Champions' League format was introduced at the quarter-final stage. The early years belonged to West and Central Africa; after 1980 the North African clubs held sway.

Eleven years after the start of the Champion Clubs' Cup, the African Cup-Winners' Cup came into being. An equivalent to the UEFA Cup, the CAF cup began in 1992.

OTHER INTERNATIONAL COMPETITIONS

Each season Uefa stages a challenge match between the winners of the Champions League and the Uefa Cup (pre 2000, European Cup Winners) to compete for the European Super Cup. Concacaf (Central American and Caribbean regions) organizes a knock-out club competition, the winners of which play the South American Champions for the Inter-American Cup. The winners of the club champions of Europe, Africa, Asia, South America and Concacaf compete for the World Team Championship.

The oldest league in the world was responsible for organizing full-time professional football in England until the advent of the Premier League in 1992.

NATIONAL COMPETITIONS

Football League

The oldest league in the world was responsible for organizing full-time professional football in England until the advent of the Premier League in 1992, an organization which satisfied the elite clubs' demand for the lion's share of television and sponsorship riches.

The League's founder was a Scot, William McGregor of Aston Villa. On 17 April 1888, three years after professionalism had been sanctioned by the southern-dominated Football Association, 12 northern and midland clubs got together to launch the competition. In 1892 it became a two-division affair, and in 1920 it took in the Southern League's best clubs to form a Third Division. In 1958 the Third Division North and Third Division South were reorganized and succeeded by nationwide Third and Fourth Divisions.

Significant changes came in 1987. Henceforward the Vauxhall Conference champions would win automatic promotion to the League, and a system of play-offs was introduced. These adjustments have added interest and boosted attendances for all clubs at all levels, especially in the Premiership.

Above: Arsenal versus Liverpool in the 1996–7 season. Both teams were to lose out in the league to a dominant Manchester United.

Opposite: At the African Nations' Cup, South Africa, in the first year of competition since the end of apartheid, won.

Right: Lee Dixon of multiple English champions Arsenal.

COMPETITIONS

Above: Aston Villa v Leeds United in the FA Cup.

Left: The FA Cup.

Opposite: Eric Cantona, the 1996 Footballer of the Year in England.

FA Cup

The FA Cup has a sense of magic and romance all of its own. While the Premier League is the most prestigious trophy, nothing can match the glamour and excitement of Wembley on a Cup Final day.

The world's oldest knockout competition was conceived in 1871 under the guidance of FA Secretary Charles Alcock. The first final was played the following year: Wanderers beat the Royal Engineers before 2000 spectators at Kennington Oval. In the early years the competition was dominated by clubs connected to public schools and London society but, as Scots came south to work in the Lancashire cotton industry, the northern clubs became more powerful. Between 1883 and 1891

Blackburn Rovers won the trophy five times.

The first Wembley final, between Bolton and West Ham in 1923, drew at least 126,000 paying spectators, and is best remembered for the white police horse which was used to guide fans off the pitch. There have been many memorable Wembley finals (although in recent years the games have promised more than they have delivered). In 1953 Sir Stanley Matthews finally held a winners' medal after Blackpool won a remarkable match against Bolton. Manchester United's 1958 defeat by Bolton, three months after the Munich air disaster had wiped out most of the team, was particularly poignant. Shocks came in 1973, when the great Leeds side of Don Revie was defeated by Sunderland, and in 1988, when Wimbledon, a

League club for only 11 years, denied the mighty Liverpool a League/Cup double.

For years the Football Association resisted sponsorship offers but financial pressures forced the inevitable – in 1994 Littlewoods became the first sponsor of the world's oldest knock-out competition. AXA are the present sponsors, paying £25 million over four years for the privilege.

INDIVIDUAL AWARDS

In any team game, individual honours are cherished. The oldest is England's Footballer of the Year, voted by the Football Writers' Association since 1948 and recently dominated by foreign players; the only Englishmen to win in the last 10 years were Shearer and Sheringham. Since 1974 English players have held their own vote and in 1984 Ian Rush collected both. There are two similar awards for managers.

In 1956 France Football magazine organized a European Players' Award (voted by journalists). This idea was copied in other continents and, in the 1990s, by FIFA, whose World Player of the Year is selected by national managers. Recently the annual Golden Shoe – the award of a golden boot to honour Europe's leading goal-scorer of the year – has been revived. The inaugural winner was Eusebio, who in the 1967–8 season scored 42 Portuguese League goals for Benfica.

The first Wembley final, between Bolton and West Ham, drew at least 126,000 paying spectators, and is best remembered for the white police horse which was used to guide fans off the pitch.

The World Cup Finals

WORLD CUP HISTORY

From unpromising beginnings, the World Cup has grown to become second only to the Olympics as a global sporting event. To give an idea of its scale, a total of 199 countries entered the 2002 World Cup tournament, 29 of which went on to join the host nations, South Korea and Japan, and the holders France in the Finals.

Brazil has won five times, Italy and West Germany three times each, Argentina and Uruguay twice each, and England and France once each. In six competitions the host country has been the winner.

1930 (Uruguay)

Uruguay 4 (Dorado, Cea, Iriarte, Castro), **Argentina** 2 (Peucelle, Stabile)

Venue: Montevideo

HT: 1–2

Top scorer (finals): Stabile (Argentina), 8 goals

Distance and disaffection meant that only 13 nations entered the first World Cup, just four braving the three-week sea trip from Europe. Yugoslavia was the sole European entrant to reach the last four, only to be crushed by Argentina 6–1. Then Uruguay, semi-final victors by the same margin over the USA, repeated the result of the 1928 Olympic Final by defeating their neighbours with three goals in the last 35 minutes. It was a fitting reward for a nation that had paid all the other countries' expenses and built a new stadium in eight months. A small profit was made and a national holiday was declared.

1934 (Italy)

Italy 2 (Orsi, Schiavio), **Czechoslovakia** 1 (Puc)

Venue: Rome

HT: 0–0

Top scorers (finals): Conen (Germany), Nedjedly (Czechoslovakia), Schiavio (Italy), all 4 goals

Much to the pleasure of Mussolini, Italy triumphed at home under the guidance of the formidable Vittorio Pozzo. This was not a pleasant tournament, however, being marred by physical matches and, off the pitch, politics. The holders, Uruguay, stayed away, piqued by the poor European attendance in 1930; also absent were the UK nations, not yet members of FIFA. The knock-out format meant that the Argentine squad travelled several thousand miles for just one game, but at least it competed in the finals. The Mexicans had to travel to Turin for a qualifier, which they lost to the USA. Even Italy, the host nation, had to qualify, as 32 entrants were reduced to 16 for the finals.

These finals made a profit substantially greater than that of the previous competition.

Above: Schiavio scores in extra time, making Italy World Champions in 1934.

Opposite near left: Paul Gascoigne in tears at the 1990 World Cup applauding the English fans.

Opposite far left: In many ways FIFA succeeded in their quest to take soccer to North America in 1994, but after a superb tournament, the final between Brazil and Italy was a turgid affair.

Left: Castro and Scarene celebrate Uruguay's victory in 1930.

Only 13 nations entered the first World Cup, just four braving the three-week sea trip from Europe.

Above: Desperate Hungarian defence in the 1938 final against Italy.

1938 (France)

Italy 4 (Colaussi 2, Piola 2), **Hungary 2** (Titkos, Sarosi)

Venue: Paris

HT: 3–1

Top scorer (finals): Leonidas (Brazil), 8 goals

The spectre of impending war overshadowed this tournament: Austria, third in 1934, had been absorbed into the German side, while Spain was trapped in a civil war. Uruguay once more refused to take part, Argentina did likewise, and the UK nations still remained aloof. Again, the tournament had a knock-out format, which meant that the Dutch East Indies (now Indonesia) had to make a long journey for 90 minutes of play and a 6–0 defeat against Hungary.

Italy, with Piola leading the line, kept the trophy, aided by Brazil's bizarre decision to 'rest' Leonidas for the semi-final against the holders. Brazil had earlier been in a savage match at Bordeaux against the Czechs, which resulted in three dismissals, a broken leg, a broken arm and various cuts and bruises.

> **Hungary figured with Brazil in the World Cup's most infamous match, the quarter-final known as the 'Battle of the Berne'.**

1950 (Brazil)

Uruguay 2 (Schiaffino, Ghiggia), **Brazil 1** (Friaca)

Venue: Rio de Janeiro

HT: 0–0

Top scorer (finals): Ademir (Brazil), 9 goals

England deigned to enter the competition in 1950 . . . and was humbled – Tom Finney, Stan Mortensen, Alf Ramsey and all – by the USA, who won 1–0 in Belo Horizonte. Among other shocks was Sweden's defeat of an Italian side depleted by the Superga air crash (see page 187).

For the Brazilian hosts, however, the biggest shock was the 'final',

Left: A last attack for Uruguay as the referee, George Reader, blows for time and Uruguay win.

1954 (Switzerland)

West Germany 3 (Rahn 2, Morlock), **Hungary 2** (Puskas, Czibor)

Venue: Berne

HT: 2–2

Top scorer (finals): Kocsis (Hungary), 11 goals

West Germany, beaten 8–3 by the 'Magical Magyars' in the group stages, surprised all but themselves by winning the re-match in the final: this was only Hungary's second defeat in five years. In fact, Hungary was 2–0 up after eight minutes, but then the side paid for having gambled on the fitness of the gifted, but injured, Ferenc Puskas.

Earlier, Hungary had figured, with Brazil, in the World Cup's most infamous match, the quarter-final encounter known as the 'Battle of Berne'. Won 4–2 by Hungary, it featured three dismissals (two Brazilian) and a dressing-room brawl, in which bottles were used. At the same stage in the contest, Switzerland – with captain and centre-half Roger Bocquet suffering from a tumour, and goalkeeper Parlier afflicted by sunstroke – lost 7–5 to Austria. In 26 matches, 138 goals were scored. England went out to Uruguay in the quarter-finals. Then the holders fell to Hungary after extra time in the semi-final.

Below: Puskas shoots at goal in the 1954 final.

in which they lost to Uruguay. The impact was all the greater as, due to the competition being staged in two group phases, Brazil needed only a draw to be the new champions. That the last match of the tournament should also prove to be the decisive one was obviously a fortunate coincidence, and the game has since been regarded as a final. Brazil, who had been cloistered in a Rio mansion for four months, drew 200,000 spectators to the Maracana stadium, but Uruguay's goalkeeper, Maspoli, and Juan Schiaffino won the match between them.

1958 (Sweden)

Brazil 5 (Vava 2, Pelé 2, Zagalo),
Sweden 2 (Liedholm, Simonsen)

Venue: Stockholm

HT: 2–1

Top scorer (finals): Fontaine
(France), 13 goals

Brazil became the first country to triumph outside their own continent. With 17-year-old Pelé alongside Didi, Garrincha, Vava and Mario Zagallo, and with Djalma and Nilton Santos behind, the side was irrepressible. Only England, depleted after the Munich air disaster and otherwise disappointing, held the Brazilians to a draw. But it was Wales and Northern Ireland who progressed furthest of the home nations, each reaching the quarter-finals. Wales, with the truly giant John Charles, beat a politically weakened Hungary and then, with Charles injured, narrowly lost to Brazil. Peter Doherty's Irish, having knocked out Italy in the qualifying rounds, had their run ended by France's Just Fontaine, who set a still-unbeaten scoring record in the tournament. The Swedes, with Nils Liedholm and Gunnar Gren still in attack (both had contested in 1950), were also impressive.

1962 (Chile)

Brazil 3 (Amarildo, Zito, Vava),
Czechoslovakia 1 (Masopust)

Venue: Santiago

HT: 1–1

Top scorers (finals): Albert
(Hungary), Garrincha, Vava (Brazil),
Jerkovic (Yugoslavia), Ivanov (USSR),
Sanchez (Chile), all 4 goals

Pelé was injured in the very first match, but nevertheless Brazil retained the trophy. In Pelé's absence, Garrincha starred, although he was fortunate to be allowed to

Right: Garrincha in full flight in the 1958 final – the Swedes were outclassed on the day.

THE WORLD CUP FINALS

play in the final after having been sent off for retaliation during the previous match, against Chile – fortunate, too, to be able to continue after being routinely kicked as well as being struck by a bottle hurled from the crowd. Earlier, Chile, the otherwise welcoming hosts, had been involved in a brutal match with Italy, during which two Italians were dismissed and another suffered a broken nose.

For the first time, Uruguay failed to make an impact; Spain, under the guidance of manager Helenio Herrera, also disappointed. The surprise of the tournament was Czechoslovakia: goalkeeper Wilhelm Schroiff was the side's hero until the final, when he fumbled the ball and opened the way for a Brazilian victory.

Below: England's Martin Peters celebrates his goal at Wembley in the 1966 final. Schnellinger looks on in disbelief.

1966 (England)

England 4 (Hurst 3, Peters), **Germany 2** (Haller, Weber), after extra time

Venue: London

HT: 1–1

FT: 2–2

Top scorer (finals): Eusebio (Portugal), 9 goals

This was a gripping tournament that mixed good with bad. The tone was set when the actual World Cup itself was lost before the off; luckily, it was found by a dog called Pickles. There followed the brilliance of Eusebio, who inspired débutants Portugal to the semi-finals, and the sadness of seeing Pelé hacked out of the tournament. North Korea shocked everybody by beating Italy and worrying Portugal. Argentina's Antonio Rattin caused uproar by refusing to leave the pitch when sent off in the match against England, whose manager, Alf Ramsey, courted criticism by omitting Jimmy Greaves from his side. Ramsey was vindicated, however, in a dramatic final. West Germany levelled in injury time, but went down to the hosts in the extra period. Geoff Hurst scored a hat-trick, the only player ever to do so in a World Cup Final, but arguments still rage as to whether his second goal actually crossed the line.

(3–2), and the side's cruel semi-final extra-time defeat against Italy (3–4) were more dramatic. The finest, however, was Brazil v England in the group matches. As a demonstration of the finest attacking and defensive arts of the time, it had few equals. Gordon Banks' save from Pelé, and Bobby Moore's tackling are remembered, but Brazil, thanks to a Jairzinho goal, claimed victory 1–0. Banks was not present for the quarter-finals because of illness, so arguably England's finest team failed to make the re-match in the final.

1974 (West Germany)

West Germany 2 (Breitner – penalty, Muller), **Holland 1** (Neeskens – penalty)

Venue: Munich

HT: 2–1

Top scorer (finals): Lato (Poland), 7 goals

Dutch brilliance went unrewarded as West Germany recovered from the shock of conceding a first-minute penalty. Finally, Franz Beck-enbauer had a winner's medal. The Dutch team, inspired by Johan Cruyff and playing 'total football', had been a revelation in their first finals since 1938. Poland, whose last appearance had been made in the same year, provided another surprise: having knocked out the English team in the qualifiers, the side finished in third place, with Gregorz Lato at the top of the list of the tournament's goal-scorers.

These finals saw the first meeting between East and West Germany; played under heavy security in Berlin, the match was won by the East German side (1–0). Brazil, playing a physical European game, disappointed.

> **The 1970 final was too one-sided to be the tournament's best match. The finest was Brazil v England in the group matches. As a demonstration of the finest attacking and defensive arts of the time, it had few equals.**

1970 (Mexico)

Brazil 4 (Pelé, Gerson, Jairzinho, Alberto), **Italy 1** (Boninsegna)

Venue: Mexico City

HT: 1–1

Top scorer (finals): Muller (West Germany), 9 goals

Arguably the best tournament of them all, and won by probably the finest team. Pelé shone brightest, but Brazil glistened with other talent: Jairzinho, Gerson, Tostao, Rivelino and the captain Carlos Alberto, who scored the last, stunning, goal.

The final was too one-sided to be the tournament's best match. West Germany's quarter-final extra-time comeback against England

1978 (Argentina)

Argentina 3 (Kempes 2, Bertoni),
Holland 1 (Nanninga), after extra
time

Venue: Buenos Aires

HT: 1–0

FT: 1–1

Top scorer (finals): Kempes
(Argentina), 6 goals

Argentina's military government
had staked everything on a
home victory in 1978, and Mario
Kempes delivered. The Valencia
striker, Argentina's only 'exile', top-
scored in both the tournament and
the final, where the Dutch were
denied again. The latter were
weakened by Johan Cruyff's refusal
to play in a nation ruled by a
murderous junta, but they still
performed with style.

Brazil and West Germany produced disappointing performances,

Peru's eccentric goalkeeper Ramon
Quiroga delighted, and Scotland's
Willie Johnston was disgraced, sent
home after failing a drugs test.
Another sour note was Argentina's
6–0 win over Peru to ensure the
hosts' place in the final; the result
is still regarded with suspicion.

Above: Rossi scores the
first for Italy in 1982.

Opposite top: The
Brazilian goalkeeper
makes a save in the face
of Italian pressure
during the 1970 final.

Opposite bottom:
Gerd Muller scoring
Germany's second in the
1974 final.

1982 (Spain)

Italy 3 (Rossi, Tardelli, Altobelli),
West Germany 1 (Breitner)

Venue: Madrid

HT: 0–0

Top scorer (finals): Rossi (Italy), 6
goals

Paolo Rossi, who was fresh from
a two-year ban following a
bribes scandal (*see* page 137), inspired the Italian side in a 24-team
competition. The world was captivated by an outstanding Italy-Brazil
match, in which Rossi scored a hat-
trick, but appalled by a savage and
unpunished semi-final assault by
the West German Harald Schumacher, which almost cost France's
Patrick Battiston his life. This
followed apparent Austro-German
collusion in Group 2 to put out an
Algerian team that earlier had
defeated the German side 2–1.
Thus, Italy's victory, even though
the final was undistinguished, was
widely welcomed.

Northern Ireland, whose side
included the 17-year-old Norman
Whiteside – replacing Pelé as the
youngest-ever World Cup Finals
player – defeated the Spanish
hosts in dramatic style with only
ten men, while Hungary trounced
El Salvador 10–1.

Left: Ossie Ardiles glides
through the Dutch
defence in 1978.

THE WORLD CUP FINALS

Maradona's famous 'Hand of God' goal, punched past Peter Shilton, will be remembered longest.

1986 (Mexico)

Argentina 3 (Brown, Valdano, Burrachaga), **West Germany 2** (Rummenigge, Voller)

Venue: Mexico City

HT: 1–0

Top scorer (finals): Lineker (England), 6 goals

Above: José Luis Brown opens the scoring for Argentina in the match against Germany in 1986.

This tournament revolved around the brilliance and knavishness of Diego Maradona, who carried Argentina to their second World Cup triumph. Germany, who were efficient rather than inspiring, lost again in the final, despite a dramatic comeback from 2–0 down. Maradona's goals against Belgium and his second against England will live in the memory, but his first against England – the famous 'Hand of God' goal, punched with his fist past Peter Shilton – will be remembered the longest.

Denmark and the Soviet Union each scored six goals in a group match, against Uruguay and Hungary respectively, then lost dramatically in the second round – the Danes 5–1 to Spain, the Soviets 4–3 to Belgium in a thrilling match. Morocco defeated Portugal and drew with both England and Poland, thereby emphasizing the fact that the African nations were making great strides in developing their footballing skills.

1990 (Italy)

West Germany 1 (Brehme [penalty]), **Argentina 0**

Venue: Rome

HT: 0–0

Top scorer (finals): Schillaci (Italy), 6 goals

After a thrilling opening, when Cameroon defeated the holders Argentina, this tournament declined towards a grim final: the late penalty that won the game was contentious, but justice was done. Argentina had been more interested in spoiling than in playing, and had had two men sent off. In the first round, Maradona had escaped punishment for an obvious handball infringement on the line when playing against Russia. Then the Argentinians scuffled by a superior Brazilian side and, on penalties, past Yugoslavia and a distraught Italy. The other semi-final also went to penalties: Germany, fading after a bright start to the tournament, hung on to defeat a resurgent English side – which, however, had struggled to overcome Cameroon.

Italy finished unbeaten, but third. Ireland reached the last eight with a mere two goals and no wins. Scotland lost to Costa Rica. It was that sort of tournament.

Above: Maradona's 'Hand of God' goal.

Right: The moment when Gascoigne was brought to tears during the 1990 World Cup.

1994 (United States)

Brazil 0, Italy 0, after extra time (Brazil won on penalties)

Venue: Los Angeles

Top scorers (finals): Salenko (Russia), Stoichkov (Bulgaria), both 6 goals

---

A good World Cup until the anti-climax of a dull final, settled, for the first time, by a penalty shoot-out. Roberto Baggio, whose genius had done so much to carry Italy to its fifth final, missed the crucial kick. Brazil was still a worthy victor: although the side was less dazzling than that of 1970, it did not betray its heritage.

Strictly enforced refereeing allowed attacking talent to flourish. Russia's Oleg Salenko scored five goals against Cameroon, and both Romania and Bulgaria prospered.

The biggest scandal of the tournament centred on Maradona again; after two manic, bravura performances, he tested positive for drugs. Tragically, Andres Escobar, who conceded an own goal during Colombia's 2–1 defeat by hosts USA, was murdered on his return home.

Above: Brazilian celebrations contrast with Roberto Baggio's despair after missing the decisive penalty in the 1994 final.

Left: Voller fouled by Sensini, the penalty that won Germany the 1990 tournament.

235

1998 (France)

France 3 (Zidane 2, Petit), **Brazil 0**

Venue: Paris

HT: 2–0

Top scorer (finals): Suker (Croatia), 6 goals

The last World Cup of the millennium was also the biggest and longest, with 32 finalists playing 64 matches in 33 days. Of their seven matches France won six outright and the seventh on penalties, and deservedly became the first host winner – and the first new name on the trophy – in 20 years. Though the side never found the right centre-forward, its defence was the best of the competition and its midfield combined industry with Gallic flair and imagination.

The competition featured a number of excellent matches and also considerable controversy, mainly over refereeing decisions but also about ticket distribution (the seating was awarded disproportionately in favour both of the French and of corporate hospitality) – further being stirred concerning the Brazilian player Ronaldo's fitness and eligibility to play in the final itself.

Most matches were watched by full houses, although the fact that the stadia were smaller kept the overall attendance figure well below that of USA 94. Moreover, many fans could gain entry to matches only by buying tickets at inflated prices from the numerous touts.

Right: World Cup hero Zinedine Zidane holds up the World Cup.

The Group Stages

The expanded entry meant the competition could revert to a simple 'top two qualify' in each group, but it also led to a visible dilution in the quality of some of the games.

The teams were split into eight groups of four, the first two in each group qualifying for the second round. Most groups followed form the only surprise being Spain's fail-ure to qualify for the next round. The last 16 comprised European and South American sides plus Nigeria and Mexico – Nigeria the only African side to do so, and Mexico for the first time in Europe.

In the second round England met Argentina. After both scored from the penalty spot, England went ahead with Michael Owen's wonder goal, but Argentina equalized, Beckham was sent off for kicking out at Simeone, and despite holding out during extra time, England lost on penalties.

In the quarter-finals France beat Italy in a penalty shootout, Brazil narrowly squeezed past Denmark, Germany suffered their worst World Cup defeat since 1954 losing to Croatia, and with ten men after Bergkamp was dismissed Holland beat Argentina in injury time.

In the semis Brazil beat Holland on penalties and France beat Croatia. Croatia went on the win the third-place play-off, Suker scor-ing the winning goal and claiming the Golden Boot as top scorer in the Finals.

The Final will be remembered for the controversy surrounding Ronaldo. The night before the final he suffered a seizure and despite originally being left off the team list was reinstated allegedly following pressure for his and Brazil's sponsors Nike. France in front of their partisan crowd won easily. So France the country of Jules Rimet, who conceived the idea of World Cup, had finally won it.

Despite success, Aimé Jacquet, the French manager, confirmed his decision to resign. Many other World Cup managers also left their jobs, but not always of their own accord.

2002
(Korea and Japan)

Brazil 2 (Ronaldo 2), **Germany 0**

Venue: Yokohama

HT: 0–0

Top scorers (finals): Ronaldo (Brazil), 8 goals

The record books will show that the two most successful nations in World Cup history contested the 2002 final. The exuberant flair of the Brazilians triumphed over a resilient German side to make it seven straight wins and install Luis Felipe Scolari's team as worthy champions. Nothing too remarkable there. And yet those bald statistics do not do justice to a competition that was full of drama, controversy and results that turned footballing orthodoxy on its head. This was undoubtedly the year of the underdog. Some of the supposed big guns of world football found to their cost that they could no longer simply turn up to beat the likes of Korea, Japan, Senegal and the USA.

The other abiding memory of the first tournament to be staged in Asia, and the first to be jointly hosted, was of the resurgence of Ronaldo. After the disappointment of France 98 and four years in which he was dogged by injury, Ronaldo chose the biggest stage to show that he was back to his best. His brace in the final took his haul to eight, which brought him the Golden Boot and ensured that the trophy was heading back to Brazil for a fifth time.

The Group Stages

The first seismic shock came on the opening day, when an exciting Senegal side ran out 1-0 winners against the world champions. Things got even worse for France when they had Thierry Henry sent off in a goalless draw against Uruguay. Zinedine Zidane, still struggling for fitness, was brought back for the crunch match against Denmark. He couldn't galvanize Les Bleus, who limped out of the tournament having failed to score a single goal. The Danes topped Group A, and were joined in the second round by Senegal. The African side almost fell victim to the comeback of the tournament when Uruguay recovered from 3-0 down to snatch a draw. It wasn't enough, and the South Americans were also on their way home.

Spain were impressive in winning Group B with maximum points. Slovenia disappointed hugely, their cause not helped by internal wrangling in the camp, notably between Srecko Katanec coach and star player Zlatko Zahovic. That left the run-

Below: Ronaldo at France 98.

ners-up spot between South Africa and Paraguay. The balance swung back and forth as the final matches were played out, but Paraguay took the honours, thanks to a terrific second half performance against Slovenia, despite being reduced to 10 men.

Group C took on a similar pattern. Brazil scored three victories, while China finished without a point, failing to match the performances of some of the other emerging nations. Turkey and Costa Rica drew, putting both sides on four points. The Turks went through on goal difference, helped by the fact that they only went down 2-1 to Brazil. That game also brought the worst example of "simulation", an offence FIFA had said would be dealt with severely. The sight of Rivaldo writhing on the ground holding his face after Hakan Unsal struck him on the thigh with the ball was one of the less savoury sights of the tournament. Worse still, the authorities imposed a fine that amounted to loose change as far as the Brazilian striker was concerned.

Portugal, the seeded team in Group D and many people's dark horses to lift the trophy, crashed out in dramatic fashion. The USA rocked them with three early goals in their opening match. The Portuguese scored twice, but couldn't emulate the great comeback of the 1966 team against North Korea. Figo and Co. then demolished Poland, but had two men sent off in their final game against Korea and went down 1-0. Korea's Red Devils, guided by Guus Hiddink, were a revelation. They played with pace, skill and style, and a refreshing lack of cynicism. They were joined in the second round by the USA. Bruce Arena's side lost to Poland in their final game, but Portugal's defeat by the co-hosts rendered that academic.

Group E always looked like being a battle between Germany, Cameroon and Ireland for the two qualifying places. So it proved. All three beat Saudi Arabia, while Ireland drew with their two big rivals. Mick McCarthy's men beat the Saudis 3-0 to ensure their progress, whatever happened in the Germany-Cameroon match. In that game the Germans went down to 10 men, yet won the match 2-0 to put the African champions out. Miroslav Klose, Germany's new star striker, grabbed the second to take his tally to five, all headers. Referee Antonio Lopez Nieto handed out 14 yellow cards and two reds, a World Cup record.

England found themselves in the Group of Death. Although all four countries looked strong on paper, few could see Argentina failing to qualify. The co-favourites had romped away with the South American qualifying group, and

started well with a win over Nigeria. But England then gave a superb performance against Marcel Bielsa's team. David Beckham put the nightmare of his red card against the same opposition at France 98 by scoring the only goal of the game from the penalty spot. A draw with Sweden in their final match wasn't enough; Argentina were out. England played out a lacklustre goalless draw in their final match against Nigeria, securing the point needed to put them through.

Italy emerged from Group G, along with Mexico, though it was a very scratchy performance from the Azzurri. After a comfortable victory over the new boys from Ecuador, the Italians lost 2-1 to a Croatia side that had looked very unimpressive in their opening match. The Italians would go down as the tournament's unluckiest side, having a number of crucial decisions go against them. These would add further fuel to the perennial debate about the use of technology to help eliminate costly errors by the officials. Mexico, by contrast, played some delightful football on their way to topping the group.

Group H, containing co-hosts Japan as the seeded side, was dubbed the "Group of Life". It seemed there was no outstanding team, and no poor one. In fact, Japan were a breath of fresh air throughout. After a pulsating 2-2 draw against Belgium, Japan recorded their first ever World Cup victory with a 1-0 win over Russia. Japan went wild, while in Russia the result was greeted with utter disbelief. It got worse for Oleg Romantsev when his team went down to Belgium. The Russian coach resigned, the Belgians went through as runners-up.

Second round

Germany were the first team to make it to the quarter-finals. An uninspiring match against Paraguay looked like heading for extra time, when Oliver Neuville scored in the 88th minute. England made short work of Denmark, who couldn't reproduce the form that had carried them to victory over the

world champions. Three first-half goals settled the match, the most emphatic scoreline of the second round. The Senegal bandwagon rolled on with the first golden goal victory of the tournament. They came from behind against Sweden, and Henri Camara grabbed the goal that ended the hopes of the team that had come out on top in the Group of Death.

The game between Spain and the Republic of Ireland also ended 1-1 after 90 minutes, Robbie Keane snatching a late equaliser from the penalty spot. Injury forced Spain to hang on with 10 men during extra time. Iker Casillas then became the hero of the hour as Ireland missed three penalties in the shoot-out. Spain also failed twice, but Gaizka Mendieta found the net with the all-important spot kick and Spain were through.

The USA ran out 2-0 winners in a bruising encounter against arch rivals Mexico. Brazil overcame Belgium by the same score, though this was closer than the result suggested. Belgium only conceded the second in the dying minutes when they were pressing forward, and they also appeared very unlucky to have a Marc Wilmots header disallowed.

Italy had yet another goal ruled out for offside in their match against Korea. It finished 1-1, and Ahn Jung-hwan headed a golden goal winner three minutes from the end of extra time. There were unpleasant recriminations as Ahn's club, Perugia, announced that his loan spell in Italy would be terminated for having the effrontery to score for his country.

Unlike Korea, Japan's bubble burst in their last-16 match against Turkey. Umit Davala scored early on, and the Turks held out quite comfortably, Japan unable to find the means to unlock a tight defence.

Quarter-finals

Germany carved out yet another 1-0 win, this time over the USA. The Americans were very unlucky, particularly when the officials failed to spot that Gregg Berhalter's close-range shot was handled on the line by Torsten Frings. Michael Ballack's

second goal of the tournament won the game, but few people were under any illusion about how fortunate the Germans had been. Franz Beckenbauer was scathing. Excluding the magnificent Oliver Kahn from his verbal assault, Beckenbauer said: "If you put all the players in a sack and punched it, whichever player you hit would deserve it."

Spain followed Italy in feeling hard done by as they went out to Korea. Spain had two goals disallowed. The second, a Morientes header, was ruled out as the ball was wrongly adjudged to have gone out of play when Joaquin crossed it. This, along with a host of dubious offside decisions, prompted FIFA to express concern at the standard of the referee's assistants employed in the tournament. The game ended goalless, and there was more bad luck for Joaquin as he missed the penalty that sealed his country's fate and put Korea into the semi-final.

England faced the new favourites to lift the trophy, Brazil. Michael Owen pounced on a Lucio mistake to give England the lead. Rivaldo equalised after a blistering run from Ronaldinho. Ronaldinho then scored one of the goals of the tour-

nament when his 35-yard free kick floated over David Seaman into the top corner of the net. Some said it was a mis-hit cross; Ronaldinho insisted it was fully intended. He completed a memorable match by being sent off, a decision which would keep him out of the semi-final.

The Turkey-Senegal match ended goalless, but extra time lasted just four minutes. That was when Ilhan Mansiz swept in Umit Davala's cross. Forty-eight years after their only other appearance in the finals, Turkey had made it to the last four.

Semi-finals

If Korea had enjoyed the rub of the green in reaching the last four, their luck ran out against Germany. The man of the hour for Rudi Voller's side was again Michael Ballack. He not only grabbed the only goal of the game, but he picked up a booking that meant he would miss the final. The midfielder was yellow carded for a trip on the Lee Chunsoo, preventing a clear scoring opportunity. It was a cynical piece of professionalism, but Ballack had done more than his share in getting his country to the final. The Koreans felt that the match against Spain had taken too much out of them.

Above: David Beckham and Trevor Sinclair celebrate after scoring the winning goal against Argentina.

Nevertheless, both players and manager received the Blue Dragon, the country's highest award for sporting achievement, for their magnificent effort in reaching the semi-finals.

Turkey's superb run came to an end as they went down by the odd goal to Brazil for the second time in the tournament. Ronaldo hit the only goal of the game just after the break. After a superb spin and burst into the box, he prodded the ball past Rustu without breaking his stride. It was a clever if unorthodox piece of finishing, something that was needed to beat one of the goalkeepers of the competition and a defence that had conceded just four goals in six games.

Turkey won an open and entertaining third-place play-off match against Korea. Hakan Sukur, who had been so disappointing thus far, finally made his mark by scoring the fastest goal in World Cup finals history. His strike, inside 11 seconds, was wiped out by Lee Eul-yong after nine minutes. Man of the match Ilhan Mansiz hit two before half-time. Song Chong-gug pulled it back to 3-2 in the dying seconds, but there was no time for the co-hosts to seek an equaliser. After the whistle, both sets of players formed a chain and ran towards the fans, encapsulating the spirit of the competition.

Final

Brazil's seventh appearance in the final, and third in succession, brought their fifth victory. Two, second half goals from Ronaldo decided the match. The first was a predatory strike after Oliver Kahn uncharacteristically spilled a Rivaldo shot. The second was a clinical finish after Rivaldo dummied Kleberson's cross. Kahn's only mistake in seven games didn't prevent him from picking up the Player of the Tournament award. Ronaldo's brace took his tally to eight, three ahead of his nearest rivals, Rivaldo and Klose. The winner of the Golden Boot now had 12 World Cup goals in all to his name, two short of Gerd Muller's all-time record.

GAZETTE

The Money Game

The administration of football, like that of most countries and businesses, is decided by the politics of money and patronage. From the earliest days, after a reluctant Football Association had been forced to accept professionalism in England, to modern times – with UEFA extending its Champions' League to non-champion clubs that came from countries with large television audiences – money has talked.

Above: **Behind the scenes, television equipment in the parking lot at USA 94.**

So, too, has patronage, with individual appointments to positions of influence and decisions about, for example, the hosting of World Cups being largely dependent upon who has most friends where it matters.

FIFA

The game is run by FIFA (Fédération Internationale de Football Association), which has grown from the seven-member body founded in 1904 in Paris to become a 198-nation organization; administered from Zurich, it has a budget larger than many countries. FIFA is responsible for the World Cup and for the overall global administration of the game. When, for example, there was a dispute between Barcelona and Internazionale over the fee for Ronaldo, FIFA (not very decisively) settled it. It was FIFA – and notably its General Secretary, Sepp Blatter – who inspired the recent changes in the laws of the game and the interpretation of those laws – for example, banning goalkeepers from picking up pass-backs, allowing them to move along the line at penalties, and making a professional foul a red-card offence.

This is not to say that FIFA can change the laws arbitrarily: it can do so only through the International Board. Formed in 1886 by England, Scotland, Wales and Ireland, the board now

Right: **The Real Thing? Advertising and commercial interests have come to dominate the game of football.**

RED CARDS The youngest player sent off in a World Cup Finals tournament was 17-year-old Rigobert Song (1994 Cameroon v Russia).

Left: **The FIFA line-up.**

has eight members, the original four (Northern Ireland succeeding Ireland after partition) plus a further four elected members of FIFA. Although in practice the four home nations do not veto FIFA's law changes, this anachronism does give them theoretical influence out of all proportion to their modern importance. Since all four are members of a single nation, their right to have four separate national teams is frequently questioned. (This is one reason why the four do not enter the Olympic football tournament. The required combined UK team might set a precedent when it came to other international contests.)

A Wealth of Football

For almost four decades only two men occupied FIFA's most senior post. When Sir Stanley Rous was elected President in 1961 his appointment was in recognition of England's football heritage and Europe's dominant position. Then, in 1974, Brazil's João Havelange engineered a coup on behalf of the more numerous but less wealthy Third World nations. Havelange has extended World Cup participation to include more countries from Africa, Asia and Central America and

has spread the game's wealth, making the sport even more widespread than ever before.

However, the power of the European television market has tilted the balance back. As long as UEFA, the European governing body, is prepared to share the riches it looks likely to take a bigger say in administration, and Havelange's retirement in 1998 precipitated an acrimonious dispute for the succession between his ultimately successful protegé, Blatter, and Lennart Johansson, the UEFA President.

Europe Dominant

UEFA is the most influential of the continental federations simply because it is the wealthiest. The recent break-up of the Soviet Union has given UEFA a number of new members (and, therefore, extra votes in FIFA's one-nation one-vote Congress), as has the outwardly bizarre decision to grant nations like Liechtenstein and San Marino full membership. UEFA organizes the European Championship, now the world's third biggest sporting event, the lucrative Champions' League and other club events. Because of enmities in the Middle East, Israel, though not in Europe, is also a mem-

ber of UEFA, having previously been an associate member of Oceania.

South America (Conmebol) North and Central America's (Concacaf), Africa, Asia and Oceania each have their own continental federations and each in turn runs its own competitions.

The hosting of the World Cup, the biggest prize in the game, is decided by FIFA. (In 1996 UEFA, in its on-going campaign to restructure the game's administration, did suggest that each federation should have the right to host a World Cup in turn but, after opposition to its claim that Europe should host both the 1998 and 2006 competitions before

the inauguration of the new system, dropped the idea.) The decision is currently made by FIFA's executive committee. They have awarded Germany the 2006 World Cup, disappointing eight other bidders after visiting and assessing each country. This process is much cleaner than the bidding for the Olympic Games, but is open to political voting and abuse.

The National Level

Below the continental federations are national associations, like England's FA. In theory these bodies have full jurisdiction over the running of the game within their own countries. In fact, clubs and players increasingly turn to

Above: **The comedy world leader three-a-side team.**

Above: **Football fan Pope John-Paul II, once a goalkeeper in his native Poland, meets officials from FIFA.**

FACT FILE

Since the advent of the penalty shootout, some of the world's best players have missed from the spot. They include:

- **Franco Baresi** and **Roberto Baggio**
  (Italy v Brazil, World Cup Final 1994, lost)
- **Mario Kempes**
  (Valencia v Arsenal, European Cup-Winners' Cup Final, 1981, won – Liam Brady and Graham Rix missed for Arsenal)
- **Chris Waddle** and **Stuart Pearce**
  (England v West Germany, World Cup Semi-Final, 1990, lost)
- **Roberto Donadoni**
  (Italy v Argentina, World Cup Semi-Final, 1990, lost)
- **Clarence Seedorf**
  (Holland v France, European

Championship Quarter-Final, 1990, lost)
- **Nadal**
  (Spain v England, European Championship Quarter-Final, lost)
- **Edgar Davids**
  (Ajax v Juventus, European Cup Final, 1996, lost)

Goalkeepers who have scored include:
- **Pat Jennings** (Tottenham Hotspur)
- **Peter Shilton** (Leicester) and **Andy Goram** (Glasgow Rangers) with clearances
- **Peter Schmiechel** (Manchester United) in open play
- **Mark Bosnich** (Australia) and **Alex Stepney** (Manchester United) from penalties
- **José Luis Chilavert** (Paraguay and Velez Sarsfield) from free kicks

the courts to settle disputes, sometimes suing the local FA in contravention of the directives issued by the relevant continental federation. Football has always felt itself to be above the law, with the right to control its own administration, but the recent Bosman case, in which the European Court of Justice made a legal decision against UEFA, showed that belief to be outdated.

The Leagues

On the step below the various national associations, each league has its own powers. The leagues – right down to the organizers of Sunday League games played at parks level – appoint referees, suspend players and operate competitions in much the same way as FIFA does at world level. At either level the vast majority of administrators are working for the good of the game out of altruism and/or professionalism, but

who you know does still help in many instances.

One of the most notorious cases of the old boys' network in action concerned Arsenal's promotion to the First Division of the English Football League after World War I. When football resumed in 1919, it was decided to extend the First Division from 20 to 22 clubs. There were obvious ways in which this could be done: the bottom two clubs of the 1914–15 season could simply not have been relegated from Division One, while the top two from Division Two could have been promoted; alternatively, the bottom two First Division Clubs could have been relegated and the top four Second Division sides elevated. Instead, bizarrely, the League relegated one and promoted the top two – plus Arsenal, who had finished only sixth in Division Two. The relegated side was Tottenham Hotspur, Arsenal's local rival, and that club was justifiably upset. Barnsley

MICHEL PLATINI I've some very bad news for you, Platini's just retired.
– Islamic hostage-taker to Frenchman Roger Auque in the movie based on Auque's kidnap in Beirut

was even more unhappy, having come third in Division Two. (Barnsley was promoted to the First Division in 1997, and remained there for only one season.) Arsenal has remained in the top flight ever since.

Arsenal's chairman in 1919, Henry Norris, was later expelled from the game on fraud charges for 'financial irregularities' by the FA. A businessman, Norris had moved Arsenal from southeast London to the better-populated north of London. His understanding of football's potential, if not his subsequent corruption, has characterized many of football's later commercial investors. Some are in the game to make money and some to gain influence; some want both, others neither. Men like Ken Bates of Chelsea,

Jesus Gil of Atletico Madrid and Silvio Berlusconi of Milan have become known across Europe through their involvement in football.

Even Alan Sugar and Sir John Hall, both noted businessmen, gained broad-based fame only after becoming chairmen of, respectively, Tottenham Hotspur and Newcastle United.

Football plc

Football is now popular with investors, and many clubs are quoted on the stock exchanges. Some companies hold an international portfolio of clubs. This surge of interest from the moneymen is, obviously, due to the rise in the game's income, which is largely underwritten by satellite and terrestrial television companies and sponsors – or, as they

are often euphemistically known, 'partners'.

Club United

Paradoxically, this development has coincided with an increase in the power of the fans – the very people whose wishes were totally ignored when their admission money was the game's chief source of income. Supporters now have a growing, albeit still very small, influence on the running of clubs and associations. One of the most dramatic examples concerns Bournemouth, a lower-division English club, which almost went bankrupt in 1997. It was rescued by a partnership between supporters, club staff and the financial administrator. Bournemouth is now run by all as a community club ∎

Glenn Moore

Bomber Aytour

In 1995 Lebanese World Cup star Oussama Aytour landed himself a 'football first' . . .

Aytour was the first player to be arrested for making a bomb! Police caught the player in Fulham where he was staying with his brother.

Perhaps the strangest thing about this potentially explosive episode came when the matter was heard in court. There, the creative Aytour explained that his reason for making the explosive device was that he was simply bored. The court were not impressed with this and fined him £300! ∎

Gerry Cox

CHRONOLOGY

1848 Rules first codified at Cambridge University

1855 Sheffield FC, world's oldest club, founded

1863 Football Association formed

1872 First FA Cup Final

1872 First international: Scotland 0, England 0

1875 Crossbar replaces tape

1878 Introduction of referee's whistle

1888 Football League formed

1891 Goal net and penalty kick introduced

1897 First players' union formed (revived 1907)

1904 FIFA founded

1930 First World Cup (won by Uruguay)

1938 Italy is first country to retain World Cup

1950 World Cup Final attracts record crowd (199,850 or 203,500, depending on sources), as Uruguay beat Brazil 2–1

1953 Hungary becomes first foreign team to beat England at Wembley

1958 Brazil is first country to win World Cup outside of own continent

1981 Three points for a win introduced in England (this system would eventually spread everywhere)

1985 Heysel disaster: 39 Italian and Belgian fans die

1989 Hillsborough disaster: 95 Liverpool fans die, toll later rising to 96

1990 FIFA make 'professional foul' a red-card offence

1995 England fans riot in Dublin, provoking first abandonment of an England international

1995 'Golden goal' rule introduced, Birmingham being the first major beneficiaries in the final of the English Auto-Windscreens Shield

1995 Jean-Marc Bosman wins European legal case, so changing the face of the international transfer market

ARSENAL One of the most notorious cases of the Old Boys' network in action concerned Arsenal's promotion, at the expense of Barnsley's, to the First Division.

Friendly international, Wembley, 25 November 1953

The Magical Magyars

England 3 (Sewell, Mortensen, Ramsey (penalty)), **Hungary 6** (Hidegkuti 3, Puskas 2, Bozsik)

This was a defining moment – or, for the purist, 90 minutes – in English soccer history. Until now the country that gave soccer to the world had never lost at home to foreign opposition

At the time the popular belief – in England at least – was that England were the best in the world. Hungary destroyed that notion. It took the 'Magical Magyars' only 60 seconds to start doing so, Hidegkuti scoring their first. Hungary – Olympic Champions the previous year and in 1954 to be runners-up to West Germany in the 1954 World Cup Final after being 2–0 up – crushed England now. Puskas' left foot seemed to control everything. Hidegkuti, the number 9, dropped back to leave the England defence confused and floundering. The men in the cherry-red shirts exhibited a combination of teamwork, ball-skills and movement rarely seen before or since. England trailed 4–2 at half-time and, although their hopes were raised when Alf Ramsey scored a penalty, two more from Hidegkuti finished them off. It didn't end there. The following year, in Budapest, Hungary beat England 7–1 ∎

Mike Collett

Above: **Stretching the Hungarian goalkeeper.**

Above: **Before kick-off at Wembley, no one rated Hungary's chances away to England.**

World Cup Quarter-Final, Goodison Park, 23 July 1966

Saviour Eusebio

Portugal 5 (Eusebio 4 (2 penalties), Augusto),
North Korea 3 (Seung-zin, Dong-woon, Seung-kook)

One of the most remarkable World Cup matches ever played left a 51,000 crowd at Goodison Park in wide-eyed astonishment on a hot, sunny Saturday afternoon as Portugal came from 0–3 down to defeat North Korea 5–3, thanks to a bravura performance from Eusebio.

North Korea, who had already caused a huge upset with a 1–0 first-round win over Italy, created a sensation at Goodison by scoring three goals inside the first 22 minutes. Pak Seung-zin, Dong-woon and Seung-kook left Portugal on the ropes – until Eusebio inspired his team to an incredible fightback. He scored his first after 27 minutes, then managed a second, from the penalty spot, just before half-time. That dented the Koreans' self-belief, which disappeared completely after 55 minutes when Eusebio equalized with a superb goal from the edge of the six-yard box. Eusebio hammered home the message with his fourth goal (his second penalty) soon after. By Augusto's goal in the 78th minute it was over ∎

Mike Collett

European Cup Final, Lisbon, 25 May 1967

Inter Unbolted

Glasgow Celtic 2 (Gemmell, Chalmers), **Internazionale 1** (Mazzola)

This, the most memorable evening in the glittering history of Glasgow Celtic, was the day Europe's love affair with attacking soccer was rekindled. The fiery Scots' ambition proved too much for the Italians' lacklustre tactics.

The Scots demolished the firmly held belief of Internazionale's coach Helenio Herrera that the catenaccio, or 'bolted door', defensive system held the key to success. Sandro Mazzola's successful eighth-minute penalty was the perfect start for a side whose whole credo was to grab an early goal and then defend in depth. But Celtic was no ordinary side. In his first full season at Parkhead, Jock Stein had fashioned a team that overflowed with attacking talent and flair: Jimmy Johnstone, Bertie Auld, Bobby Murdoch and Tommy Gemmell – an attacking fullback who scored the equalizer from 20 yards (17m) after 62 minutes – provided a diamond-hard backbone to the side. With half an hour to play and the scores level, Celtic were in total control. Internazionale's tactics backfired: they simply could not cope with the constant attacking pressure. They eventually caved in six minutes from time, when a Murdoch shot was deflected in by Chalmers. As Celtic became the first UK side to win the European Cup, even Herrera admitted: 'Celtic deserved to win and their win was a victory for the sport.' ∎

Mike Collett

England, 1994–5

The George Graham 'Bung' Scandal

George Graham was Arsenal's most successful manager, bringing six trophies to Highbury in eight years, but he was sacked in February 1995 for accepting unauthorized payments ('bungs') on transfer deals.

In all, he pocketed £425,000 from Norwegian agent Rune Hauge following the transfer to Arsenal of Norwegian Pal Lydersen from IK Start and Dane John Jensen from Brondy, in 1991 and 1992 respectively. Hauge's methods were questionable, but not illegal. His company profited by negotiating a difference between the buying and selling prices involved in a transfer deal, and Graham accepted a share of that difference. Graham eventually handed all the money, exactly half the 'profit' – he called it an 'unsolicited gift' – back to the club, with interest. He was still sacked by Arsenal and banned by the FA for 12 months, but later managed Leeds United and Tottenham. Hauge was suspended from working as an agent ■

Above: George Graham during his time as manager of Arsenal.

Penang, the Mayalasian Cup, 1994

The Malaysian Betting Scandal

Allegations of fixed matches, bribery and betting scandals abound in Asian football – but one case was blatant enough that a club sacked its own players for cheating so obviously.

That team was Penang, in the Malaysian League, who blamed four players for accepting bribes after the team conceded 12 goals in two games and surprisingly failed to reach the quarter-finals of the Malaysian Cup. In 1994 the authorities finally acted on some of the corruption blighting the game: 102 players, coaches and club officials from dozens of teams, not to mention various book-makers, were suspended for match-rigging. Seven of those involved were eventually banned from soccer for life ■

Mike Collett

World Cup qualifier, 1962

The Battle of Santiago

When Chile met Italy in 1962 it led to scenes never witnessed before at a football ground.

Poaching of Chilean players by Italian clubs and a vicious press campaign led to Giorgio Ferrini being sent off after eight minutes. Sanchez broke Maschio's nose and Mario David drop-kicked an opponent: all very nasty ■

Teamwork Sports Agency

Above: **Bruce Grobelaar in his days with Liverpool.**

England, 1994–7

The Trials and Tribulations of the Three

The most protracted soccer court case in England since the 1960s involved Bruce Grobbelaar, John Fashanu and Hans Segers. These three were alleged to have thrown a number of matches between 1992 and 1994, instigated by Mayalasian business interests.

They were charged along with Malaysian businessman Heng Suan Lim, who was alleged to have been the link between the players and gambling syndicates in the Far East. Among the matches in question were Liverpool's 3–0 defeat at Newcastle in November 1993 and Wimbledon's game at Everton on the last day of the 1994 season, which Everton won 3–2 after trailing 2–0. The story broke when Zimbabwean businessman Chris Vincent, angry with Grobbelaar over the failure of a joint business deal, publicly alleged he had given Grobbelaar money to throw matches in order to make huge profits through Malaysian bookmakers. After one jury failed to reach a verdict, a second cleared the defendants.

Although the players were innocent, the scandal occupied the headlines of various tabloid newspapers for many a long month and cast a shadow over the integrity of the game. Grobbelaar, though with Southampton when charged, is best known as a member of Liverpool's 1984 European Cup winning team. Fashanu, then retired through injury, had achieved fame at Wimbledon where he was a team-mate of Segars ∎

Mike Collett

Above: **John Fashanu.**

Money, Soccer and Fame

With football at the peak of sporting fashion, the game has become part of show business, with a lot in common with pop music and sopa operas. Indeed, at the moment the relationship could be said to be symbiotic – one feeding off the other.

After all, it is not uncommon for young women celebrities to be romantically linked with famous players. Victoria Adams, better known as 'Posh Spice' of the Spice Girls, married Manchester United's David Beckham, solo singer Louise has married Liverpool's Jamie Redknapp and Ulrika Jonsson of

Gladiators and *Shooting Stars* fame has dated Aston Villa's Stan Collymore, before the Aston Villa striker notoriously assaulted her in a French bar during the 1998 World Cup.

Sometimes famous names play an active part in their favourite clubs. As Watford chairman, rock star Elton John was instrumental in attracting Graham Taylor to the club and triggering the Hertfordshire side's remarkable rise that took them from the

Fourth Division to the First in only five seasons. Prince Albert, heir to the 900-year-old Grimaldi throne, is the number one supporter and effective owner of Monaco, the French League club.

Other famous fans include singer Rod Stewart, who has travelled round the world in support of the Scotland international side, and Noel and Liam, the Gallagher brothers of rock band Oasis, who are avid Manchester City supporters ∎

Pickles the Celebrity Dog

The first star of the 1966 World Cup had four legs not two.

Three months before the start of the tournament, Pickles, a black and white mongrel, found the Jules Rimet trophy in South London after it had been stolen from an exhibition in Westminster. A ransom demand was made and led to the arrest of a 47-year-old dock labourer.

However, the Cup was still missing and it was not until Pickles, out on a walk, sniffed at a mysterious bundle under a bush that the trophy could be returned to embarrassed FA officials.

Pickles became an instant celebrity and was given a film role, and a year's supply of food ∎

England vs Argentina

England's quarter-final with Argentina at Wembley will go down as one of the most turbulent matches in World Cup history.

It was a rough affair from the start and the German referee Herr Kreitlein was soon busy taking Latin names. The Argentinian captain, Antonio Rattin, cautioned for a foul, was then ordered off when he objected to the booking of a colleague. The central defender, towering over the official,

refused to go and for nearly ten minutes disorder reigned as it appeared at one stage that all his team would leave the field. The controversy rumbled on after the game with Alf Ramsey, the England manager, labelling Argentina 'animals'. It was revived for the 1986 and 1998 World Cup meetings ∎

FA Cup Final, Wembley, London, 18 May 1923: Bolton 2, West Ham Utd 0

The White Horse Final

Perhaps the most famous match of all-time, the first FA cup final to be staged at Wembley, has become legendary, not for the football, but for the events which went on before the kick-off.

The organizers had not made the game all-ticket and had badly underestimated supporters' interest. The new stadium, built as part of a complex to house the British Exhibition, had a capacity of 125,000 – but nearer 200,000 turned up on the day and forced their way into the ground. The crush was so severe that thousands of fans spilled on to the pitch.

It took an hour to clear the crowds and most of the work was done by Constable George Scorey and his white horse Billy. Thus the match was named after the horse, and Bolton went on to win it 2–0. Scorey was not even a football fan ∎

Very, Very Superstitious

Superstition has been part of football since the game began. Players, managers, supporters – few wrapped up in the emotion of the sport are able to resist a lucky charm that, as illogical as it sounds, could just make the difference between winning and losing.

The Newcastle team of the early 1900s believed they would win if they saw a wedding on their way to a match, and lose if they saw a funeral. Ipswich put their run of victories in the 1953–54 season down to the seven-leaf clover given them by an American fan.

RABBIT'S FOOT
Dave Sexton not only wore the same jacket when winning two cups with Chelsea and while presiding over League title challenges with QPR and Manchester United but also kept the same rabbit's foot in his pocket.

DANCING SHOES
Jimmy Melia wore his white dancing shoes to the FA Cup final with Brighton in 1983. The story goes that the manager forgot to change his shoes before one Cup-tie that followed a dancing session and ended up wearing them all the way to Wembley.

PUDDING EQUALS POINTS
After the 1927 FA Cup final when goalkeeper Dan Lewis blamed his slippery new jersey for the goal that denied Arsenal the trophy, it became a tradition for the club's keepers to wash new jerseys before playing in them. Some players have 'lucky' pre-match meals. The Derby goalkeeper in the 1890s was always provided with rice pudding in response to his prediction: 'No pudding, no points.'

ALL IN THE MIND
Weird and wonderful methods have been used in the treatment of injuries. One particular trainer believed that muscle strains were best relieved by sleeping with a nutmeg in-side a red-spotted hankie placed beneath a pillow. Then there was the club doctor who told of the player whose imagined ankle in-jury was treated by weekly injections of sterilised water instead of pain killers. 'It was all in the mind' said the doctor.

MONKEY-GLANDS, SPATS AND HORSESHOES
Monkey-gland injections were a much-publicized feature of Wolverhampton Wanderers' preparations for the 1939 FA Cup final against Portsmouth whose manager Jack Tinn sported a pair of lucky white spats, Tinn insisted they were fastened before each game by winger Fred Worrall who himself carried a lucky sixpence and a miniature horseshoe ■

Gerry Cox

Milla's Strange Idea

Cameroon legend Roger Milla organized one of the most unusual and, probably, most distasteful events in footballing history.

During 1993 he ran a tournament at the Omnisports stadium for teams of pygmies. Around 120 pygmies turned up, but the tournament wasn't a success. Criticized for keeping the pygmies imprisoned, under guard and under-fed, only 50 spectators turned up – and these just wanted to shout abuse at the players. Milla had gained global fame at the 1990 World Cup ■

Curse at Elland Road

As the Leeds manager, Don Revie was deeply superstitious, wearing the same suit for as long as his team avoided defeat.

When he learned of an ancient curse on Elland Road he brought in a gypsy fortune-teller from Blackpool who claimed to sense something evil in a brown presence and in particular in Revie's suede overcoat. Revie was told that the coat had to be lost, not given away, so he left it in a restaurant cloakroom. Leeds' many detractors felt it was not the coat that was being referred to ■

Abundantly GOALS!

Some days there seem to be goals being scored in abundance. The record victory for a British Club side came on September 5, 1885, when Arbroath beat Bon Accord 36–0 in the Scottish FA Cup.

But for anyone who watched the match, it must have been a bizarre spectacle: Bon Accord were a cricket team moon-lighting as a football club, playing in their working clothes without a single pair of proper football boots between them. While the Arbroath goalkeeper didn't touch the ball the entire match, Bon Accord's goalkeeper, who had never played before, was injured and had to be replaced at half-time by a defender. This was the match in which John Petrie scored thirteen goals, a record haul for a single game.

Incredibly, on the same day, Dundee Harp beat Aberdeen Rovers 35–0, missing out on the record set that day by one ■

Nick Callow

Team Awards

UEFA Cup
(known as Fairs Cup until 1972)

1958	Barcelona	1969	Newcastle
1960	Barcelona	1970	Arsenal
1961	Roma	1971	Leeds
1962	Valencia	1972	Tottenham Hotspur
1963	Valencia	1973	Liverpool
1964	Real Zaragoza	1974	Feyenoord
1965	Ferencvaros	1975	Borussia Mönchengladbach
1966	Barcelona	1976	Liverpool
1967	Dinamo Zagreb	1977	Juventus
1968	Leeds	1978	PS Eindhoven

1979	Borussia Mönchengladbach	1992	Ajax
1980	Eintracht Frankfurt	1993	Juventus
1981	Ipswich	1994	Internazionale
1982	IFK Gothenburg	1995	Parma
1983	Anderlecht	1996	Bayern Munich
1984	Tottenham Hotspur	1997	Schalke 04
1985	Real Madrid	1998	Internazionale
1986	Real Madrid	1999	Parma
1987	IFK Gothenburg	2000	Galatasaray
1988	Bayer Leverkusen	2001	Liverpool
1989	Napoli	2002	Feyenoord
1990	Juventus	2003	Porto
1991	Internazionale		

European Championship
(European Nations Cup 1960–68)

1960	Soviet Union	1984	France
1964	Spain	1988	Holland
1968	Italy	1992	Denmark
1972	West Germany	1996	Germany
1976	Czechoslovakia	2000	France
1980	West Germany		

African Nations' Cup Finals

1957	Egypt	1980	Nigeria
1959	Egypt	1982	Ghana
1962	Ethiopia	1984	Cameroon
1963	Ghana	1986	Egypt
1965	Ghana	1988	Cameroon
1968	Congo Kinshasa (Zaire)	1990	Algeria
		1992	Ghana
1970	Sudan	1994	Nigeria
1972	Congo	1996	South Africa
1974	Zaire	1998	Egypt
1976	Morocco	2000	Cameroon
1978	Ghana	2002	Cameroon

European Cup Finals

1956	Real Madrid	1980	Nottingham Forest
1957	Real Madrid	1981	Liverpool
1958	Real Madrid	1982	Aston Villa
1959	Real Madrid	1983	Hamburg
1960	Real Madrid	1984	Liverpool
1961	Benfica	1985	Juventus
1962	Benfica	1986	Steauna Bucharest
1963	AC Milan	1987	FC Porto
1964	Internazionale	1988	PSV Eindhoven
1965	Internazionale	1989	AC Milan
1966	Real Madrid	1990	AC Milan
1967	Celtic	1991	Red Star Belgrade
1968	Manchester United	1992	Barcelona
1969	AC Milan	1993	Marseille
1970	Feyenoord	1994	AC Milan
1971	Ajax	1995	Ajax
1972	Ajax	1996	Juventus
1973	Ajax	1997	Borussia Dortmund
1974	Bayern Munich	1998	Real Madrid
1975	Bayern Munich	1999	Manchester United
1976	Bayern Munich	2000	Real Madrid
1977	Liverpool	2001	Bayern Munich
1978	Liverpool	2002	Real Madrid
1979	Nottingham Forest	2003	AC Milan

World Club Cup Finals

1960	Real Madrid	1982	Penarol
1961	Penarol	1983	Gremio
1962	Santos	1984	Independiente
1963	Santos	1985	Juventus
1964	Internazionale	1986	River Plate
1965	Internazionale	1987	FC Porto
1966	Penarol	1988	Nacional
1967	Racing Club	1989	AC Milan
1968	Estudiantes	1990	AC Milan
1969	AC Milan	1991	Red Star Brigade
1970	Feyenoord	1992	São Paulo
1971	Nacional	1993	São Paulo
1972	Ajax	1994	Velez Sarsfield
1973	Independiente	1995	Ajax
1974	Real Madrid	1996	Juventus
1975	not played	1997	Borussia Dortmund
1976	Bayern Munich	1998	Real Madrid
1977	Boca Juniors	1999	Manchester United
1978	not played	2000	Boca Juniors
1979	Olimpia	2001	Bayern Munich
1980	Nacional	2002	Real Madrid
1981	Flamengo		

Copa Libertadores

1960	Penarol	1982	Penarol
1961	Penarol	1983	Gremio
1962	Santos	1984	Independiente
1963	Santos	1985	Argentinos Juniors
1964	Independiente	1986	River Plate
1965	independiente	1987	Penarol
1966	Penarol	1988	Nacional
1967	Racing Club	1989	Atletico Nacional
1968	Estudiantes	1990	Olimpia
1969	Estudiantes	1991	Colo Colo
1970	Estudiantes	1992	São Paulo
1971	Nacional	1993	São Paulo
1972	Independiente	1994	Velez Sarsfield
1973	Independiente	1995	Gremio
1974	Independiente	1996	River Plate
1975	Independiente	1997	Cruzeiro
1976	Cruzeiro	1998	Vasco da Gama
1977	Boca Juniors	1999	Palmeiras
1978	Boca Juniors	2000	Boca Juniors
1979	Olimpia	2001	Boca Juniors
1980	Nacional	2002	Olimpia
1981	Flamengo		

Copa America

1910	Argentina	1947	Argentina
1916	Uruguay	1949	Brazil
1917	Uruguay	1953	Paraguay
1919	Brazil	1955	Argentina
1920	Uruguay	1956	Uruguay*
1921	Argentina	1957	Argentina
1922	Brazil	1959	Argentina
1923	Uruguay	1959	Uruguay
1924	Uruguay	1963	Bolivia
1925	Argentina	1967	Uruguay
1926	Uruguay	1975	Peru
1927	Argentina	1979	Paraguay
1929	Argentina	1983	Uruguay
1935	Uruguay	1987	Uruguay
1937	Argentina	1989	Brazil
1939	Peru	1991	Argentina
1941	Argentina*	1993	Argentina
1942	Uruguay	1995	Uruguay
1945	Argentina	1997	Brazil
1946	Argentina	1999	Brazil
unofficial tournaments		2001	Colombia

European Cup-Winners' Cup

1961	Fiorentina	1981	Dinamo Tbilisi
1962	Atletico Madrid	1982	Barcelona
1963	Tottenham Hotspur	1983	Aberdeen
1964	Sporting Lisbon	1984	Juventus
1965	West Ham United	1985	Everton
1966	Borussia Dortmund	1986	Kiev Dynamo
1967	Bayern Munich	1987	Ajax
1968	AC Milan	1988	Mechelen
1969	Slovan Bratislava	1989	Barcelona
1970	Manchester City	1990	Sampdoria
1971	Chelsea	1991	Manchester United
1972	Rangers	1992	Werder Bremen
1973	AC Milan	1993	Parma
1974	FC Magdeburg	1994	Arsenal
1975	Kiev Dynamo	1995	Real Zaragoza
1976	Anderlecht	1996	Paris St Germain
1977	Hamburg	1997	Barcelona
1978	Anderlecht	1998	Chelsea
1979	Barcelona	1999	Lazio
1980	Valencia		

Olympic Games Finals

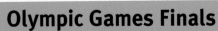

1908	England	1936	Italy	1964	Hungary	1988	Soviet Union
1912	England	1948	Sweden	1968	Hungary	1992	Spain
1920	Belgium	1952	Hungary	1972	Poland	1996	Nigeria
1924	Uruguay	1956	Soviet Union	1976	East Germany	2000	Cameroon
1928	Uruguay	1960	Yugoslavia	1980	Czechoslovakia		
				1984	France		

The Japan and Korea 2002 World Cup

First booking in finals: Petit (France)

First goal in finals: P B Diop (Senegal)

First penalty scored: Quentin Fortune (South Africa)

First Hat-trick: Miroslav Klose (Germany)

First player to be sent off: Boris Zivkovic (Croatia)

First win for S Korea in five World Cups: South Korea 2 Poland 0

First player to play in three Final matches: Cafu (Brazil, 1994, 1998, 2002)

First ever meeting of the two most successful countries: Brazil v Germany: 2002 Final.

Argentina eliminated after the First Round for the first time since 1962.

France first holders ever to go out finishing bottom of their group and without scoring a goal.

France first holders to not reach the Second Round since Brazil in 1966.

Most club players come from: 1st AC Milan, 2nd Arsenal

Most players come from the English Premiership

Statistics 2002

Games: 64   **Goals:** 161 **Yellow cards:** 267 **Red cards:** 17

Average goals per match: 2.52   **Goals in first half:** 69 **Goals in second half:** 89

Golden goals: 3 **Penalty shoot-outs:** 2

Leading scorers:

8   Ronaldo (Brazil)

5   Rivaldo (Brazil), Miroslav Klose (Germany)

4   Jon Dahl Tomasson (Denmark)

    Christian Vieri (Italy)

All time appearances in Final matches

25   Lothar Matthaus (Germany)

23   Paolo Maldini (Italy)

21   Diego Maradona (Argentina)

     Wladoslav Zmuda (Poland)

     Uwe Seeler (Germany)

20   Grzegorz Lato (Poland)

All time top scorers in Finals

14   Gerd Muller (Germany)

13   Juste Fontaine (France)

12   Pele (Brazil)

     Ronaldo (Brazil)

11   Sandor Kocsis (Hungary)

     Jurgen Klinsmann (Germany)

10   Gabriel Batistuta (Argentina)

     Helmut Rahn (Germany)

     Gary Lineker (England)

     Teofilio Cubillas (Peru)

     Grzegorz Lato (Poland)

Golden Boot Winners

2002   Ronaldo (Brazil) 8

1998   Davor Suker (Croatia) 6

1994   Hristo Stoichkov (Bulgaria) 6

       Oleg Salenko (Russia) 6

1990   Salvatore Schillaci (Italy) 6

1986   Gary Lineker (England) 6

1982   Paolo Rossi (Italy) 6

1978   Mario Kempes (Argentina) 6

1974   Gregorz Lato (Poland) 7

1970   Gerd Muller (Germany) 10

1966   Eusebio (Portugal) 9

1960   Florian Albert (Hungary) 4

       Leonel Sanchez (Chile) 4

       Valentin Ivanov (USSR) 4

       Vava (Brazil) 4

       Garrincha (Brazil) 4

       Drazan Jerkovic (Yugoslavia) 4

1958   Juste Fontaine (France) 13

1954   Sandor Kocsis (Hungary) 11

1938   Ademir (Brazil) 7

1934   Ledinas Da Silva (Brazil) 8

1930   Oldrich Nejedly (Czechoslovakia) 5

Fastest Goal in World Cup Finals 2002:

Hakan Sukur, 10.8 secs, 3rd/4th place play-off.

Index

Contributors

GLENN MOORE
Football correspondent of the *Independent* and author of *Soccer Skill and Tactics*.
A Gillingham fan who would love the chance to be called a glory-hunter.

TIM BARNETT
Former *Sunday Express* football reporter, now freelance. Author of *European Soccer Who's Who*
and *Fantastic Football phenomena*. Puts up with the joys of watching Crystal Palace.

NICK CALLOW
Co-owner of Teamwork Sports Agency. Writes for various newspapers from the *Independent on Sunday*
to the *News of the World*. Edited the *Arsenal Year Book* as a labour of love.

IAN CRUISE
Former reporter for the *Sunday Mirror* and *Shoot*, now Head of Content at Premium TV,
which owns the digital rights to 80 clubs.

MIKE COLLETT
Football editor of Reuters and author of the *Guiness Record of the FA Cup*. A Tottenham fan whose greatest
moment came when Ricky Villa scored the FA Cup-winning goal on Mike's birthday.

GERRY COX
Football writer for the *Observer* and chairman of the Football Writers' Association.
Author of *Tottenham Hotspur: The Supporter's Guide*, for which he is amply qualified.
Managing Editor of Teamwork Sports Agency.

TREVOR HAYLETT
Former football reporter for the *Daily Mail* and the *Independent*, now freelancing
for newspapers and magazines. A Norwich City supporter.

CHARLOTTE NICOL
Became the first woman broadcaster on BBC Radio Sport in 1990. Took over as football
producer in 1991. A Leicester City supporter.